CRISIS OF ECONOMY AND IDEOLOGY:

ESSAYS ON WELSH SOCIETY, 1840 - 1980

Edited by
GLYN WILLIAMS

S.S.R.C./B.S.A. Sociology of Wales Study Group

First published in 1983
by British Sociological Association
Sociology of Wales Study Group

Printed at Coleg Prifysgol Gogledd Cymru, Bangor, Gwynedd

British Library Cataloguing in Publication Data

Crisis of Economy and Ideology : essays on Welsh society 1840–1980
1. Wales - Social conditions
I. Williams, Glyn
942.9'081 HN398.W26

ISBN 0 9508890 0 8

CONTENTS

Page

CONTRIBUTORS

PHILLIP COOKE: Department of Town Planning, U.W.I.S.T., Cardiff.

CHARLOTTE AULL DAVIES: Department of Anthropology, Duke University, North Carolina, U.S.A.

COLIN FLETCHER Department of Social Policy, Cranfield Institute of Technology, Cranfield, Bedford.

JOHN LOVERING School of Advanced Urban Studies, Bristol University

E. GLYN LEWIS Her Majesty's Inspectorate, Retired

DAI MICHAEL Department of Sociology, Coleg Harlech, Harlech.

RICHARD H. MORGAN: Department of Social Administration, University College, Swansea.

PHILLIP M. RAWKINS: Department of Politics, Ryerson Polytechnic, Toronto, Canada.

GARETH REES: Department of Sociology, University College, Cardiff.

TERESA L. REES: Department of Sociology, University College, Cardiff.

CATRIN ROBERTS: Department of Education, Manchester University, Manchester

GLYN WILLIAMS: Department of Social Theory and Institutions, University College of North Wales, Bangor.

JOHN WILLIAMS: Department of Economics, University College of Wales, Aberystwyth.

ACKNOWLEDGEMENTS

Many people have contributed to the preparation and publication of these papers. The seminars from which they derive were supported by the Social Science Research Council to whom thanks are due for their efforts to stimulate interests in researching Welsh problems. The participants in these seminars, not all of whom are contributors to this collection, made valuable contributions in the various discussions and their views appear throughout the texts. The papers were expertly typed by Karen Jones.

CHAPTER 1

INTRODUCTION

Glyn Williams

Marx conceptualized major shifts in the organization of economic production in terms of modes of production. Within each mode of production there occur economic changes which involve a significant restructuring of social and political organization. Such periods of change are often portrayed as periods of crisis which involve far reaching political responses associated with the reproduction of the social formation. There is little doubt that the industrial revolution of the late eighteenth and early nineteenth centuries represented precisely such a period. For many the restructuring of capitalism since the second world war represents a similar period. Yet social scientists often fail to avail themselves of the opportunity to understand the complexity of such crises, partly because certain paradigms play down the influence of the economic, while others focus attention upon the individual as the unit of study thereby overlooking structural change. It is part of a general tendency to fragment society into 'areas of interest' which inhibits a holistic view. Frequently it is when sociologists divorce themselves from their immediate research area through the teaching of courses such as 'The Sociology of Modern Britain' that they allow themselves the 'luxury' of more generalized statements. A recent development which is an exception involves an awareness of what is significantly referred to as the 'regional problem'.[1] It obliges the sociologist to consider the holistic perspective. Furthermore, when the 'regional problem' is understood as a manifestation of the crises referred to above the sociological approach to the study of Wales assumes a different relevance.

Until recently a global view of Wales was restricted to geographers! Several commentators have drawn attention to the fact that whenever sociologists paid attention to Wales, which was not very often, their studies tended to be conducted at the community level either as part of the search for a society and culture not entirely integrated into 'civilization', or of the romantic desire to understand and document the Welsh community in its condition of cultural purity prior to its inevitable contamination by external, alien influences (Day, 1979, Williams, 1977). However, as Michael points out in the second chapter, there was another quasi-sociological interest in Wales prior to this period of community studies. Among these students of Wales, Lleufer Thomas stands out. His work in relation to the Commission on Agricultural Labour and the Royal Commission on Land in Wales during the 1890s constitutes the earliest of modern rural sociology and its importance has scarcely been surpassed in subsequent rural sociologies. In tracing these early contributions to the sociology of Wales, Michael's chapter makes a useful addition to our knowledge about the link between social science research and policy in Wales.

Recent studies have focused upon social, cultural and economic change in Wales within a wider context. This is itself a response to the present crisis with sociologists increasingly confronting the issues which they study as much as involved social actors. It is hardly surprising therefore that, given the persistence of a need within Wales to look to the past in order to find security in the meaning of the present, a historical perspective is central to such studies, and it is no coincidence that the contributions in this volume mix the present with the past in their analyses of Welsh society.

Yet the past and the present often seem to have a great deal in common. The process of economic restructuring during the industrial revolution bears many similarities to the recent economic changes in Wales, especially insofar as changes in social formation and hegemonic and legitimation responses are concerned. Such intense changes in the social formation generate a crises of hegemony, which

> ... requires and precipitates a consequent 'recomposition' of the whole social and ideological integument of the social formation (C.C.C.S., 1978:255).

Changes in economic structure involve changes in the social formation, changes which have to be legitimized by ideological forces which can in turn generate significant economic responses. It is towards understanding this complexity of change in Wales that the contributions to this volume strive.

The relationship between capitalism and the state in the nineteenth century was encapsulated by the role of liberalism as the predominant feature of the legitimizing ideology. It argued that within a 'free' market economy no producer could ignore competition from other producers and consequently it was claimed that the only role of the state involved the creation of the juridical basis for this economic competition. In reality of course, the state played a central role in the emergence of the very concentration of capital which has served to supress liberalism. Rather than organizing competition the state stimulated it to the extent that monopolistic tendencies emerged. Thus the large industrial enterprises which appeared in the nineteenth century served to eliminate the petty commodity producers who were so central to the earlier economy. It was only those enterprises which offered complementary benefits to the new industrial production which survived. Evidently some economic interests were being eliminated while others were being advanced. In a sense we witness the articulation of economic forms which in many respects resembles the articulation of distinct modes of production since the relations of production in each economic 'system' are substantially different. In reality of course the relations of production in each are essentially capitalist relations. It is the early form of monopolism and its influence upon the social formation which needs to be highlighted.

The ownership of the means of production associated with the industrialization of Wales during the first half of the nineteenth century was almost exclusively English. It was not until the development of anthracite coal, which required far less capital, that we see the emergence of a native bourgeoisie of any size. There were examples of early Welsh capitalists such as Thomas Williams of the Anglesey copper industry or the quarrying interests of the Penrhyn family. Many of these were 'classified' as English in that they had distanced themselves from the indigenous language and culture. This was part of the ideological ploy of the emergent nationalism of the first half of the nineteenth century which sought to label industrial capitalism as an alien, English phenomenon, so that all of the associated social problems which accompanied it were blamed on the English. This much is evident from an analysis of the nationalist philosophy of Michael D. Jones, the leading nationalist of the nineteenth century (Chapter II). This nationalism was a reaction on the part of those who felt excluded from, or influenced by, the industrial developments. It is hardly surprising therefore that its underlying ethos was a form of equality based upon the persistence of petty commodity production and a 'small is beautiful' element which advocated the universal ownership of sufficient land and livestock to guarantee family subsistence.

The relationship between the economic developments and the occupational structure are outlined in Chapter 3. It is here that we begin to comprehend the disparate forms of social and cultural contradictions and antagonisms with in such developments. They were particularly manifest during the 1830s at which time labour organization and the ownership of capital were in direct confrontation. This heralded a less violent struggle involving the rising bourgeoisie and the established aristocracy. The location of these class fractions in the changing economic struggle is important in our understanding of the nature of the confrontation. The native petit-bourgeoisie was expanding and some of its members expanded into a fully fledged Welsh bourgeoisie later in the century. The aristocracy on the other hand were struggling to retain their position and found themselves being displaced by the new bourgeoisie of the industrial sector. Not that this separation of fractions of the bourgeoisie was deep rooted for we do find members of the aristocracy who played a central role in the industrial process, and members of the new industrial bourgeoisie integrated into aristocratic institutions and married into aristocratic families. Any antagonism between them appears to have been short lived.

A central feature of Lovering's discussion of the economy in Wales in Chapter 4 is the link between modes of production or phases of a single mode of production. In his reference to the nineteenth century he considers the relationship between the residual, feudal and the capitalist modes of production. Evidently the persistence of what were essentially feudal relations of production was of benefit to the owners of the means of production. It is unfortunate that such a persistence has tended to be discussed in terms of a romantic 'tradition of Welsh culture'. This is particularly true of medieval legal structures (Williams n.d.). Despite the persistence of feudal forms into the nineteenth century a more crucial relationship was that between the new industrial economy and the residual petty-commodity production. While both were phases of the capitalist mode of production there is little doubt concerning the determinate ascendancy of the former over the latter. Unfortunately we know little about the changes in the social formation which resulted from this form of articulation. Williams' discussion of the changing occupational structure in Chapter 3 is a useful contribution but we must realise that there is a significant difference between occupation and class. As our understanding of the relevant changes develops we should recognise that history consists of economic development and under-development as a drama being acted out by collective actors who are locked in a struggle to maintain or change a system of dominance and exploitation. Furthermore we should accept that there are as many features of exploitation as there are dimensions of inequality and to discuss change exclusively in terms of class exploitation is a gross over-simplification.

The nationalism which developed in mid-century was influenced by the sweeping developments in Europe during the second quarter of the nineteenth century but to treat it simply as a feature of the diffusion of ideas will not get us very far. The ideology which served as the basis for this nationalism is analyzed in Chapter 11. It was argued that the development of an externally owned industrial capitalism and its impact on the residual petty-commodity sector was responsible for generating a reaction in the form of a philosophy which emphasized the small self-sufficient entrepreneur. It was a petit-bourgeoisie nationalism led by a fusion of the new petit-bourgeoisie of the emerging commercial sector and the petit-bourgeoisie of the declining petty-commodity sector. It is hardly surprising therefore that in the long run it was transformed into a vibrant liberal radicalism, thereby losing much of its nationalist flavour. Certainly the explicit nationalism never penetrated very far into the popular consciousness. This liberalism was an opposition to the ownership of the large agricultural estates and advocated the liberation of the small tenants who worked the land. Opposition was to the ruling artistocratic class rather than to the new industrial bourgeoisie.

While the land issue would appear to appeal to the rural peasantry it would seem that there might be less appeal to the associated political movement among the industrial proletariat. On the other hand, as several sociologists have recently emphasized, the distinction between rural and urban/industrial may well constitute a false dichotomy. Certainly the structure of rural and urban societies was, in many respects, similar. Much of the industrial proletariat was integrated into single industry communities where the ownership and managerial staff were the leaders of the non-conformist chapels while also holding close links with Liberalism. There is also some evidence that there was an overlap between this leadership and that of the unions. Within such communities the link between economic ownership and religious and political leadership extended to patronage ties which linked work and politics. Under such circumstances it is difficult to develop a political opposition to economic ownership. It is perhaps significant that apart from local gains at the turn of the century the Labour party does not gain universally in industrial Wales until ownership in the coal industry takes the form of a depersonalized combine. While such a suggestion is tentative there is little doubt that our analyses of the shift of political ascendancy between the Liberal and Labour parties must move beyond the simplistic interpretation which involves a polarization between non-conformism and trade unionism.

The focus of the struggle for the support of, and control over, the proletariat and peasantry was religion which, as a consequence, became polarized between the various non-conformist sects on the one hand, and the Church of England on the other. This opposition was accommodative in the sense that, unlike the link between Chartism and non-conformism in the 1830s, it was not a debate about capitalism and alternatives to capitalism, but rather about the form which capitalism should take and which action should control it. Industrial capitalism appears to have entered the realm of the 'taken for granted' by mid-century. Thus the liberal ideology was central to the development of the relationship between non-conformism and nationalism. The emergence of non-conformism in Wales generated a crisis of hegemony which was much more far-reaching than in England. Since the sixteenth century which saw the simultaneous introduction of the Reformation, the Act of Union and the translation of the Bible into Welsh, religion had served as the main agency of the state's ideological control, with the Welsh language in Wales being the medium of ideological transmission. Central to this hegemonic order in Wales was the legitimation of the territorial state which had been consolidated by the Act of Union but which found its legitimacy in Wales challenged during the nineteenth century. Non-conformism was not under state control, indeed for some sects control was vested in the individual congregation. A new institutional structure was established which not only trespassed into the traditional domain of state ideological control but which was also capable of transmitting an ideology which challenged the state. Furthermore, in Wales, it could occur through the medium of a language which was not under state control in terms of its agencies of reproduction. This revolutionary potential of a minority language had become evident as early as the 1830s and 1840s when an alliance between Chartism and non-conformism was imminent. It emphasized the need for an alternative agency of ideological control. The Welsh language had either to be expropriated or eliminated. Thus we recognize the importance in Wales of the emergence of a system of compulsory education, a system carried out exclusively through the medium of English. Thus the domain restriction of the Welsh language and its subsequent reproduction within a restricted institutional context which focused upon civil society was no coincidence but was a manifestation of a changing power relationship. It is not surprising that such an interpretation of education in nineteenth century Wales has been slow in developing and the chapter by Catrin Roberts (Chapter 14) goes a long way towards reorientating our understanding of education in Wales away from the received wisdom of education as the basis for individual 'progress'. The shift away from a view of inequality in economic terms to its discussion in terms of 'educational opportunity' meant that Welsh people came to strive for recognition on the very terms which were the basis of their oppression, both in economic and in ethnic terms.

A similar interpretation can be made of that feature of the popular culture of the time which has subsequently been interpreted in behavioural terms as the Welsh peoples' 'love of music and literature'. Some sociologists (Clarke, Critcher and Johnson, 1979) see popular culture as the basis of ideological control which also has the potential of developing into a 'counter culture'. It tends to contrast with a 'high culture' which is seen as the prerogative of the dominant classes (Bourdieu, 1973), serving as the basis for differentiating and distancing the social classes from one another, thereby serving to legitimize the reproduction of the class structure. Rarely is the congruence of 'popular culture' and 'high culture' given any attention. This was precisely the case in nineteenth century Wales with musical and literary ability being reproduced within the community. A case can be made for this phenomenon being viewed as the basis for ideological control. There are examples of industrialists and members of the gentry purchasing instruments and encouraging the choral activities in the belief that it served as the basis for good work habits while the creation of literary societies in the community by the gentry was seen as an explicit creation of ideological interests which countered those produced in the non-conformist institutions. This is less true of the poetic tradition which was reproduced in the community and which was integrated, together with other features of what is generally regarded as 'high culture', into the eisteddfod tradition. It is only recently that the basis for the reproduction of this 'high culture' in Wales has shifted from the community and its institutions to the formal institutions of state education with the result that the overlap between 'popular culture' and 'high culture' has weakened. This would appear to be a topic that is worthy of further study in Wales.

The most obvious consequence of the emergence of industrial capitalism was population growth, geographic mobility and the associated spatial redistribution of population. There has been an unfortunate tendency to discuss migration in non-structural terms, the emphasis being upon the individual propensity to migrate or not to migrate. Fortunately, such an approach is much less accessible to the historian. In Chapters 7 and 10, Rees and Rees and Lewis respectively consider the relationship between economic developments and migration trends. At first the migration consisted of movements to the new industrial areas from adjoining rural areas but as industrialization intensified the in-migrating population was drawn from further afield. For a time the south Wales industrial area represented a 'core' area in the sense that there were abundant employment opportunities with skilled workers being paid particularly high wages. These high wages derived from a competition for a limited pool of skilled labour between different industrial areas in Britain. Also evident was a process of step-by-step migrations in which local agricultural labourers moved to the adjoining industrial area to be replaced by a workforce drawn from the south west of England. This was an important factor in the rapid erosion of the Welsh language in the Vale of Glamorgan. Within the coalfield the large number of Welsh speakers, together with an institutional structure within civil society which was organized on the basis of the language countered the attempts on the part of the state to eliminate the language through its domain limitation. This relationship between migration trends and the salience of the Welsh language is discussed in the chapter by Lewis (Chapter 10).

It remains for someone to consider in detail the relationship between language reproduction and social reproduction in the nineteenth century. As a consequence of the consolidation of the domain limitations, a process which is discussed in Chapter 10 and 14, the Welsh language was eliminated from the domains and institutions of primary social reproduction. Associated with this development, which served to denigrate the native language and its speakers, was an ideology which countered the emerging Welsh nationalism. This ideology emphasized the relationship between the dominant language and a social mobility which was presented in terms of the characteristic liberal notion of the enterprising individual. English was presented as the language of reason which left Welsh as the language of something other than reason, spoken only by the 'unenterprising individual'. In addition to stressing the hegemony of the English language the ideology laid the basis for a strong British nationalism which was presented as the converse of a parochial Welsh nationalism. At this time the British nationalism was explicit and in contrast to the 'common sense' nature of the present day British nationalism.

Yet the idea of Wales persisted. Having emerged in the nineteenth century out of changes in the social formation associated with the economic changes of the industrial revolution, it coincided with a more explicit state ideological involvement in which a sense of British identity associated with the idea of Empire was diffused through new state-controlled agencies of ideological control. The tension between the two ideologies was a manifestation of the struggle between classes and class fractions striving to mobilize support among the masses. We are only beginning to understand the nature of these tensions within the context of sociological analysis and it would be useful if historians could shift from a consideration of 'when was Wales?'[2] (Williams, G. A., : 1979) to the question of 'why is Wales?'.

The economic changes which have occurred since 1936 have, in some respects had similar effects as the profound changes which occurred as a consequence of the industrial revolution. The two significant factors associated with these more recent changes are monopolism and the associated state intervention. It involves an attempt to re-structure the economy following the disaster of the 1920s and the 1930s when half a million people were obliged to leave Wales. The change which is outlined in Chapters 4 and 5, involved a shift from primary production to an economy which emphasized manufacturing and an associated service sector. Within the labour force heavy manual labour performed by males has been replaced by semi-skilled, assembly work and non-manual jobs performed by a female labour force. It seems that, apart from the financial incentives offered by state intervention, the existence of a cheap non-unionized female labour force was the main attraction for many of the firms which were located in Wales within the context of the 'regional development programme'.

In Chapter 4 Lovering draws upon the work of Quijano Obregon (1974) in drawing up a typology of the economy in Wales. He suggests the existence of three sectors: firstly an 'enclave' which is divisible into two parts, a monopology sector of large and medium sized firms which are predominantly owned outside Britain and medium sized enterprises owned in parts of Britain outside of Wales. An increasing number of firms are owned outside of Britain, being part of what Rawkins identifies in Chapter 13 as part of the process whereby Britain, within the world economy, is relegated from a 'core' to a 'semi-peripheral' position in which it serves as both exploiter and exploited. It is manifest in the recent process whereby simultaneously the economy within Britain is becoming increasingly de-industrialized while its external economy is expanding. There is little doubt that the shakeout associated with the present recession will increase the monopolistic tendencies. A feature of these developments is the increased state intervention, with public money being employed to finance the location of non-British firms close to the European market where the cost of labour is reduced by this grant aid. The British firms owned outside of Wales are equally monopolistic and are generally branch extensions. These two groups of enterprises form an enclave of high productivity employing high wage unskilled labour, having weak linkages with Welsh enterprises, and with advanced production functions located outside of Wales. As a consequence of growth pole policies and the locational needs of certain establishments the tendency has been for the 'enclave' to be spatially limited to areas close to the major communication arteries and at specific growth poles.

A consequence of such 'enclave' development is the progressive marginalization of enterprises which are not included in this integrated sector. It is a consequence of the monopolistic effect and its relationship to social and economic policy. It constitutes Lovering's third sector. The enterprises within this sector tend to be small, consisting often of family labour, self-employed personnel and workers with relatively low remuneration. It reveals a tendency towards occupational pluralism as well as substantial mobility between the self-employed and skilled worker occupational categories. It is a consequence of marginalization that small enterprises are eliminated and the petit-bourgeoisie proletarianized. Those enterprises which do survive do so as a result of their limited ability to survive as capitalist enterprises, often as a result of their integration as providers of cheap services in their articulation with the integrated sector.

In Chapter 5 Cooke elaborates upon this structure in his discussion of the uneven development of capitalism. He outlines how the regional division of labour serves to stratify the spatial organization of capitalism. He indicates how, by 1975, Wales had developed a threefold division of labour involving deindustrialized regions, branch plant regions and what he terms 'archipelago' regions. Associated is a tendency to elaborate a tertiarization and feminization of the economy. Thus he develops on Lovering's conceptualization in specifying the dynamic nature of the changing economic and labour force structures especially as related to the role of the female in the labour force. One needs only proceed a step further in order to recognize the link between gender, ethnicity and space as three crucial inter-related dimensions of inequality. The dynamics of this inter-relationship begin to emerge in Cooke's chapter.

Given the extent of the restructuring of the economy it is inevitable that there will be significant repercussions. The two papers by the Reeses and Morgan (Chapter 6 and 7) tell us something about the manner in which the circulation of capital has generated specific patterns of population movement. What is interesting about these contributions is that they focus upon a marginalized area in the south Wales valleys on the one hand and on a comparison of a rural growth pole and a rural marginalized location. Morgan looks at patterns of out-migration from a rural area in west Wales and underlines the tendency for young people with high educational qualifications to leave such areas. Unfortunately while considerable attention has been given to out-migration, studies of population in Wales have told us little about in-migration. Morgan's chapter begins to remedy this deficiency. He indicates that much of the in-migration consists of people of retirement age and, in the case of the growth pole centres, of skilled workers from outside of Wales. This is part of the process which tends to polarize the residual native population and the in-migrants which, in general, tend increasingly to be associated respectively with the marginalized and 'enclave' sectors. This is substantiated in the observations made by Grant (n.d.) and Carter and Williams (1978) of the correlation between social indicators and the ability to speak the Welsh language. It is here that we witness animosoties which assume an ethnic dimension and which further complicates the process of economic development. The work of Rees and Rees on migration patterns in the south Wales industrial area deserves a wider audience than it has thus far received since it tells us a great deal about the responses of those most directly affected by the process of marginalization that has been developing in the valleys. In their chapter they show how

> ... migration is in itself an integral element in the determination of both the strategy adopted by capital in respect to restructuring and the nature of the worker's response to it.

Their study assumes particular importance in light of the continued running down of the south Wales coalfield and the phasing out of steel production in south Wales.

Perhaps we should look to changes in the class structure which derive from the economic restructuring for the most revealing indication of political and ideological developments. Unfortunately we know too little about the class structure in contemporary Wales. It is unfortunate that the S.S.R.C. sponsored studies of social mobility in England, Scotland and Ireland were not extended to include Wales. In the English study (Goldthorpe, 1980) Wales was treated as part of England which, together with the inability to fund a Welsh study, tells us a great deal about the way in which Wales is conceptualized, or rather not conceptualized, within the same 'common sense' of most British sociologists. As a consequence the contributions in this volume which refer to class are obliged to operate from a limited amount of empirical data.

Chapter 9 refers to a discussion about class in Welsh rural society which has generated considerable discussion in recent years. During the 1950s Dafydd

Jenkins (1960) claimed that within the rural community which he had studied the significant social division involved the idea of 'buchedd' which was claimed to have a greater salience than social class. This was criticised by Day and Fitton (1975) who disagreed. The debate in Chapter 9 underlines the fact that 'buchedd' is nothing more than an explication of the Weberian concept of status group, in this case, a division which draws class fractions together across class lines. Once this is recognised the significant question involves the circumstances under which status groups achieve such a salience. Perhaps the most obvious feature is that since the Welsh language was restricted during the nineteenth century to domains and institutions of language reproduction which were marginal to social reproduction, class varieties of both language and culture - seen as the ideological basis of social reproduction - were but poorly developed. The direct cultural reproduction which reinforced class divisions were related to the dominant language and culture. It is hardly surprising therefore that the institutional structure within which both the Welsh language and culture were reproduced were akin to status groups nor that 'emic' class reference was weak. This in no way implies that class did not exist, nor that Welsh culture was irrelevant to social reproduction. Also relevant to this question is the impact of the process of marginalization upon class in that it serves to fragment the class structure and separate actors from their 'natural' class allies. Within the marginalized sector the process of making a living tends to be individualized, there is also an exaggerated opportunity for self-employment, for work to be organized in small enterprises and for the employed to show a considerable mobility between the skilled worker (proletariat) and self-employed (petit-bourgeoisie) employment categories in both directions. Given the perilous nature of employment within the marginalized sector and the existence of most of the ethnic cohorts of bourgeoisie status in the very public sector which serves to compensate for the marginal status, alliances between this bourgeoisie - which contrasts with the non-Welsh bourgeoisie who dominate the private sector - and the proletariat of the marginalized sector makes sense. Most evident of course is that we should abandon the rural-urban/industrial dichotomy and replace it with the enclave/marginalized distinction.

Within the private sector, given the external ownership of the means of production, the management and middle management will tend to be non-Welsh, consisting of spiralists whose period of residence in Wales is limited. Their mobility patterns contrast with patterns of burgher mobility among the native population. Fletcher (1978) has discussed such spiralists elsewhere. In this volume (Chapter 8) he focuses upon burgher mobility by reference to the relationship between position within the hierarchical structure of the 'works' and position in civil society. The link between them is held to be crucial in understanding local social mobility. In a sense it can be seen as a defence mechanism against the intrusion of outsiders in that local mobility patterns can be controlled through the exerting of closure in civil society rather than within the work setting. This fascinating discussion certainly lends new insight into the relationship between social mobility and the wider class structure.

The period which Fletcher described was the optinum period for steel and the subsequent gutting of the industry has had a profound impact upon the essence of community and cross-class alliances in the threat of external power.[3] Indeed rather than the conceptualisation of community in geographical and interactional terms it is time that we began to see it in terms of the principal that where there is power there is resistance. Thus community is not more than the social practice of resistance in the face of the power of the state while this, and the form of inter-class alliance which Fletcher describes, will not please orthodox Marxists and welfare liberalists it does extend the analysis away from the limitations of class reductionism. It also leads to a realisation that the failure of state intervention in the form of 'regional development' or 'cowboy capitalism' which Fletcher (1978) has previously discussed together with the associated undermining of the 'nationalised' (sic) sector leaves the community little choice but to act in its own defence. The implications of individual life for social life are profound.

In Chapter 5 Cooke discusses variation in the incorporation of labour within a historical context. He shows how different patterns of work control in different industries and the emergence of craft unionisms are crucial in understanding intra-class divisions. The issue of relationships between spheres of production and reproduction in constituting class relations are also considered. His chapter is an important contribution to our, thus far, limited understanding of social class in Wales.

Given the accelerated redistribution of population which results from the economic reorganization it is not surprising that we have witnessed the collapse of the previous tendency for marriages to be endogamous by language group in areas where the proportion of the population which spoke Welsh was high. This, together with the decline in religious involvement, means that the two institutions which served as the agencies of Welsh language reproduction no longer fulfill that function. The erosion of the language leads to a concern on the part of those class fractions which are threatened by this development and demands are made for the reinstitutionalization and religitimization of the Welsh language in new domains and institutions. This is most evident with reference to education and the mass media (Williams and Roberts, 1983). However, since these are institutions which are firmly located within the ideological domain of the state rather than in civil society it would appear that such an extension constitutes a form of language expropriation. As a consequence it is conceivable that the language will survive but that it will be employed to transmit and reproduce the ideology of the state and the associated dominant ethnic group. Thus while the language survives, the culture will disappear. Some of the circumstances surrounding this process are discussed in Chapters 10 and 14.

Since the 'major' parliamentary parties have been responsible for the reorganisation of the economic structure in Wales it is to be expected that any reaction to such economic policies would come from outside of these parties. Evidently the reaciton will come from those classes and class fractions most adversely affected by the developments. Furthermore, we should also recognize that the changes place demands on all political parties regardless of their philosophies. Yet the issue of nationalism has its own appeal in terms of sociological analysis to the extent that it is in danger of being misunderstood through reification. In the past, nationalism was integrated into the philosophies of both the Labour and Liberal parties where it remains, and in many respects it is naive to conceive of nationalism simply in terms of voting behaviour and support for an explicitly separatist platform. Nonetheless, it is interesting to consider the emergence of Plaid Cymru as a political force in Wales and the nature of its support and appeal. Unfortunately, such an analysis has tended to rely heavily upon the concept of 'cultural nationalism', the tendency being to correlate what are held to be the diacritica of culture - most often the ability to speak Welsh or the frequency of religious participation - with voting behaviour and thereby to 'explain' political behaviour in terms of culture. The origin of this 'culture' is unexplained except in terms of a residual form of atavism while the relationship of political behaviour to social structure is unnecessary given the culturalist nature of the argument.

The two chapters by Aull (Chapter 12) and Rawkins (Chapter 13) seek an alternative viewpoint on nationalism. Aull emphasises the role of the increased penetration of the state into the lives of the masses with the growth of the welfare state. An associated feature has been the decentralization of the administrative apparatus which has served to legitimize the idea of Wales. Morgan (1980) makes a similar point in his valuable discussion of regional policy with reference to Wales and the British state, claiming that it was pressure from within Wales which was responsible for the granting of concessions not available to other regions. While there is considerable value in this point, we should recognize that it is not simply a matter of the state granting concessions. It is no coincidence that this process of decentralization occurred at the same time as direct state intervention in the economy took the form of 'regional development'. It was also inevitable that, in time, the two processes should unite in the form of the creation of the Welsh Development Agency. In a sense the processs of decentralization can be seen as a product of the administrative feature of democratic state ideology (Williams and Roberts, 1983). Within the democratic framework the state cannnot be seen to be over-centralized and dictatorial. An appearance of democratic liberalism is conveyed by decentralization. While an impression of the decentralization of power is conveyed, in reality it is only responsibility that is devolved, power remains firmly located in the centre. Nonetheless the effect is to convey the impression of the disassociation of the state from responsibility for any consequences which emerge as a result of its economic policies while also making any of the state's resources which are distributed appear to be a consequence of the state's altruism towards the 'region'. Furthermore, any conflict which emerges as a consequence of state policy tends to be acted out within the region, or even locally, rather than being related to the role of the state. It is this complexity which makes it difficult for nationalism to be seen as an opposition to the state. On the other hand there is no doubt that decentralization not only legitimizes the idea of Wales but also generates further demands for functional 'autonomy', demands which, as a consequence of the image of democracy which it represents, the state is obliged to respond to insofar as they do not present a threat to its ultimate authority.

Rawkins relates his discussion of nationalism in Wales to Wallerstein's (1979) conceptualization of a capitalist world economy. He claims that the shift in the status of Britain from that of a 'core' state to a 'semi-peripheral' state has significant repercussions for inter-regional relationships within Britain. Among these repercussions are the increased concentration of investment in the south east of England and the process of 'enclave' development within Wales which was referred to in Chapter 3. He underlines the point made in this introduction, that nationalism emerges as a manifestation of crises associated with periods of economic transition in both the nineteenth and twentieth centuries. He further emphasizes that as a periphery within a semi-periphery the politics of Wales reflects the '... pattern of dependency that its economic structure would lead us to expect.' The essence of nationalism is to develop a philosophy which allows the integration of people across class lines, the recognition of which should lead us to ask the question: under what structural conditions are such alignments likely to develop? I believe that they involve the fragmentation of classes which derives from marginalization, the associated employment patterns and the extent to which features of ethnicity can be employed to mobilize actors across class lines as a form of defence (Williams, 1981).

Finally we should be wary of thinking that all struggles involving different fractions of the social formation are operating at the level of infrastructure. There is also the struggle for hegemony involving conflicts over access to ideological and political resources. This is emphasized by Roberts in the final chapter when she points out that one of the major contributions of recent developments in the sociology of education has been its emphasis upon the role of education as a central aspect of the production and reproduction of ideological control. This should be nowhere more evident than in Wales where this function must relate both to the legitimization of the state in the face of the threat presented by nationalism and also to the legitimization of class relationships.

CHAPTER 2

BEFORE ALWYN : THE ORIGINS OF SOCIOLOGY IN WALES[1]

David Michael

> The first sociological studies undertaken in the principality developed as an aspect of social anthropology in the Department of Geography and Anthroplogy at the University College of Wales, Aberystwyth. The pioneer study of the rural parish of Llanfihangel-yng-Ngwynfa - Life in a Welsh Countryside (1950), by Alwyn D. Rees was followed by similar studies of several other rural communities.
>
> Jac L. Williams (1968)

> Early British social anthropologists, under the stimulus of the imperial tradition, and the conviction that primitive societies were somehow simpler and easier to understand, had been largely concerned with cultures and societies outside of Britain. But Aberystwyth was very far removed from the imperial ideal . . . . The result of this remoteness, physically and culturally, from the imperial tradition was the application of anthropological methods in a local context and the beginnings of the scientific study of Welsh society, particularly of the rural communities. Most of this work was directed by Alwyn D. Rees.
>
> H. Carter & W. Davies (1976)

> . . . . . The Aberystwyth School appears to have been the only academic tradition in Wales with an institutional and unified basis for social scientific studies specifically on aspects of the social structure of Wales.
>
> Glyn Williams (1978)

The above statements are provided as illustrations of the received view of the origins of sociology in Wales. Rather than discuss them directly I would prefer to examine the evidence for early social movements and research to establish that Rees' work did not appear as if by some immaculate conception, and as a corollary of this, to suggest Life in a Welsh Countryside may in important respects represent a divergence from the emerging mainstream of British sociology, as practised within Wales and beyond its borders in recent decades.

If at first sight, the activities presented here may seem to possess no theoretical cohesiveness since they embody a range of intellectual practices, social speculation, and empirical enquiry, they indisputably share this feature with the entire early sociological movement. In Wales, as elsewhere,

> . . . . sociological empiricism in bourgeois sociology was in its origins closely associated with movements of social reform - the Protestant origins of the Chicago School in the United States, the Fabians and early twentieth-century research in Britain, the Vereinfur Social-politik and similar developments in Germany. (Birnbaum, 1979)

The young sociological movement in Britain reflected many intellectual cross-currents - 'the condition of the people question', 'the quest for national efficiency' of the Social Imperialists, the concerns of the Labour Movement, and the response to and synthesis of these within the New Liberalism.

In the early twentieth century, with the reproductive functions of the State growing through increasing governmental intervention in social welfare, many Welshmen were drawn to serve in the new machinery. If some like Thomas Jones moved to London to participate more centrally in Lloyd George's service, many others remained loyal servants of the New Liberalism and advocates of reconstruction within Wales. Thomas Jones, amelioristic social engineer par excellence, achieved much of his influence through an extensive network of state functionaries and wealthy industrialists, not least of whom were David Davies, Daniel Lleufer Thomas, Percy Watkins, and other like-minded Welshmen in social movements paralleling those already existing in England.

Some Early Welsh Social Movements

For heuristic purposes we can do no better than to follow Halliday's (1968) categorisation of the early British sociological movement into three schools:

> (1) A school of ethical or social work sociologists - 'which owed much to the political and ethical philosophy taught at Balliol. This kind of sociological thinking was dominant in the Central Office of Statistics, the Christian Social Union, The Social Institutes Union, and in the ethical movement as a whole'. According to this school '. . . sociology established the fact that society and its co-operative institutions was largely a product of man's rational

capacity. Hence sociological investigation was necessarily involved with an application of co-operative ideals and social responsibilities, questions of value could not be kept out, and practical sociology implied doing social work in furtherance of co-operative ideals'. (Halliday, 1968:390). The practical and vocational aspect involved settlement work, efforts to establish professional training for social work, and providing sociological expertise for those engaged in voluntary and charitable endeavours. Typical figures were C. S. Loch, Charles Booth, L. T. Hobhouse and Henry Jones.

(2) A school of racial sociologists, represented by the Eugenics Education Society, and such scholars as Galton and Karl Pearson.

(3) A school of civic sociologists or town planners, associated with the names of Patrick Geddes and his collaborators who were '. . . . attempting to reassert the importance of environmental factors in human evolution and to refute any sociology or biology which set heredity and environment in opposition to each other. For this reason, it was a school concerned to popularise the sociological method of Le Play and to establish the City as a natural phenomenon . . . . Hence, for this school, sociology was the science of man's interaction with a natural environment; the basic technique was the regional survey, and the improvement of town planning the chief practical application of sociology' (Halliday, 1968:380).

In the early years of its existence from 1903, the Sociological Society inadvertantly became a battleground for the three schools, failing to advance the civic sociology its main founders propounded. As Halliday shows us, the Ethical School was able to successfully impose its definition of sociology upon new university teaching departments, initially at Liverpool and the London School of Economics, with the other two schools being shunted into specialised disciplinary sidings, although civics exerted some influence over another embryonic university subject, Geography.

Within Wales, Galton's variant of sociology was encapsulated in the anthropometric investigations and correlative studies of Fleure's Aberystwyth School of cultural geography. Desite what we now know to be its dubious scientific basis, its ideological significance, as a recent author suggests (Stepan, 1982) is not inconsiderable. In the skillful hands of E. G. Bowen and Alwyn Rees, the translation of their mentor's biologically based classification into a socially based one, became a means of 'naturalising' Welsh culture. This alone suggests an extended analysis of the Aberystwyth school of racial sociology - written from 'outside' - is long overdue. Whilst not attempted here, I will return to its implications for sociologies of Wales in the conclusion.

The examination begins with a description of two organisations, alike in their normative concerns and with a considerable coincidence of leadership and membership, yet sufficiently distinct in their main emphasis to support the view that they represent in the early sociology movement in Wales, Halliday's first and third categories 'ethical' and 'civic'.

I have already introduced the name of D. Lleufur Thomas (1863-1940), a man who stood astride both organisations, indefatigable in his activities as initiator, propagandist, officer, spokesman, '. . . . the most important social thinker in Wales of that era' (Stead, 1977; Jones, 1942; Jenkins, 1940). As a young man Thomas served his apprenticeship in social research as an investigator and officer of those uniquely British institutions, the Royal and Parliamentary Commission, institutions respected, even envied by researchers in other European nations. He emerged with credit from his duties on behalf of the 1893 Commission on Agricultural Labour and the Royal Commission on Land in Wales, 1893-6.

The Welsh School of Social Service / Cyfysgol Gwasanaeth Cymdeithasol dros Gymru

When D. Lleufer Thomas addressed the 1910 Assembly of Welsh Independents, traditionally the most politically radical of Welsh non-conformist sects, at Lampeter, he urged that the churches of Wales constructively study the problems of modern society. The socially oriented Christianity growing in influence across the border had, he thought, relevance to a Wales in the grip of a Calvinistic theology so emphatically spiritual in character that it insulated believers from the more unpalateable aspects of poverty and squalor. From Thomas' call there emerged in 1911 the School of Social Service. It promptly issued a bilingual manifesto on the principle of a living-wage, a concern evident in the Second School of 1912 where Thomas Jones spoke on 'The Problem of Expenditure : Personal, Domestic, Social' and there was an exhibition devoted to the 'sweated trades'. The early organisational work fell on Thomas, the Rev. Gwilym Davies, and Professor Miall Edwards of Brecon Theological College. Whilst it had no trouble in attracting distinguished social activists from outside Wales to address its Schools with Will Reason, Tom Bryan, Arthur Greenwood, Arnold Rowntree, J. J. Mallon being amongst them, the burden was carried by hundreds of local members ready to give informed papers on urban and rural social questions of every description. Silyn Roberts, Edgar Chappell, R. Stapledon Cotton, T. Gwynn Jones, Abel J. Jones, Alwyn Lloyd, William George,

Percy Watkins, Alun Roberts, Bryner Jones, Saunders Lewis, F. W. Gilbertson, and David Thomas are names outstanding for their wide-ranging activism as public men.

Prior to the war the School was primarily a forum, its gatherings a 'clearing house for ideas' and 'moulders of opinion on social issues'. In the immediate post-war period it became, predictably, preoccupied with matters of reconstruction. Gradually, it then came to place a greater emphasis on encouraging professional social investigation and local community surveys such as that undertaken by its Aberdare branch during the war-years, rather than upon the formation of public opinion. This shift was not unconnected with the social changes which rendered the pre-war 'social season' enjoyed at the Welsh spas by middle-class Welsh 'influentials' a thing of the past. It was this rare opportunity to corner a select audience that explains the School's early choice of Llandrindod Wells as a venue until 1925. One officer tells us that ". . . . its impressive array of nine vice-presidents could be relied upon to choose the better boarding homes and superior hotels . . . .' of the fashionable watering places. The decision to change course in the mid nineteen twenties is reflected in the change of venue, first to Caerleon Training College in south Wales, then to the newly opened Coleg Harlech in 1927 and 1928, perhaps seeking converts amongst a new audience of adherents to the dynamic new secular religions of labour politics, trades unionism, and adult education.

This latter development did not meet with any great success. The School remained in existence until the out-break of War when, in 1940, the Council of Coleg Harlech ". . . . accepted the invitation of the Council of Management of the Welsh School of Social Service to continue its work and to undertake responsibility for its future development", deciding ". . . . the name of the new organization be The Coleg Harlech School of Social Studies". This was not to be.

The Welsh Housing and Development Association

In Wales, as in England, ". . . . the town planning movement was a small pressure group drawing support from the professions . . . . with little mass support. Its closest connections were with other groups such as the Fabians, the Sociological Society, and the Housing Reform Council" (Mellors, 1977:127). The earliest major expression of this movement was the north Wales based Welsh Housing Association (Cymdeithas Cartrefdai Cymru) emerging in 1909 under the Presidency of Lord Kenyon, followed in 1912 by the South Wales Garden City and Town Planning Association, headed by David Davies and D. Lleufer Thomas. The north Wales body was primarily engaged in building development whereas its southern counterpart directed its energies into political lobbying and propagandist activity. Both these early organizations desired an investigatory role, as one of the objects of the Welsh Housing Association reveals:

> To inquire into the conditions affecting housing and town planning in Wales and its borders; to collect, tabulate, and collate the results of scientific and economic observations, and to apply the same to the housing and cognate conditions of life in Wales.

Collaborations began in 1913 when they united to form a public utility, the Welsh Town Planning and Housing Trust, influenced by Ebenezer Howard in its goal of providing garden villages for workers. Together with officers already mentioned were Lady Boston, Lord Aberdare, F. W. Gilbertson and Edgar Chappel as Secretary. Garden Villages were constructed at Wrexham, Cardiff, Llanidloes, Machynlleth and Burry Port.

When in 1916, the south Wales group desired to expand its activities to include rural housing, this was achieved by a merger with the Welsh Housing Association to form the Welsh Housing and Development Association. This new organization was divided into north and south Wales branches, the northern branch including William George, Dr. Lewys Lloyd, (Medical Officer for Health, for Meirioneth), Mrs. Silyn Roberts, Sir Harry Reichel, and quarrymen's and other union representatives. Later council recruits were Stapledon-Cotton, David Thomas for the north Wales Trades Council and Patrick Abercrombie.

Assiduously seeking to bridge class-barriers, official trade union involvement was sought from the outset by the original south Wales organization. It successfully involved figures as notable as Sam Fisher of the Cardiff Coaltrimmers Union and S. O. Davies and Arthur Jenkins of the South Wales Miners' Federation. In 1917 the trades unions staged a conference on post-war housing policy at Cory Hall, Cardiff, with D. Lleufer Thomas in the chair. Later the Association extended its support to the ill-fated Guild Socialist Movement, much of whose strength came from building workers. These dispositions highlight a central aspect of the philosophy of the planning movement, an aspect with a good Victorian pedigree. As expressed in the Wales Report of the Commission on Industrial Unrest (1971), chaired by Lleufer Thomas, with Chappell as Secretary:

> The conviction that Capital and Labour are necessarily hostile, a conviction engendered by conflict on industrial matters, has been accentuated by the fact that the social conditions of the working

> classes are of an unsatisfactory character . . . It is clear . . . that unsatisfactory surroundings and the inadequacy of housing accommodation in Wales and Monmouthshire, and especially in the south Wales coalfield, is a factor of great importance in the causation of unrest.

As a disseminator of information and opinion its Welsh Housing Yearbook is impressive in its range and the quality of the contributions, whether it is E.T. John deliberating on the future of Welsh agriculture or the socialist planner George Unwin writing on hillside-siting. Unwin went on to design the Town Hill Council Estate at Swansea, an exemplary model for such developments. It would, though, involve some considerable research in order to attempt any assessment of the influence exerted over local authorities, the building industry and public opinion through this organisation and related activities.

Limitations of space restrict the discussion to noting some of the Welsh Housing Development Association's interventions as a pressure group. In 1916 it made bold representation to the Reconstruction Committee of the Cabinet, calling for a unified attack on the housing problem in rural Wales under the aegis of a new Welsh Board of Agriculture designed to co-ordinate a comprehensive reconstruction programme for rural Wales. Later, it more successfully encouraged the Local Government Board and its successor, the Ministry of Health to initiate a Welsh Regional Enquiry into Housing conditions. This resulted in 1920 in the establishment of the South Wales Regional Survey, amongst whose members the Association would count five supporters, in addition to Edgar Chappell as Secretary. Another representation which ultimately bore fruit was the Royal Commission on the University of Wales, where D. Lleufer Thomas and Alwyn Lloyd put the case for the teaching of architecture and town-planning in the University.

It may be that the Association did achieve some advances in raising the level of consciousness of the professional and growing white-collar strata including labour leaders with regard to standards of housing, health and environment, and thus contributed to the formation of Welsh political support for the later growth of state involvement. Whether limited ameliorative policies of class incorporation such as were embodied in the planning movement could in themselves achieve much is doubtful. The Coal Dispute and the General Strike could be taken as negative or positive evidence; ten years earlier Geddes had believed the frustration of his plan for modern workers' housing in Dublin had aborted the only measure capable of averting the 1916 Easter Rising! Certainly, after examining the Glasgow evidence on reconstruction housing policy, Butt (1979) concludes that, given the inadequacy of central and local government response ". . . about the question of whether housing policy actually made a contribution to a general 'programme' of incorporating the working classes and reducing class awareness and identity (he) can only express doubt". This does not, however, preclude the conclusion that this movement was, like Thomas Jones himself, an important articulator of 'a Welsh social Darwinism that mostly took itself for granted' (Smith, 1980 : 229). A satisfactory analysis of these two movements would require a much fuller consideration of the dynamics of class and status in the social structure of early twentieth century Wales. Here it is only possible to make some tentative preliminary points. From the evidence, it appears that, like elements of the American intelligentsia of a slightly earlier period, the rural background and non-conformist upbringing of many participants disposed them to seek secular forms of expression for an essentially Christian ethic. In so far as some of the key figures were clergymen having a reference group experiencing downward mobility as part of a secularisation process, there is value in restating Hofstadter's (1955) thesis,

> . . . it may not be unfair to attribute the turning of the clergy towards reform and social criticism not soley to their disinterested perception of social problems and their earnest desire to improve the world, but also to the fact that as men who were in their own way suffering from the incidence of the status revolution they were able to understand and sympathise with the problems of other disinherited groups.

At another level, the constituent propaganda on behalf of the regional development and devolution of central government functions to Wales, may well reflect no more than the experienced self-interest of this new governmental elite.

As organisations, the School of Social Service and the Housing and Development Association display many of the features familiar to the student of the natural history of social movements. The increasing differentiation between the role of 'organizer' and 'enthusiast' is evident in the career of Chappell, and the failure of the School of Social Service to acquire a vocational leadership through financing Davies as a full-time officer was a debilitating handicap.

From the outset, the influence of Patrick Geddes' civics was clear in the activities and rhetoric of the Welsh Housing and Development Association. The passing of the 1909 Town and Country Planning Act and the great Town Planning Exhibition and Conference, London, 1910 helped shape the immediate climate of opinion amongst public men in which the housing movement could flourish. Geddes had influenced the Act and was undoubtedly the star of the Exhibition. The Association strived to keep his thinking before a Welsh audience. His plans and surveys were displayed at an exhibition mounted by the Assocation for the 1921 School of Social Service at Llandrindod, his associates Unwin, Abercrombie and Fleure were enthusiastic supporters and D. Lleufer Thomas showed keeness for the idea of establishing a demographic survey display on Geddesian lines at the National Museum of Wales.

In the Housing Association's political statements we see many similarities with Geddes advocacy of Le Plays' Third Force Sociology, that is the new sociology and the new Liberalism as the theory and practice of a last stand against socialism. Eighty years earlier arithmetic had been the social scientists answer to politics, now it was town planning' (Abrams, 1968).

Most important in accounting for the decline of these movements is the ideological blow delivered by Lloyd George's enforced retreat from Reconstruction. Under Conservative and National Government's favouring unregulated capitalism, the Third Force, as distinctive politics or sociology was seriously impaired. Keynes, Beveridge, and the newer men of the Conservative and Labour Parties appropriated its thinking, with Lloyd George remaining in the political wilderness. The middle opinion in the thirties helped set the scene for the emergence of the welfare statism of the 1940s. Occasionally, we catch glimpses of the New Liberal and Geddesian panaceas in Welsh political life now re-clothed in the guise of the most novel contemporary synonym for regionalism and planning, 'T.V.A.'. For both movement, the most representative work, to appear was, paradoxically, by a non-member. Hilda Jennings' Brynmawr (1934) was the one excursion into Wales of the unadulterated Geddesian technique of a community self-survey, guided by the Sociological Institute at Le Play House, London and promoting Quaker ideas of co-operation in the face of what was perceived as unreasonably polarized attitudes on the part of labour and capital. This book can be viewed both as an early forerunner of action-research and community development, and as a monument, or if we prefer, a headstone, to a largely forgotten tradition of social research.

The decline of the voluntary effort in sociology coincides with the fulfillment of one of its aims, the growth of professional research, social work and town planning. As social investigation simultaneously acquired the form of natural science, and became professionalized, researchers increasingly disclaimed moral-political concerns. The ethical and civic schools of sociology may be appreciated as staging posts in this process. However, such an interpretation of the advance from 'pre-scientific' unrealistic reformism to 'scientific' sociology obscures the real character of the strategic shift of reformers from the spas to the academies of

Wales. The scientific trappings underwrote the relegitimation of the reformers' moral enterprise in the face of advancing secularisation.

Professional Social Science in Wales

At this point, there are advantages in introducing an important source of documentation on positions taken up by the Welsh radical intelligentsia. I refer to the Report of the Royal Commission on the University of Wales (1916), chaired by that major New Liberal, Lord Haldane, accompanied by another reconstructionist Sir Daniel Hall, and by Sir Henry Jones.[2]

In seeking a new paradigm for a higher education conceived differently to that of Oxbridge, the Germanophile Haldane had for a time turned away from the previously admired Prussian model to an enthusiasm for American mid-Western institutions. During the Commission proceedings it emerged that this interest was shared by certain witnesses, notably D. Lleufer Thomas. The most scrutinized American academy of the day was Wisconsin, a land-grant college. These institutions originated in the 1861 Act of Congress designed to improve agrarian communities, Wisconsin being the institution most closely associated with a progressive state regime, that of Robert la Follette. It boasted on its faculty a pioneer of university economics, friend of labour, and champion of academic freedom, Richard T. Ely (1854-1943), along with his own recruits, promising scholars including Frederick J. Turner, and John R. Commons. We can usefully view Ely as the American counterpart of many British radicals, his German education imbuing him with a respect for intellectual excellence and rigour that fused with American populist values into an appealing progressivism. Much of Wisconsin's reputation came from the international standing of such teachers, its record of service to its local community, grounded on research and extension work, its fostering of social as well as natural sciences, and its robust revolution against the social elitism and effete bookishness of the Eastern colleges.

Lleufer Thomas presented arguments, influenced by his reading of the Wisconsin experiment, designed to counter a perceived failure of the Welsh University Colleges to serve the people. With Thomas Jones and F. Llewellyn Jones, he propounded the idea of a social and administrative science faculty. "Do you look to the University to direct sociological investigation?" asked Haldane of Thomas. "Very largely, I do, and . . . I should like . . . . to cite the very remarkable work which is done in the University of Wisconsin . . . where all the sociological enquiries . . . are conducted directly for the State by people holding academic appointments". Haldane apparently, was now less optimistic about a system where academic standards may have been diluted in the achievement of democratic goals. However, if no consensus on future paths for the University existed, there is evidence of shared disatisfaction with its previous performance. The plea of C. Bryner Jones for a humanistically-directed agricultural education for Welsh farmers in place of the available scientific pot-pourri could be taken as an advocacy of teaching after the Wisconsin or Danish models.

The commission took the question of further extending university teaching to the community to heart, with action following from the University with the foundation of the Extension Board. If some of the other proposals advanced by witnesses were lost without trace, progress was made in at least one other direction. In 1919 the Government made £2 million available for agricultural education in Britain, with another £1 million derived from the Corn Production (Repeal) Act. As Chairman of the Council of Agriculture for Wales, C. Bryner Jones was determined to ensure Wales received a proper allocation to underwrite some of the changes he considered desirable.

A. W. Ashby, Pioneer of Rural Sociology

The achievements of a newcomer to Wales deserves attention. A. W. Ashby was brought to Wales by developments arising from the Government's increased expenditure on agricultural teaching and research, a man with special skills and commitments, some derived from his early upbringing, others from exposure to American social science in one of its formative stages.

Son of a small-holder in the English Midlands, Arthur W. Ashby (1886-1953) grew up in a rural society marked, in his own words, by ". . . . intellectual, moral, and social ferment . . . . when all sorts of people were asking questions and attempting to provide answers. In a way my family was one of the subjects of this ferment". His early manhood spanned a period remarkable for the intelligence and authority of the debate on agrarian isues, perhaps its golden age, with monumental Royal Commissions, the scholarly and polemical outpourings of Caird, Hasbach, Ernle, Hall, Rider Haggard, Rowntree, Vinogradoff, the Hammonds, Tawney, and others too numerous to mention, standing as testaments to its brilliance.

The young Ashby received a grass roots political education from his self-educated father, stomping the countryside in a red campaign caravan of the Land

Restoration League. His sister Mabel would later describe how, at the time of the highly controversial 1909 budget,

> Arthur stuck a copy of Lloyd George's Limehouse speech in the frame of the rosewood and gilt mirror, laughing for the terseness of the attack on wealth and privelege and obstinacy. That feudal business must be finished now! (Ashby, 1974)

Joseph Ashby was also a studious man, with publications in the Economic Journal and the local press to prove it a passion transmitted to the son and developed through correspondence courses and wide reading whenever the demands of farming and coal-carting permitted.

Entry to Ruskin College in 1909 allowed Ashby to escape the fate of Jude. It was his good fortune to attend one of the few institutions where social sciences, including sociology, figured predominantly in the curriculum. This very fact had precipitated an ideological struggle within the college making it, for the period Ashby was there, the storm-centre of a historical dispute in the Adult Education and Labour movements over the control and content of the working-class educational provision. Such an education, wedded to his previous life and later experiences in America, must have ensured a catholicity of outlook possessed by few professors of more orthodox origin and schooling. Following his Oxford Diploma success, a spell of pioneer extra-mural teaching, and research and publication, he became a student at the newly-founded Agricultural Economics Research Institute, Oxford, where he was again fortunate. Acting as guide to Professor Richard T. Ely studying European land reform in Britain, he received an invitation to Wisconsin - ". . . . one of the three universities then strongly pioneering agricultural economics . . . . The approach at Wisconsin was from economic history and economics. Besides Dr. Ely, Dr. H. C. Taylor was teaching general agricultural economics and C. J. Galpin taught rural sociology. The Wisconsin approach fitted Asby's own. There was not a more exciting period in the formative years of rural sociology; the first text, Gillette's Constructive Rural Sociology had just appeared and in 1915 the Wisconsin Agricultural Experimental Station published Galpin's Social Anatomy of a Rural Community, later recognised as a work of first importance and seminal influence on Chicago ecological studies. No doubt a bonus for Ashby during his eighteen month stay was the presence in Ely's Department of Economics and Sociology of his protege, E. A. Ross, progressive writer and politician, author of Social Control, and later, friend of the Russian refugee sociologist Sorokin.

The Wisconsin sojourn was to leave a lasting impression on Ashby's academic outlook, one of the earliest indicators being his delivery of the public Plunkett Foundation Lectures in Rural Sociology at Barnett House, Oxford in 1919. In these he addressed himself to such questions as the Social Relation between Town and Country and recommending texts by Gillette, MacIver, Ellwood, Galpin and Rowntree. Meanwhile, at Oxford and on attachment to the Food Production Department of the Ministry of Agriculture he had busied himself researching into small-holdings, rural industries, rural education and agricultural wages. Also, he completed his initiation into the politics and government of agriculture through service on the Royal Commission of Agriculture, 1919, the Linlithgow Committee, the National Agriculture Wages Board, and in 1924 as Economic Advisor to Noel Buxton, Minister of Agriculture in the first Labour Government. Anyone aware of the depths of economic depression into which Wales was plunged in the 1930s will appreciate the significance of Ashby's mature advice to the former Liberal Reconstructionist Christopher Addison, Minister in the Second Labour Government and Architect of the Marketing Acts. It could be argued that in terms of social importance, the resultant cushioning of Welsh farming against even greater privations outshines even Asbhy's life-long championing of the interests of agricultural labour.

It is likely that Ashby's wartime service brought him into contact with a fellow member of the Food Production Department, C. Bryner Jones. A man confident in his own analysis of Welsh needs and well able to ensure the attainment of his designs, Jones may have ensured that when the Ministry and the Development Commission established Advisory positions in Agricultural Economics, Ashby was appointed to Aberystwyth. If Cardiff/Barry was the power-house of social thinking in urban-industrial Wales, this small Cardiganshire seaside town was fast becoming its equivalent for agrarian Wales. To the company of C. Bryner Jones, Ministry of Agriculture, Professor G. Stapledon, grassland scientist, and now Ashby, we must add the presence of the headquarters of the Welsh Agricultural Organisation Society (Cymdeithas Trefnu Gwledig Cymru).[3] Over the next fifteen years the desire expressed by witnesses at the Royal Commission on the University of Wales that higher education serve the local community came as near fulfillment as ever. Ashby's co-operative links, his affinity to the agricultural trade union movement, and his overall advisory role in Wales afforded him an unrivalled opportunity to develop the preparation of researchers, investigative projects, and extension and related adult education efforts. The advantages of his strategic position are more fully appreciated if we pause to remind ourselves that most contemporary social research in the 192Os was accomplished by men of independent means like Rowntree, researchers supported by philanthropic bodies, and by social movements. The only Sociology chair proper was at the London School of economics then occupied by Morris Ginsberg, a provision not improved upon for another thirty years. Ashby's main duty was to engage in economic researches. However, given his dispositions and training it was not unexpected that he should seek to devote to the analysis of human and social factors in agriculture all the resources he could spare. He seized his opportunities with alacrity. In the words of Tom Lewis, Secretary of WAOS:

> He seemed to look at rural Wales as a priest looks at his parish, and nothing that happened in it was outside his active interest . . . . within three years of his arrival at Aberystwyth, he had established a network of extension classes for farmers in five counties and had contacts with every type of rural organisation in the principality. He had initiated researches into a wide range of economic problems, and had succeeded in making hundreds of working farmers his willing collaborators.

Later, he was to receive encouragement in these efforts from a new Principal, Ifor L. Evans, another student of agrarian affairs and eventually Ashby's co-author for the standard Agriculture of Wales (1944).

In 1924, the newly arrived Ashby had confidently given the reader of Welsh Outlook an exposition of the tasks facing students of rural society, which in retrospect can be read as a blueprint of the programme he set himself,

> Of speculation on the future of rural society or knowledge of routes of development there can be little practical value until we have organized experience of the existing system. We have to master the social inheritance of our rural communities as we are mastering our natural environment . . . In inquiry and the organization of experience, in speculation and social experiement or creative action, is a new field of self-realization for some of the adventurous spirits of the countryside.

These adventurous spirits he found and trained himself from amongst the Welsh-speaking farmers' sons he recruited as students and research officers. At this point it would not be inappropriate to name some of them, J. Morgan Jones, H. J. Meredith, J. Llefelys Davies, W.H. Jones, E. Llewellyn Harry and J.R.E. Phillips.

The University College of Wales at Aberystwyth already had a tradition of Agricultural Economics teaching within its Department of Economics and Political

Science before Ashby joined, so within this degree structure Ashby commenced internal university work. Soon there was a course in Rural Sociology; an early student recalls Ashby's apparently uninfectious enthusiasm for MacIver's book Community. Rural Sociology was also to feature in the Extension and Extra-mural work undertaken throughout mid-Wales and more occasionally in Glamorgan and Caernarfonshire.

Although in 1929 Ashby's status was recognised and confirmed by election to Britain's first Chair of Agricultural Economics, he increasingly expressed frustration at the 'official' definition of his advisory role with its subordination of the 'more human aspects of agricultural organization'. By 1935 he was entering clear pleas for a broader approach, for

> . . . . as there is no academic organization in Great Britain specially charged with research in Rural Social Organization; as this college is, so far as is known, the only institution in Great Britain which has provided a university course in the subject; and as the rural communities of Wales offer special opportunities for original work in this field, facilities for research in rural sociology would be very specially appreciated.

This call was never answered for there was no finance comparable to the post 1945 Clapham money to foster social sciences teaching, no Social Science Research Council, as general sociology also, with few exceptions, languished in an academic limbo.

Despite this, much was accomplished. The long-standing concern of Ashby's, the small-holder, and the immediate post-war debate on land-settlement for demobilized soldiers led him to acquire material on how men gained access to farming careers. With J. Morgan Jones mounted on a motorcycle, data was collected from all but two Welsh counties, this later being supplemented from research by J. Llefelys Davies. For all their lack of methodogical sophistication, these early studies of social mobility were recognised as valuable by Sorokin and Zimmerman when they reprinted reports in their classic Source Book (1930). Further recognition of Ashby's standing with U.S. rural sociologists came with his appointment alongside Sorokin, Galpin, Taylor, et.al. as a contributing editor to Rural Sociology, launched by the American Sociological Association in 1936. After assisting Hilda Jennings with her Brynmawr study, the Department continued to cultivate an interest in industrial south Wales in response to the growing influence of the Agricultural Marketing Acts, productive of a need to know more about consumer behaviour. It embarked on an ambitious series of surveys in city, mining valley, and village communities. These were more tightly organized than the earlier mobility studies, the researchers having the advantage of a well-established social scientific tradition of family budget surveys stretching back through Zimmerman, Rowntree, Booth and Engel, to Le Play, and reflect a considerable methodological advance, not only on the mobility studies but on budgeting surveys by researchers elsewhere in Britain. They attracted scant attention outside Wales. Work on demography was also fostered, especially upon rural migration and depopulation. Since Ashby was the leading British critic, of the theory of selective migration, the equivalent of Sorokin's role in the U.S.A., his student D. J. Davies not surprisingly wrote what remains the most authoritative examination of the question. In all this work Ashby drove his associates as hard as himself, 'Ashby never asked if you were tired'.

Due to the lack of resources to expand such research, it was too delicate a growth to withstand later pressures. Thus, the consumption and dietary work was first of all overtaken by the emergence of the Government's National Enquiry on Household Expenditure and then by war-time measures modifying the market operation via food controls and by tight Ministry control of all officially gathered data. More serious was the staffing problem. Technically, Ashby as Professor was the only departmental member with a recognised University teaching status. Officially, his assistants were Ministry of Agriculture advisory staff. Early on, J. Morgan Jones had moved off to the Ministry in London with others like J. Llefelys Davies later taking up leading posts in the new marketing boards. With the outbreak of war, the remainder were transferred to service with the Ministry or the County War Agricultural Executive Committees.

The war produced a further narrowing and specialization in Agricultural Economics as emergency duties required an almost exclusive concentration on the topics of farm organization and management. It seems that abandoned research areas were never fully reoccupied after the war at either Aberystwyth or Oxford, where Ashby migrated in 1946. Gradually the advisory role of the department was lost as the Government's National Advisory Service appeared, retaining the services of some of Ashby's former staff. Agricultural economics became a fully recognised university subject, staffed with full-time teachers but showing only a fitful interest in rural sociology.

In attempting a brief assessment of Asbhy, we might reasonably say that of all workers in agricultural economics and related agricultural science disciplines, he came nearest to viewing rural life as a totality, a view consistently without nostalgia for what was in reality a difficult past. His contribution thus stands uniquely free of the debilitating effect of a utopian romanticism which, as Raymond Williams (1973) so cogently argues, mars so many otherwise admirable contributions to our understanding of the country and the city. If Agricultural Economics has retained any of the breadth of Ashby's vision it is encountered only rarely. Not long before his death, Ashby was drawn into the activities of the young British Sociological Association and to the end he was ever the sociologist manque. We cannot justly claim his contribution to rural sociology esablished an on-going tradition in Wales or elsewhere in Britain. No one else has that distinction either. Eventually a native empiricism fused with American and continental theory to produce a Sociology, that appeared at other University Colleges in Wales during the 1950s and 1960s, if not immediately at Aberystwyth. Of Ashby's contribution, all that is left to say is that in his relationship to co-workers, students, farmers, farmworkers and rural dwellers of Wales, he remained true to Le Play's 1879 dictum that '. . . . social science is truly transmitted only by the scholar who lives it for the earnest men who listen to him'.

Conclusion

Despite the rapid speed of social transformation in inter-war Britain, social thought remained characteristically ante-bellum. Theoretical advances on the continent hardly impinged on British intellectual life, except for a minority Marxian tradition. The necessity of the state's role in social amelioration was so widely accepted as to seem unremarkable. Certainly there was no great impetus to make its theoretical underpinnings explicit or to fundamentally question the compatability of capitalism and social reform. In such circumstances, and given the range of other constraints already noted, it is no surprise that the sociological movement in Britain as a whole made little progress until the 1950s. Today, in reviewing the figures and movements discussed in this paper and their inheritors the non-socialist intelligentsia of post-war Labour and Tory Governments, it daily becomes harder to disagree that

> . . . . the ideology which attempted to side-step ideology, to tread the middle ground of realism and rationality, has lost its credibility as British society moves out of the euphoria of post-war growth and stability into an era in which class ideologies are reasserted. (Meillor, 1977)

Where the reformers had toiled, whether as philanthropists, planners, social workers or rural sociologists, the failures as much as the successes helped forge a society uncongenial to some Welshmen. To these, a devotion to the modernising impulse - liberal, statist, or socialist, could be interpreted solely as a betrayal of the native culture. To these sharers in a new cultural consciousness which reflected a Welsh ethnicity, the modernizers now appeared as the assimilated agents of an alien centralising English power. When one of the early exponents of this nascent cultural identity embarked on his anthropological fieldwork in rural Montgomeryshire, he was set to become the last great ideologue of a decadent Welsh weltanschauung, equipped to bestow the cachet of academic social science upon his version of the O. M. Edwards' myth.[4] The success of Alwyn Rees' project went far in producing a cultural division of sociology within Wales and between Welsh university colleges, a state of affairs which has long obscured other sociological traditions.

CHAPTER 3

THE ECONOMIC STRUCTURE OF WALES SINCE 1850

John Williams

Anyone rash enough to write about the Welsh economy in modern times is immediately brought up against what can only be described as a fundamental problem. Namely, that there must be serious doubts as to whether there has been, in modern times, any such thing as 'The Welsh Economy'. Certainly, it seems permanently to have been the case that the economic links of the various parts of Wales run east-west to England rather than north-south to other parts of Wales. South Wales looks to Bristol or Birmingham, north Wales to Merseyside and Liverpool. All this is a matter of simple observation and, in the absence of such constraints as customs barriers, reflects basic geographic realities.

The implications for historical studies of Welsh economic development are, however, formidable and deep-seated. For example, in attempting to compile a set of historical statistics for Wales it was a repeated source of frustration to discover that there were for the past no existing figures for the railways of Wales or the Welsh iron industry or the Welsh coal industry or the level of public expenditure in Wales. The basic reason for such gaps was simple: in the past statistics were mostly collected, not for their own sake, but to meet a separate need or problem, to serve as a basis for decisions of some sort. The implications of the gaps were thus clear: figures over a wide range of industries and economic activities were not collected for Wales because no-one was being asked or felt the need to answer questions or make decisions in these areas on an all-Wales basis. Thus, as we look back across the past, the economic existence of Wales is a genuine and serious problem. The argument is not that because the figures do not exist, therefore Wales was not a meaningful unity. The emphasis is really the other way round. Nobody felt any compulsion to gather statistics because Wales was not the relevant basis.

However, the force of this contention varies according to the particular issue under consideration. For many aspects of social history it is not a major concern. It does, however, raise acute problems for the economy of Wales. It is certainly highly plausible to argue that until quite recently - the 1930s at the earliest - the concept of the Welsh economy has little empirical content, it is a mostly empty abstraction. There is no need or wish to press this too far, but it is meant as a cautionary reminder that lurking behind much of what follows is the bleak question: 'Did Wales - for these economic purposes - exist?'

One consequence of the kind of circumstances which have been mentioned is that there is no direct measure of the economic structure of Wales until the 1950s. It is contended, however, that a reasonable proxy does exist in the form of information about the occupational pattern of the people living in Wales. The argument here is that the occupational distribution does serve as a fair indicator of the economy as a whole: what people do, how they earn their living, does give a rough guide to the kind of economy and society in which they work.

One substantial drawback to such an approach is that no very secure start can be made to analysis on these lines before 1850. The basic source for information on occupation is contained in the decennial census returns. But although the first census was taken in 1801, the information which the censuses contain on occupation is badly deficient before the census of 1851. The early censuses, for example, took the family as the occupational unity so that the whole family was categorised according to the work done by the head of the household. The difficulties raised by such a procedure are, in any event, enormously compounded because the early censuses simply evade all questions of occupational detail. They only divide occupations into three exceedingly broad categories: Agriculture; Trade; Manufacturers and Handicrafts; and Others. Of these, only agriculture can be said to constitute a useful and meaningful category. Fortunately it is, in the context of the period, the most significant single occupation so that, despite the crudity of the material, its indication that about half the working population in the first half of the nineteenth century was engaged in agriculture was probably broadly correct. So, probably, was the only other reasonably clear conclusion to be drawn from these early censuses - namely that the proportion in agriculture was slowly declining. But, given the uncertainties, neither statement is particularly useful. Of course it is possible, from other evidence, to attempt more specific estimates of, for example, the number of coal miners in Wales in, say, 1820. But such estimates necessarily rest on fairly heroic assumptions.

The present survey starts with the 1851 census for two main reasons. It is at that time that the census material on occupations becomes both reliable and useful; and also because the use of what is essentially the same source over a period of more than a century gives more confidence to the long-run comparisons which will be made.[1] The basic material can be fairly rapidly summarised by dividing it into two main periods. Although the break appears conveniently at the middle it is hoped to show that the division is not simply an arbitrary one, but that each of the periods is reasonably distinct in its trends and flavour. The first period covers the years from around 1850 to the first world war; the second covers the half-century following 1920.

So far as male occupations were concerned most were, in 1850, to be found either in Agriculture or in Mining and Quarrying. Over half (fifty-two per cent) of the occupied male population of Wales worked in one or other of these two industries. In this respect there was relatively little change before 1914. Nearly half (fourty four per cent) of the men were still engaged in 1911 in either Agriculture or Mining. Indeed, the dominance of these two industries was even greater than such figures indicate. Why? Because many other occupations only existed - or only existed on the scale that they did - in order to service these sectors. In transport, for example, the essential occupation of most railwaymen was to shuttle the black wagon-trains back and forth to the sea. And certainly many dockers and all the coal-trimmers existed to shovel this energy to the four corners of the earth. The same was to a greater or lesser degree true of several other occupational groups - building, or retailing. The jobs were created by the needs of Mining or Agriculture.

There is another significant aspect to the dominance of these two industries. It meant that a century-and-a-half after the traditional starting date of the so-called British industrial revolution, manufacturing was still, relatively, a fringe occupation in Wales. The Welsh economy was still essentially about primary production; it was not mostly concerned with mechanised manufacturing production. This emphasis had consequences for the outlook and mores of Welsh society, making it different from that of Birmingham or Manchester.

It is right to stress the continued dominance of Agriculture and Mining during the sixty years or so after 1850, but it would be wrong if this was allowed to create an impression that the period was, therefore, one of relatively little change. On the contrary, firstly there was an enormous increase in the total numbers employed. There were more than twice as many men at work in 1911 (808,000) as in 1851 (386,000). Indeed, this remarkable expansion makes the continued dominance of just two of the twenty two occupational groups even more notable. The second point, however, is that the relative steadiness of this dominance disguises very sharp changes in the two basic primary-producing sectors themselves. Indeed, their relative positions were totally reversed. In 1851, Agriculture accounted for thirty five per cent and Mining for seventeen per cent of the occupied male population of Wales; sixty years later, thirty two per cent were in Mining and twelve per cent in Agriculture. Moreover, during this time the actual numbers in agriculture had declined from 135,000 to 96,000 whilst those in mining had increased in a most spectacular fashion from 65,000 to 256,000.

By 1911 the size and scale of the mining sector was sufficient to influence all else. Thus changes in the composition of the army of miners assumed a special importance. In general, the mining sector of the Welsh economy before 1914 was becoming steadily more homogenous and steadily more concentrated. In 1851 less that sixty per cent of those in the Mining sector were employed in coal mines. These were comparatively evenly spread between north and south, since the output from south Wales was only about three times as great as that of the north Wales coalfield. But by 1911 almost ninety per cent of those in Mining were in coal-mining, and nearly all of these were now in the south, where output had become fifteen times as great as that of north Wales. The other mining sectors - lead, iron, slate, copper - which had accounted for over two-fifths of the employment in the group in 1851, had become relatively insignificant. Even in the slate industry, where the total number employed had increased between 1851 and 1911, the share of the sector had dwindled to less than five per cent. The most dramatic shift, however, was in iron-mining. In 1851 one out of every six Welsh miners had been searching for iron; in 1911 there were only 169 iron miners in the whole of Wales.

Thus, the occupational pattern of Wales before 1914 was dominated by Agriculture and Mining; but, at the same time, there were sharp shifts both in the relative importance of these two sectors and within the sectors themselves. What else should be said, at this broad aggregate level, about the work men did, in Wales up to 1914? Perhaps three other aspects are worth emphasizing.

First, the only two other major occupational groups in Wales, each of which gave work to almost as many as Agriculture, were Metals, Machines, etc., and Transport. A large part of the Metals sector was engaged in Iron and Steel production. Thus each of these other large sectors was closely associated with coal production, and their employment was concentrated around the coalfields. Much the same could also be said of Building and Construction which was the next largest group.

Second, the only other sectors to experience any significant expansion before 1914 were: Food, drink, tobacco; Commercial; and Professional. Of these three, two - Commercial and Professional - were portents of the future or, at least, they can, with the advantage of hindsight, be seen as such. At the time they still seemed pretty small beer. All the professions - doctors, lawyers, teachers, the military, the clergy, central and local government officers, engineers, the literary (though in Wales most bards probably still retained their amateur status), the scientific, artists, and, a nice incongruity among such serried ranks of respectability, fairground showmen - all these professions amounted to less that three per cent of the occupied population. Furthermore all the commercial occupations - merchants and agents, including accountants and salesmen and commercial travellers; the growing army of insurance men (who, by 1911, were beginning to acquire bikes for their weekly rounds) and what the Census terms 'dealers in money'; ammounted to a little more than three per cent. The reputed Welsh passion for education, if it existed at all, had not allowed many to escape from the pull of the pits and the grip of the soil.

Thirdly, the British census procedure identifies twenty two broad occupational groups before 1914. In Wales nearly half of these basic groups were insignificant. The total number of men employed in ten (of the twenty two) occupational groups accounted only for five per cent of the total occupied population of Wales. What did this imply for Welsh society? It meant that, in terms of work experience, there was relatively little diversity. Many occupational groups - Textiles; Paper; print and books; Chemicals, oil and soap; Brick, cement and pottery; etc., - were hardly to be found in the economy and society of Wales before 1914. Evidently all the talk of Welsh flannel was precisely that - relatively speaking. This reinforces and emphasises, from the bottom end of the occupation structure, what we have already seen fom the top - the substantial dominance of Agriculture and especially Mining.

What of women at work? In this brief survey, attention must be confined only to issues of the broadest social consequence. At that level of generality the most noticeable feature is the very narrow range of occupations taken up by women in Wales. Indeed, the dominance by just two sectors was even greater for women than it was for men. In 1851, sixty per cent of all working women were either in Agriculture or in Domestic Service; in 1911 these two groups still accounted for more than half (fifty one per cent) of the women in employment. Whereas in 1851 this proportion was fairly evenly divided between Agriculture and Domestic Service (twenty seven per cent to thirty three per cent), by the eve of the first world war

Domestic Srvice had become easily the most important source of female employment with forty two per cent of all employed women being employed in this single sector, compared to nine per cent in Agriculture. Thus the typical Welsh working woman before 1914 was a domestic servant. This typicality was, for women, even substantially more marked than was that of the typical Welsh working man being a miner.

The over-riding truth of that does, however, obscure another important factor. Namely, that the peak of employment in Domestic Service had already been passed before 1914. Both absolutely and relatively, 1891 was the peak year for the employment of women in this sector, from then on the number of women so employed was falling. Moreover, it has already been indicated that the number of women engaged in Agriculture had also fallen. From these two facts an important conclusion emerges about the work done by women in Wales before 1914; the occupational structure was dominated by two groups, both of which were rapidly declining.

Only four other occupational groups were large enough to be worth mentioning. These were Dressmaking which by 1914 was a larger source of work for women than was Agriculture (34,000 as against 20,000); Food, drink, and tobacco; Professions; and Textiles. The other sixteen occupational groups between them gave work to less than ten per cent of the total occupied women in 1911. Thus, during this period, the degree of occupational concentration was even more marked for women in Wales than it was for men. Did this high concentrtaion of occupational experience make for a more homogeneous economy and society? If it did, were the presumed social advantages of this more significant than the possible economic costs of a lack of diversity?

This is not the place to attempt an answer to such questions. In any event, perhaps of even greater significance is a prior, and simpler point. There was a relatively slow growth in the number of women at work. The total number of working women did, of course, increase (from 126,000 to 216,000), but this increase was at a much lower rate (seventy one per cent) than both the general increase in the population and the increase in the number of men at work. There were thus proportionately fewer women working in Wales in 1911 than there had been sixty year earlier.

Why was this? There seems to be little doubt that it was associated with the rise in the relative importance of Mining in the Welsh economy. Why, it may be asked, should the growth of mining reduce employment opportunities for women?

Broadly because it had unfavourable effects on both the demand for, and the supply of, female labour. The demand was less, because mining was overwhelmingly a male occupation, especially after the Act of 1842 forbade the employment under-ground of women and children under 10. Although the employment of women on the surface was quite legal, custom, especially in the newer mining districts, soon made the practice relatively rare. John Griffiths, a Rhondda collier giving evidence to a select committee in 1866 stated categorically that women had never been employed in his neighbourhood and, even if employers had wanted to employ women, the colliers would not have allowed it.[2] In any event, the supply of women available for work in mining areas was constrained because the daily need for baths and hot water in the home, often for several men in a household, who may have worked separate shifts, added substantially to the normal burdens of trying to combine a job with housekeeping.

Any doubts as to whether the existence of mining had so direct an impact on women's work may be reduced, if not removed altogether, by looking at the inter-county variations. The reduction in the female activity rate that has been emphasised emerges clearly in the six counties, which contained the new mining and industrial areas. It emerges most sharply in the two major mining counties of Glamorgan and Monmouth. Moreover, because these are the counties with the largest populations, they determined the trend for Wales as whole. Nonetheless it is significant that in seven, mainly rural counties the female activity-rate actually increased during this period. This means that the employment of women before 1914 was falling proportionately in the mining districts, but rising in the countryside.

Of the many social and economic consequences of the overall fall in employment oportunities for women, just two will be mentioned. First, it is perhaps this factor more than any other which gave rise to the legendary Welsh 'Mam'. The emergence of the dominance, especially within the home, and especially in the mining valleys, of the mother-figure so extravagantly and romantically extolled in literature by the men both husband and sons and fathers, who so remorsely exploited them in life. As in so much else, Richard Llewellyn presents the full-blown sick-sweet myth in <u>How Green was my Valley</u>. But in some respects more telling, because it occurs casually and incidentally, is the brief portrait in one of Rhys Davies' short stories. The men, husband and sons, are back from the pit and at their meal:

> Jaw stuck out, she worked about the table, shifting on to each plate four thick slices of bacon, a stream of sizzling fat, ladles of potatoes and tinned tomatoes ..... She poured the thick black tea

> out of a battered enamel pot, fit enough for a palace or a workhouse ..... She got the tarts ready, full-sized plates of them and they slogged at these ..... Oddments followed: cheese, cake and jams. They only stopped eating when she stopped producing .....
>
> ..... At once, after the meal, the table was shoved back. She dragged in the wooden tub before the fire. The pans were simmering on hob and fire ..... and she was out and in with towels, shirts and buckets .....
>
> (When the men were finished she was). Left alone with the piles of crusted pit clothes, all waiting to be washed or dried of their sweat, she stood taking a cup of tea and nibbling a piece of bread, looking out of the window. Except on Sundays her men seldom saw her take a meal, though even on Sunday she never ate bacon.

These formidable 'Mams', organising and ruling their houses, loving and, what often seemed to be the same thing, feeding their progeny, proclaiming their family's respectability by kneeling in their chapel pews and on their door-steps, emerged not from something inherent in the character and temperament of Welsh women, but from a lack of opportunity to work outside the home. The same cause must also be a substantial part of the explanation for the high level of births in the colliery districts. The birth-rate in the mining areas was higher than the rate for the country at large; and it remained high for several decades after the general U.K. birth rate began to fall from the 1870s.

When attention is turned to the past fifty years, the most striking impression is one of being met by a series of dramatic reversals. For men, this emerges in its most primary sense in a decline in the total number occupied. In sharp contrast to the doubling of the number of occupied males in the half-century or so before 1914, the half century after 1920 saw an overall fall of about 100,000 in the number of employed males. In addition there are marked shifts in the occupational structure. There is a general lack of realisation of just how dramatic have been the occupational changes, both in terms of who is doing the work in Wales, as well as in the kind of work which they are doing.

Even the most obvious shift, involving the decline in the dominance of Agriculture and Mining, is imperfectly appreciated. This is largely because the enormous scale of the shift is usually overlooked. The nature of the change is very inadequately conveyed by the information that the percentage of males employed in Mining and Agriculture fell from forty two to ten per cent between 1921 and 1971. Nor even that most of this decline was concentrated on Mining where the percentage fall was from thirty one per cent to less than five per cent. What has to be grasped is the sheer magnitude of the numbers involved. For mining, the twentieth century fall was even more dramatic than the nineteenth century rise. In the fifty years after 1920 over one quarter of a million men have left mining, and a further 50,000 have left agriculture.

There was also a large decline in the number occupied in Transport, and smaller, but still significant, declines in Sales workers, and those employed in Clothing and Building. On the other hand, there were important expansionary groups. Metal Manufacturing and Engineering saw the biggest increase (99,000 to 160,000) and it became the largest single occupational group, accounting for one-fifth of all occupied men in Wales. There were also substantial increases in Professional; Clerical; Administrators and Managers; Service, sport and recreational; and Warehousemen. The combined effect of all this was, firstly, to spread employment more evenly within the occupational structure reflecting the change from a traditional dependence on primary production towards an emphasis on service occupations. In a social sense, whatever arguments might range around the myth of Welsh classlessness in the past, there can be no doubt that Wales now has a numerically significant middle class.

For women, the occupational changes over the last fifty years have differed from those associated with men. While the total number of occupied males fell during this period, that of occupied women rose by 175,000. On the other hand, the degree of occupational diversity open to women is still mostly limited. By the 1970s the top four male occupational groups accounted for less than half (forty six per cent) of all occupied males; but for women the top four groups still accounted for nearly three-quarters (seventy three per cent) of all occupied females. Moreover, there was little change in the important occupational groups. In 1921 these had been Services; Sales; Professional; and Clothing: fifty years later the only change was that Clerical had ousted Clothing in the top four having dramatically leapt into second place. Services was still the largest group, but its total numbers was stable, indeed, almost exactly the same number of women were employed in this sector in 1971 as in 1921. The real shift here is hidden; the numbers were much the same; what had changed was the place of work. There had been a move out of private homes and into such public institutions as offices, hospitals and hotels.

The above remarks are meant to provide a brief and rapid summary of the last half century or so. It is important, however, that despite their brevity they should convey a strong impression that it was these years, the years since 1920, and especially since 1950, which saw the most remarkable shift in occupational patterns in Wales. For this reason it might be helpful to emphasise, or re-emphasise, a few very broad aspects of these changes. The nineteenth century witnessed a substantial expansion, but in some essential ways its second half was relatively stable. Most of the major characteristics of the Welsh occupation structure in 1914 were already clearly in evidence by 1850. The dominance of primary production, especially, mining; the lack of diversity; and the predominance of men in the total work-force. Up to 1914 each of these characteristics was being increasingly re-inforced.

After 1920, however, there were decisive and fundamental changes of direction. Enormous numbers have been shifted out of agriculture and mining, and these primary-producing sectors have become much less important in the Welsh economy and Welsh society. There has been a considerable increase in the diversity of work done by Welsh men although this development has not been marked so for Welsh women, most of whom are still engaged in a narrow range of occupations. Moreover, both men and women have moved in considerable numbers into the Professional and Service occupations, the expansion of which is often taken as the hall-mark of advanced modern societies.

Perhaps, paradoxically, the most pervasive changes have been in the aggregates. Paradoxically, because the total number of occupied persons hardly changed at all in the fifty years after 1921. Indeed, the 1951 total was almost exactly the same (1,093,000) as that in 1921, and in the two decades after 1951, it only increased slightly (by about 70,000). Such relative stability was itself in marked contrast with the years before 1914, when the total number of occupied persons had more than doubled (from 512,000 to 1,025,000) between 1850 and 1914. However, the differing experiences of men and women before and after 1914 are even more striking. Before 1914 the number of occupied men rose substantially, much more rapidly than the number of occupied women. Since 1921, and especially since 1951, the absolute number of men in the Welsh workforce has actually fallen, whilst that of women has risen substantially. Indeed, if it were not for the greater participation by women, the total Welsh workforce today would be smaller than it was fifty years ago, despite the modest increase in the total population. This is a most significant shift. It means, to give but one example, that there are now far more women clerical workers than there are coal miners.

Such occupational shifts are necessarily fraught with significant economic, political and social consequences, which cannot be taken up here. Instead, they will be used as a background against which attention will be drawn to three major turning points in the recent economic history of Wales and to offer a few brief comments on each. The suggested turning-points are: the 1890s; the 1920s; and the 1950s. The particular dates have, as is evident, a neat periodicity which would seem to make them amenable to the currently fashionable cyclical treatment. This is not the intention here.

Of the period around 1890 two basic factors are evident. The one is the apparent contrast in the economic experience of Wales to that of Britain generally. For the British economy as a whole the decade immediately following 1890 is commonly characterised as a climacteric. Loosely speaking, this outlandish term is meant to convey that the economy faltered in its confidence, failed to respond positively to the challenge of German and American competition, and shifted to a long-run slower growth. There is some discussion about the dating of this melancholy process, and much more about who or what was responsible for it, but that there was a lapse in the resilience of the British economy commands general acceptance. This was in sharp contrast to the Welsh experience, and especially the south Wales experience, at this time. Wales naturally shared in the short-run fluctuations of the British economy, but there was no denying that the atmosphere and the under-lying trend was one of expansion and buoyancy.

The other factor is more conjectural. The occupational figures have already decisively indicated that the economic structure continued to be dominated, right up to the First World War, by the primary-producing sectors of Agriculture and, overwhelmingly by Mining. Moreover, the major Mining sector was, of course, heavily export-orientated. These were characteristics which loom large in developmental and dependency literature. It is argued, however, that the interpretations of backwardness, inferiority and, possibly, exploitation which are commonly placed on these characteristics might need to be modified by such considerations as the scale and pace of change. Certainly the development of the Welsh economy between 1890 and 1914 was rapid and large. It was not simply that the basic demand for coal grew so strongly that output almost doubled between 1890 and 1913, nor even that the absolute amounts involved were so large. The 1913 output was twenty seven million tons greater than in 1890. Beyond this, however, the declining productivity of the industry and the obstacles to mechanisation meant that the demand for men was even greater. In the mere decade or so between the Boer War and the First World War the industry's male labour force in south Wales rose by over 100,000. The suggestion is that the momentum of the pace and scale of such expansion dragged Wales into an irreversible modernity which belied the continuing predominance of primary production.

It has already been suggested that a major feature of the occupational structure after 1920 was that many of the major pre-1914 trends were reversed. One aspect of these reversals raises important questions for neo-imperialist interpretations of Welsh economic development, but it raises them in a highly ambiguous manner. This is the reversal of the migration flow. The shift was quite abrupt. Even in the decade preceding 1921 the rate of population growth in Wales was over twice as great as that of England (9.7 per cent against 4.7 per cent). During the inter-war years the population of Wales actually fell in absolute numbers; the first time that this had occurred since the official census was introduced in 1801. Migration out of Wales during this period removed, numerically, not only the entire natural increase of a quarter of a million but also an additional 90,000. So drastic a shift in so strategic a variable naturally had wide repercussions. The present purpose is simply to direct it in the form of questions rather than answers, towards a particular point. Can theories of 'exploitation' accommodate migration flows as large as these, and also reversals as abrupt as this?

In part, of course, they can, by pointing to the precariousness induced by the high degree of specialisation in the pre-1914 economic structure of Wales. Such an approach, however, tends to slur over one aspect of that precariousnes which was more or less peculiar to Wales. Because of the geological conditions the south Wales coalfield has always been an area of high production costs, but the effect of this has either been persistently ignored or it has not been understood. Thus in the nineteenth century Welsh coal-owners and miners wallowed in pride at the superior quality of Welsh coal, as if it somehow reflected and magnified their own virtues. The higher quality, it was said, ensured that Welsh coal would stay in high demand. In fact the causation ran, and continues to run the other way. The nineteenth century saw the emergence of new demands for coal, especially for steam raising, for which Welsh coal just happened to be particularly well-suited. The steam-raising qualities of Welsh coal were sufficiently marked to ensure a demand for it despite the fact that it necessarily cost more to produce. Once the special demand declined, much of the industry was then doomed: since its higher quality would not be able to offset the greater cost of extraction. The fate of the anthracite area since 1945 bears eloquent testimony to the force of this consideration.

The 1950s was a totally different scene. Brinley Thomas (1962) surveying the position at the close of that decade was positively, and reasonably, euphoric. It is true that events since then make far more sober, if not more sombre, judgements. Nonetheless, it was a period in which the manufacturing sector became, for the first time, a significant part of the structure. It was a time in which the basis of greater diversification was laid, and it was a time in which productivity in Wales seemed to be growing rapidly. All of this required substantial investment. Much of the investment was government sponsored, but there was still a strong slice of private finance. These different sources, however, had one aspect in common. They were each partly activated by the adoption of regional policies, policies which, perhaps for the first time, made some sense of the concept of a Welsh economy.

These policies made a timorous start in the 1930s with the setting up of the early trading estates. In the 1940s, with the strategic needs of the war forcing many factories to move westwards, Wales received a special boost, and the tight control of Industrial Development Certificates gave the government a powerful lever to push private investment in the same direction in the early 1950s. It can, moreover, be plausibly argued that the two sources of the investment essential for these developments were largely external, although there is some ambiguity about public investment in this context. A more important qualification, however, would be that the mostly external nature of the post-1945 investment cannot simply be pushed backwards. Certainly there would be large doubts whether the same could be said of the half century before 1914.

In any event, it may be that the period ushered in around 1950 is coming to an end. The cut-backs in regional policy may come to be seen as making a new phase begining around 1980 - elevating the years between 1950 and 1980 into another excessively neat thirty-year period. But that, it need hardly be emphasized, is mere speculation.

The necessarily modest intention of this paper has simply been to provide some background and, it is hoped, some additional perspective. More particularly the object has been to stress the very large changes which have taken place in the structure of the Welsh economy over the last century or so, and to direct attention towards three more recent turning-points as indicators of the relatively abrupt way in which shifts can occur. Any general explanations will need to encompass and accommodate such changes and such shifts. Of course, behind many such explanations is the counterfactual: suppose Wales had been, more or less, self-governing. Historically at least, it is difficult to see any possibility of being able to specify so enormous a counter-factual in any way which would give it any operational content which, perhaps, simply brings the discussion back to where it began: 'Was there - is there - a Welsh Economy?'

CHAPTER 4

UNEVEN DEVELOPMENT IN WALES : THE CHANGING ROLE OF THE BRITISH STATE

John Lovering

Despite the fact that Wales, a distinct country within the British system, has long played a key role in British economic development there were until recently very few attempts to come to grips with its political economy. Partly this was a result of the fact that none of the three power groups involved in Welsh politics recognised that there might be any point in doing so; south Wales labourism tended to operate within a British nation perspective. Welsh nationalism disavowed any great concern with economic matters, and the state apparatus was able to conduct its activities through a mesh of institutions which had no clear Welsh identity. In the event, however, it was from that third source that a new perspective developed. By the 1960s the state had restructured in a form that specifically recognised a Welsh entity and a new literature on Wales began to emerge.

The reasons for the transformation in state forms cannot be dealth with here, but were clearly bound up with the particular 'compromise' between capital and labour which crystallised after the war, and the way in which this consolidated or generated a regional alliance of interests (Gough, 1979). Under the pressure of wartime decentralisation and post-war Labour and Nationalist campaigns a series of measures gradually created a set of agencies and structures of government with a Welsh reference: by the end of the war fifteen government agencies had set up in Wales; a Minister for Welsh Affairs was created in 1951, a full-time Minister of State in 1957, and a Secretary of State for Wales in 1964. This partly reflected the success of a Labour party 'Parliament for Wales Campaign' from 1950, but it also owed much to the arguments of the Council for Wales and Monmouth that a full Welsh Office should be created on the Scottish model to coordinate the various government departments. The threat that failure to implement some sort of national machinery might damage Labour's election prospects was a major factor (Osmond, 1977).

In parallel with the growth of 'Welsh' state institutions research work began to reflect a new analytical perspective, premised on the existence of a real object corresponding to 'Wales'. At this time Wales was widely regarded 'especially by the people who wrote or sponsored most of these studies' as the site of an impressive new industrial transformation, and indeed, if the administrative framework could be perfected, this might become even more impressive.

It was not until the mid 1970s that any serious attempts were made to offer an alternative to this 'social administrative' orientation. Curiously the major stimulus to this reappraisal was derived from a source alien to the mainstream of European political or economic analysis. Michael Hechter's (1975) 'Internal Colonialism' began with a discussion not of Welsh working class history, or even of the language, but with Black liberation in the United States of America. The author, who had never set foot in the British Isles identified the key to understanding Wales as the alleged fact that "large sections continue to define their culture as being 'Celtic' rather than British'. Despite the somewhat arguable empirical basis for this claim, the lack of territorial definition, and an analytical hotchpotch, Hechter's work became a landmark in the field.

One of Hechter's central themes was the argument that Wales paralleled in many respects the condition of underdeveloped countries. This perception clearly did have something to offer, although there can be no doubt that the main reason for its widespread popularity was that it dovetailed with a range of ideological preconceptions. The notion of 'dependence' is comforting to conservative nationalist thinkers, and provides an effective political slogan. In the case of Wales, however, it has little meaning and serves mainly to obscure similarities between regions within the unitary state-system.[1] The more specific notion of 'internal colonialism' advanced by Hechter was even less fruitful, and served both to romanticise and obscure local processes of social reproduction while reducing the analysis of state intervention to little more than a conspiracy theory (Lovering, 1978a). Nevertheless, the analogy with 'national underdevelopment' or 'peripheral development' did raise new questions about economic structures and social institutions (Day, 1979, Lovering, 1978b). Moreover, as the world economy has become more internationalised and new transnational divisions of labour increasingly cut across national boundaries, the problems which first drew analytical attention in third world contexts have become increasingly important in the 'first world'. The causes and effects of uneven spatial development now occupy centre stage, and it is becoming increasinly urgent to understand the interconnections between the international context and the internal structuring of territorial units. In this context an account of Wales must situate its uniqueness, in terms of processes of more general application. This paper is an attempt in that direction.

The first part presents, in highly summarised fashion, an outline of early industrialisation in Wales. It is intended to demonstrate that Wales was industrialised in a manner similar to that of many colonial or nominally independent third world countries, and that this had analagous effects on subsequent economic development. Part two, which is the nub of the paper, contrasts this with development since the Second World War. In this period the attempt to draw an analogy between Wales and an industrially advanced 'third world' country, is misleading because of what it misses out, and this is the ameliorative and modifying role of the unitary British state. In a schematic fashion this section attempts to indicate the effects that this has had on economic and social development in Wales. The British state is currently undergoing a far reaching transition and the conditions of the post-war period are being dismantled. The conclusion comments on the implications of this restructuring.

Capitalist Industrialisation and the Creation of Dualism

The political conquest of the Welsh by the English in 1281 and again in 1409 did not have a major economic rationale. Its effect was to secure the English state militarily, and to preserve two distinct economic and social systems in Wales. In the 'Englishry' manorial relations were imposed, including the extraction of surplus by direct feudal labour, while traditional pastoral activities continued to dominate the 'Welshry', and dues were periodically paid in money or food (Clapham, 1966). From the eighteenth century, however, a new relationship emerged in which economic activities became closely interdependent. The mobilising principle was capitalist industrialisation.

The first wave involved the reorganisation and expansion of the copper, slate, tin, coal and iron industries. In each case the process was initially more a matter of administrative and organisational innovation than of technological change. Ownership was concentrated in the hands of a few magnates, prominent amongst whom were Thomas Williams (copper - Anglesey), Asheton Smith and Richard Pennant (slate - Caernarfonshire), John Wilkinson (coal and iron - north east Wales), the Crawshay family (coal - Cyfartha) and the Guest family (iron - Dowlais). Much of the capital employed came from outside Wales, merchants in

Bristol and London playing a particularly influential role in the south. The Hirwaun furnace was set up by Thomas Williams together with Henry Morgan, a Bristol linen merchant, and the Ebbw Vale forge was set up by Jeremia Homfrey, from Staffordshire, with Bristol capital. In the north the slate owners styling themselves 'Penrhyn' (after their Irish estates) derived much of their capital from slavery in Jamaica. Indeed, Hobsbawm (1969 : 295) has summarised the whole process of early industrialisation as 'something done to Welshmen rather than by Welshmen'.

The secondary economic effects of industrialisation were mostly felt outside Wales. Since capitalist penetration took the form of controlling larger and larger numbers of workers, (rather than of increasing worker productivity through technical change), it did not create a large local demand for new innovation.

This, together with the preservation of traditional social institutions, inhibited the emergence of manufacturing industry, and in any case manufacturing in England was already in the lead. In south Wales, the boundaries of the enclave were less tightly drawn, largely because the growth of iron and coal was eventually accompanied by large scale in-migration leading to the forced growth of new communities and a capitalist labour market with accompanying opportunities for entrepreneurship. Consequently, by the early nineteenth century 'there was in existence a body of industrialists and an increasing number of people in the subsidiary trades and professions called into being by their activities' (John 1950 : 31).

The concentration of the new fortunes in the hands of the mine and factory owners led to imports of luxury goods. 'The first step of the rising Cambrian businessman tended to be to assimilate to the only pattern of an upper class there was, namely the English' (Hobsbawm, 1969 : 296). This use of surplus became embodied in the landscape - Bethesda, the workers' town, is bleak and grey, while the Penrhyn estate is luxuriant, green, and adorned with exotic vegetation imported from across the world, and a superfluous mock castle.

The demand profile emerging from this kind of industrialisation was critical for the future pattern of development. It was reinforced by the limited transformation of the production apparatus. In farming, for example, ownership remained concentrated in the hands of large estates while tenants undertook immediate production. This was largely a consequence of the pattern of part-time farm employment which characterised the early development of both coal mining in the south and slate in the north-west. While this minimised the wage cost of labour, and reinforced the control exercised by capitalists who were simultaneously landowners, it inhibited the emergence of bourgeois farming and maintained backward technical and social institutions. Significant agricultural improvements were avoided for fear that they would provoke rent increases, which the land-hungry population waiting off-stage would be willing to pay if the tenants themselves could not (Howell, 1977).

In south Wales, especially in the Vale of Glamorgan - farming did eventually develop a modern face, with farms of between 200 to 300 acres, but elsewhere archaic patterns of ownership and control remained. One per cent of the population owned some 60 per cent of the land, while 91 per cent owned 12 per cent of the land. Some 62 per cent of the land was thus worked by a conservative tenantry (Davies, 1974). Absentee landlordism, especially where this was policed by unsympathetic agents who were often Irish or Scottish in origin, as a deliberate precaution against over friendly relations, maintained a climate of insecurity inimical to improvement. Meanwhile markets were constricted by legal and customary restraints; in Caernarfon in the 1820s fines were still levied on farmers who took their grain to other than the mills of their local lord (Barnes, 1970). This combination of factors explains why shopkeepers in Anglesey, traditionally the 'granary of Wales', began to import flour from the new steam mills in Liverpool.

Capialist expansion in Wales, especially in the north, was thus initially a matter of transforming the scale of production while retaining several of the institutions of the earlier society. Consequently the industrial revolution in Wales "impoverished, but did not disrupt, agrarian society" (Howell, 1977 : 69). The effect of the spread of capitalism was <u>not</u> to remodel Wales in the image of the country from whence that force came, that is, England. On the contrary, since capitalism took the line of least resistance in each situation it encountered, the local form varied widely.

North Wales in the late eighteenth century provides a remarkable example of the preservation of the old, indeed, the revival of the old, within the shell of the new. In Llanddeiniolen the growth of slate quarrying was associated with the reappearance of 'boon tenancies'. These were 'a curious form of semi-medieval tenure' in which rent was paid in the form of a direct 'boon' of harvest service on the landlords estate (Howell, 1977 : 63). This was a vivid example of the incorporation of pre-capitalist by capitalist social relations. Less vivid, but more widespread, was the general practice that quarrymen were simultaneously tenant smallholders, usually occupying farms of well under twenty acres (Morgan, 1981). In short, capitalism penetrated especially in the north, by transforming the context, not the substance, of the productive activity. This had a profound effect on the subsequent development of supply flexibilities and demand profiles and this consolidated the new industries as enclaves, and fixed a rigid pattern of economic specialisation.

In terms of class formation a major effect of this pattern was the non-emergence of a Welsh industrial bourgeoisie. In the rural areas Welsh gentry, subject to quite different forces, 'opted out of their position as leaders of the community and expended much of their energies in shooting, hunting, fishing, and coursing and attending petty sessions and vestry meetings (Smith, 1980 : 215). In the industrial south, especially following the massive population explosions of the later nineteenth century, the main niche for domestic capital was in commerce. The extractive industries were monopolistically organised and oriented towards the outside, and as a result no significant secondary development emerged - not even shipbuilding, despite the ample opportunities offered by geography (Mathias, 1969).

The rapid industrialisation of Wales was a consequence of expanding markets in the British Empire. Slate demand grew as the stock of U.K. housing trebled in the century as did the demand for domestic coal and industrial production for home and foreign markets. South Wales became as prime an investment area as American railroads or African gold mines (Furtado, 1974) leading to a consolidation of the specialised role. Profits tended to be reinvested elsewhere, rather than in modernising local production, and also tended to be channelled through a small capitalist elite which diverted enough to establish its own distinct style of luxury. By the end of the century not only had the Welsh economy failed to diversify but those industries which generated the wealth were stagnating technically. Germany and U.S.A. extractive industries emjoyed twice the output per man, thanks to extensive investment. Symptomatically, the Thomas 'basic' method of steel production, invented by a Welshman in 1879, was only very slowly adopted by Welsh industry, despite its potential advantages (Morgan, 1981).

In short, early accumulation in Wales imposed a pattern of economic specialisation which became intensified through the nineteenth century. This 'dualistic' and rigid structure was a result of the fact that capital accumulation was initially based on the ability to control large masses of labour and exploit low wages. This permitted the preservation of earlier social institutions, especially in rural areas, and inhibited the emergence of an autonomous capitalist class. In short, the transformation wrought upon Wales from the late eighteenth to late nineteenth century echoed that of many countries in Third World or colonial contexts. Furtado's description of Latin American experience suggests many similarities:

> The result, was almost always to create hybrid structures, part tending to behave as a capitalistic system, part perpetuating the features of a previously existing system . . . . increased economic productivity, resulting from exports of raw materials, caused an increase in and a diversification of the consumption of the well-off minority which was geared to the cultural values of the central countries. This process gave rise to a peripheral capitalism which was unable to generate innovations and was dependent upon decisions coming from the outside. From the economic point of view this appeared as a discontinuity of demand, and industrialisation transformed this discontinuity into the structure of the productive apparatus (Furtado, 1974 : 162).

This 'dualism' of income and production patterns disguised a unity, in that both the 'archaic' and the 'modern' sectors were reproduced by the process of capital accumulation. Indeed, there was often a clear link where the backward sector provided cheap labour, and cheap goods and services, to the advanced sector.

Transition - and the Emergence of the State

Like many Latin American economies Wales was hit especially hard by the depression of the inter-war period, when the broader context which had nurtured expansion in the nineteenth century dramatically disappeared. For the Welsh economy was heavily dependent upon exports, both to England and to newly industrialising countries abroad. This was particularly so for coal: "more than any other section of the British coal industry south Wales was sensitive to overseas competition", (Morgan, 1981 : 213) but slate in the north was also heavily involved in exports and became vulnerable to imports from America and Europe after the turn of the century (Lindsay, 1974).

The narrow economic base, and the high involvement with foreign markets, meant that central governments and international trade policy became particularly important. Until the 1930s the ideological and practical orientation of the British state was unreservedly towards free trade, and this meant that Welsh interests were only secure so long as no substantial competitors emerged abroad. The period from around 1900 to the 1930s was one in which competition emerged rapidly, and at the same time markets shrank with the onset of recession. Consequently, the fact that the state never implemented a protectionist policy, or any compulsion to restructure, had profound economic and political implications in Wales. Indeed, not only did central state policy ignore the interests of labour and industrial capital in Wales, it intervened to sacrifice them in favour of the interests of finance capital centred on the City. In 1901, an export tax was imposed on coal, although this was repealed following vociferous protest. In 1925 Churchill restored the gold-standard and in effect imposed a 10 per cent surcharge on the price of exported coal (Macmillan, 1933). The General Strike and the defeat of the miners perhaps marked the high point of that tendency in state policy which made no concessions to the predominant interests represented in Wales.

There is no space here to trace in any detail the transition from the nineteenth century pattern to that which prevailed after the 1940s, but two themes must be indicated. Firstly the British state acquired a new and more visible role in the economic field, both in general macroeconomic policy and through a number of interventions which had direct spatial consequences. The imposition of protectionism in the 1930s was the thin end of a wedge that widened with direct controls in theh 1940s and a number of new policies after the war. This was not unique to the British state, as virtually every capitalist economy was transformed by radically new forms of state intervention in this period. What was particular to the British state, however, was the feebleness and lack of direction in this transformation. Changes were made and, given the advantages which British firms continued to enjoy over still embryonic competitors, these insured that the impact of recession was mild compared to that which was felt in other countries (Lipiet, 1982). The opportunity was never taken to modernise industry in the way that those other countries did. This was essentially a matter of responding to finance capital and established industrial monopolistic firms rather than innovative new ones. Politically it has been convincingly argued that this reflected the fact that the British state was sufficiently strong to be able to continue to assert imperial priorities and the domination of the south-east. Tom Nairn (1979) suggests that containment, was followed by the defeat of industrialism by an older, more powerful, and more political bourgeoisie. This was of course, the southern, London-based elite, first mercantile and then financial in its interests.

The second theme in the transition to a new pattern concerns the emergence of a centralised labour movement, in which Wales, particularly south Wales, of course played a major part. For a time this had little direct impact on the economic policy pursued by the state despite the alarm calls sounded by those like Macmillan who called for industrial planning to avoid revolution (Macmillan, 1933). Its impact after the war, however, was enormously significant, especially for Wales.

Post War Development Patterns

The early basis for industrialisation had primarily been the extension of exploitation. It is convenient to contrast this with the new pattern which became generalised the following century. In this system the basis of accumulation lay in 'deepening' rather than in 'widening' capital, and in increasing productivity rather than the number of workers employed. This also entailed orienting production towards affluent elite consumers rather than the larger numbers of low-income consumers. Where those elite consumers were the very workers whose productivity was increased by rising investment, the result was to create a system, Fordism, in which the life-style of wage earners underwent a dramatic change (Mandel, 1975).

One of the major effects of the new regime was to differentiate labour markets. As capital per worker was raised, the rate of expansion of the industrial labour force was slowed down, and a dualism was created "between a small high wage, high productivity sector in advanced countries and a large low-wage, low-productivity sector in the less advanced".[2]

This dualism might have remained one between countries if firms retained their production facilities in their home nation and served markets abroad solely by exports, but from the mid-twentieth century a new pattern began to emerge. Direct foreign investment became increasingly important as a means of penetrating foreign markets when nation states imposed installed protectionist tariff barriers, especially during the depression (Helleiner, 1972). After the war rising domestic incomes, especially in Europe, perpetuated this tendency, and the multinational company became the 'determinant organisational form of big capital' (Quijano, 1974 : 415).

As a result a new dualistic pattern was inserted in most national economics (Wright, 1976). This has brought about a rapid industrialisation of some Third World nations and has led to a de-industrialisation of those nations which had earlier been in the vanguard. These changes were smothered during the long post-war boom by the transient advantages which countries such as Britain and the U.S.A. enjoyed but they emerged with full force after the 1960s.

The combined effect of capital deepening, direct foreign investment, de-industrialisation. and the concentration of capital was to create new national patterns. This was first identified by analysts working in 'Third World' contexts, who noted that the implantation of advanced manufacturing often created "an enclave in as real a sense as a foreign mine ever did" (Hymer, 1979 : 60) since the level of activity in the sector was virtually independent of local markets. A most important consequence was that the demand for labour within this sector became largely unresponsive to the local supply of labour. Only the locally-oriented and controlled sectors would respond to local conditions. Routine labour in the externally oriented or internationalised sector is characterised by high productivity, and can therefore be paid wages above the ruling local rate, but that rate is governed by the low productivity and high level of unemployment in the localised sector. In effect the result has tended to generalise the 'Reserve Army of Labour' on a global scale, increasing the international interdependence of wage rates for similar work functions. At a national level, the effects can be traced in the separation of labour markets. Quijano Obregon (1974) has suggested that this kind of system tends to exclude a 'marginalised' section of the potential work force. A growing sector of the labour force is produced which with regard to the employment needs of the monopolistically organised hegemonic levels of activity is superfluous; and with respect to the intermediate levels organised under the competetive form and consequently marked by permanent instabilityof its weakest enterprises . . . . this labour force is floating, since it tends to be intermittently employed, unemployed or underemployed. Where this marginalisation is severe the labour concerned is pushed out of the direct labour market into non-surplus producing subsistence activites and becomes an 'excluded labour force.

In the earlier pattern of industrialisation wages were controlled both by the direct threat of unemployment and by the dependency of wage-earners on non-market inputs, that is, on the produce of their tenancies and the unpaid labour of their wives and children. In the emergent pattern wage earners are fully immersed in the market, and the local cost of goods and services (housing, food, welfare, etc.) and by organised labour movements. These factors in turn are influenced by the existence of a surplus population. In other words, the control of labour costs is now mediated through a complete spatial and hierarchical fragmentation of the working class, rather than through a direct confrontation with a homegenous class. These new structural relations read-out in myriad patterns of spatial and social differentiation. Prominent amongst these are balkanised labour markets, core-periphery systems with the firm, and inter-firm dependencies, all of which have begun to attract attention in 'advanced' economies. (Quijano Obregon, 1974).

In extremely stylised form we might represent the social implications of this model in terms of the allocation of classes to broad economic sectors. For the sake of simplicity it is convenient to condense the classes to four. I prefer Wright's (1976) solution to the problem of categorising class and opt for the category 'contradictory class locations' for those intermediate between capitalist and working class. The excluded or 'marginalised' groups form an 'underclass'. The dynamic core of the economy, the 'monopolistic' sector, may be differentiated from the 'competetive' sector by virtue of its indirect dependence, via corporate decisions, on non local market and supply conditions. The loci of agency - control centres - are situated according to 'global' criteria', that is, normally the monopolisation of resources limits the scope for accumulation in the competetive or localised sector and this implies that a portion of the local labour force may be ejected downwards into the 'excluded labour force' if its supply is excessive. The class formation associated with this model is represented as in Figure 4:l:

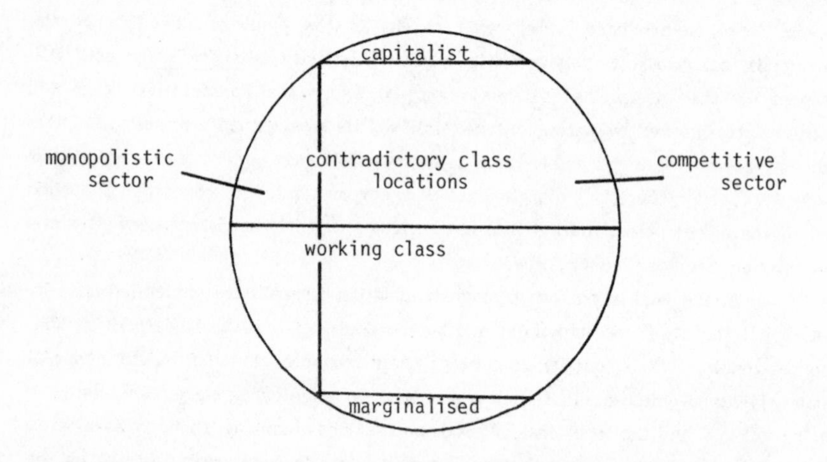

Figure 4:l NATIONAL DEVELOPMENT PATTERN IN LESS DEVELOPED INDUSTRIAL COUNTRIES
(Emergence of 'excluded labour force' or 'marginalised population' due to limited employment opportunities in both the 'monopolistic' and the 'competetive' sector.

Development in Wales During the Long Boom

At first sight the differences between what may be observed in Wales today and the features of this model are far more notable than the similarities. The purpose of this section is to trace 'some' of the evidence for a 'hidden' pattern of the sort described. The subsequent section suggests that the extent to which that pattern has emerged has been profoundly modified by the unitary British state.

a) The 'Monopolistic' or 'Internationalised' Sector

A high proportion of branch-plants of international firms, branches or subsidiaries of U.K. firms which behave in an analogous way, nationalised industries and public sector establishments which are integral to activities on a U.K.-wide scale, and other state establishments, have no direct connection to resource or labour conditions in Wales. These establishments share certain features of ownership and control, employment content, research and development, wage structure, and input and output linkages.

The development of modern manufacturing, and extractive industry in Wales has been almost entirely undertaken by non-locally owned business. Overseas firms account for around 16 per cent of manufacturing employment, and are most important in the larger establishment size groups, with 70 per cent of employment in overseas firms is concentrated in those employing over 500. These firms have been concentrated in the sectors of engineering; metal manufacture; electrical and instrument engineering; vehicles and related trades, and oil. 40 per cent of U.S. firms produce office and industrial machinery and equipment, or chemicals and plastics, and another 18 per cent produce automobiles and components, and oil. The consumer goods produced are electronic items, some clothing, processed foods and Japanese electronic products. Virtually all the foreign firms produce for markets outside Wales, either in the U.K. as a whole or the E.E.C. (Davies and Thomas, 1976). There is an emphasis on exports, one study found that only 4 per cent of output went to other firms in Wales, while 20 per cent of sales were directly exported out of the U.K. and the evidence consistently suggests that 'overseas firms do not regard Wales as a regional outlet for their products'. The composition of employment reflects the fact that these are mainly subordinate plants or subsidiaries within corporate systems: most firms did not come to Wales to recruit skilled labour, and there is a general absence of higher management and R & D personnel at these plants. Unskilled labour accounts for 58 per cent of all jobs created, and the establishments are concentrated in those sectors where female has been growing fastest. Also, in 1977, R & D expenditure was on average only 77 per employee and half the firms did not undertake any R & D at all. One study describes these as units in which 'the benefits of R & D in the companies' headquarters are embodied in product design, a somewhat ingenuous way of referring to their lack of innovation and subordinate status (Davies and Thomas, 1976).

The other 'foreign' firms, those owned or controlled elsewhere in the U.K., are less well documented. They probably account for about two-thirds of all manufacturing employment and are most important in the middle size ranges. Welsh firms predominate in the smaller size ranges and overseas firms have their greatest presence in the largest ranges (Tomkins and Lovering, 1973).

TABLE 4:1 Overseas-owned manufacturing establishments in Wales

Year	Number	Employment Provided
1949	16	14,OOO
1959	3O	18,3OO
1969	82	34,6OO
1974	127	52,817
1977	177	5O,3OO
1978	168	-

Source: 1949-74 Davies and Thomas (1976)
1978 Welsh Economic Trends, (198O)
1978 Development Corporation for Wales (1978)

Few non-Welsh establishments are able to exercise much autonomy over investment decisions. On the whole U.K. firms and overseas companies delegate little initiative to their Welsh plants, which are basically assembly units. Migration patterns tend to corroborate this impression. Most out-migrants have been managers of large firms, or professional, intermediate or junior non-manual workers. In-migration has brought in the self-employed, small-scale managers, own-account workers, and foremen. By 198O only 6.4 per cent of Welsh male heads of households held administrative or technical jobs compared with 11.2 per cent in south east England. Branch-plant development in Wales in the 197Os is also reflected in the fact that female employment grew by twice the U.K. average, that is, at 1.5 per cent annually, and male employment fell by eight times the U.K. average.

The evidence on worker productivity is also indicative of new style enclave development. In the 197Os net output per worker in Welsh manufacturing was higher than that for the U.K. as a whole and second only to the south east England region. In metal manufacture and engineering it was very much higher than the national average. Wales developed a concentration of high productivity employment, cancelling out, on aggregate, the effect of the fringe of low-productivity sectors. The net result was an overall decline in the total of well-paid (male, skilled) jobs, and a rise in lower-paid (female, unskilled) employment. This qualitative shift took place within a more or less unchanged total employment of around a million workers.[3]

An indication of the limited development of a genuine industrial leadership is the fact that there are relatively few high income earners and wealthy people in Wales. In Great Britain the wealthiest 5 per cent of the population possess abount a third of the wealth over 5,000 (in 1966 prices). In Wales the top 5 per cent owned only about a quarterof the similar wealth. Investment income in Wales, which is a major source of income only for the capitalist class, is proportionately even smaller (Revell and Tomkins, 1974).

The benefits of manufacturing growth have been concentrated on selected areas and particular groups of workers. This is a pattern of nodes of limited development and is reflected in the transport network, which has expanded to re-emphasise the orientation towards England. By the late 1970s, 70 per cent of overseas firms setting up in south Wales did so within ten miles of existing or proposed motorways, and all those in north Wales have been close to the arterial link to Cheshire and the north west of England. Later arrivals, including Japanese electronics factories, have intensified this pattern.

In historical perspective the growth of manufacturing in Wales into the late 1970s was remarkable. Investment in manufacturing in Wales was continually greater, proportionally, than in the U.K. as a whole - thus in 1975 some 7 per cent of U.K. investment in manufacturing went to Wales, while only around 4 per cent of U.K. manufacturing output came from Wales. Even after the onset of recession in 1980 the imbalance remained, at 6 per cent and 4 per cent respectively. In this limited sense it was not completely wrong to talk of a 'new industrial revolution' in Wales. However, the spread effects in terms of employment, market stimuli and incomes in other activities were not at all 'revolutionary' in this apologetic sense.

b) The 'Competetive' or 'Localised' Sector

In many cases, activity is governed by local demand and accumulation is controlled by locally-owned capital. These sectors consist of small establishments and utilise relatively labour-intensive technologies. The classic instances emerge within the categories of construction and tourism and both of these are particularly important in Wales.

Some 16 per cent of jobs lie within construction and miscellaneous services. In addition some 25,000 people are self-employed in retailing and a further 120,000 work in shops with an average of 4 employees per establishment.[4] Part of the 'localised' sector might also lie within the industrial heading of Manufacturing; almost 3,000 manufacturing establishments employ less than ten persons each, with a further 500 employing between ten and twenty persons (Welsh Economic Trends, 1977). While many of these are undoubtedly peripheral contractors to firms we would regard as being in the 'monopolistic' sector, some may be small capitals conditioned by local markets.

The presence of a 'localised' sector might also be inferred from data on incomes. Despite the high wage, high productivity strategy of leading firms, Wales has a higher proportion than the U.K. of workers receiving incomes below the regional average. The sectors which probably contain the greatest 'localised' content, especially tourism, miscellaneous services and construction notoriously pay low wages.

The impression given by ownership patterns and income levels is reinforced by data on technical interdependencies. The sectors in which the highest proportion of inputs came from within Wales, other than coke ovens, iron and steel and coal mining, were the localised activities of construction, building and distribution and services. The same study found that the communications, distribution and services sectors had an 'essentially local quality' (Iveson, 1978) in the sense that an increased activity in these sectors tended to 'leak' out of Wales, in the form of demand for U.K. firms, to a lesser degree than any others except coal mining[5]

The disarticulation between levels of the territorial economy is not solely a matter of technical interdependencies, nor of incomes or ownership. The fragmentation of the labour market affects demand profiles, which reinforce the fragmentation of the productive apparatus. A remarkable example was discovered in a study of the economy of Anglesey. Taking into account the combined effects of technical linkages and of the demand patterns characterising different income levels it was found that an increase in the income of medium-income professional and managerial workers could <u>reduce</u> income and output in the rest of Anglesey. The significance of this finding is best made in the words of the authors of the study:

> . . . . this is the type of income increase that one can expect with modern industry and associated activity, and the implications are quite clear. The introduction of modern industry alone is not sufficient for the regeneration of the regional or subregional economy . . . . the industry and its attendent labour will gradually become an enclave in an economy to which it has little economic relation (my emphasis added) (Sadler, Archer and Owen, 1974 : 78).

In short a lot of circumstantial evidence consistent with the view that Wales, like many less developed countries, has experienced the disintegration of the production systems lying within its borders. As a very rough rule of thumb we might guess that at least one quarter of the working population is engaged in the 'monopolistic' or enclave sector, and most of the remainder in the 'localised' sector.[6] The 'marginalised' would include the unemployed, 'disposable' female workers lost to unemployment statistics, and young people on state 'make-work' schemes. The discovery that Wales has a highly dualistic economy should not be taken as proof that Wales is an underdeveloped country. For one thing, this pattern of fragmentation is observable elsewhere in the U.K. and in advanced countries generally. More pertinently, when we look at the role played by the British state we are bound to conclude that it has transformed this process in a manner that has no conceivable equivalent in an independent less developed nation.

The Role of the State

A major conceptual difference between regional and 'national' development arises from the presence of an overarching body which embraces a region together with other areas. A unitary state is able to redistribute activities and incomes, within limits, and this may govern development at a regional level. These effects derive partly from the application of universalistic policies which the region in question is disproportionally qualified to draw upon (for example, welfare services), partly from deliberate interventionist measures designed with regional or industrial goals in mind, and partly from the general regime of accumulation which state decisions influence. From the point of view of a sub-region these effects alter the local level and pattern of effective demand - the purchasing power in the hands of different classes in the local population - and influence the composition of the local production apparatus.

In Wales the immediate effect of the presence of a unitary state has been to generate a net inflow of income. This is quite the reverse of the external relationship experienced by most independent peripheral countries which have to allocate a large part of domestic output to repaying interest and royalties on foreign capital. Aggregate spending has been greater than aggregate production by some 10 per cent, throughout the 1970s representing an inflow of some thousands of millions of pounds (Tomkins, 1972; Welsh Economic Trends, 1976). In effect this is a disguised Central Government subsidy for an indefinite balance of payments deficit (Moore and Rhodes, 1975).

If there is any outflow of private capital, which seems unlikely, it is greatly counterbalanced; if there is an inflow of private capital, which seems likely, it is still dwarfed by this inflow of public funds. We may visualise two dimensions to this effect; firstly, it puts money in the hands of workers and employers in Wales; secondly, some part of the flow is directly connected to measures which aim to influence the structure of the productive apparatus. The 'consumption' impact and the impact on the productive apparatus each have a different significance.

The former immediately influences the size of the 'localised' sectors via the increase in purchasing power - especially since much of it is distributed spatially across the whole of Wales through, for example, grants to the personal sector, public investment in, construction, and subsidies to local authority employment. The latter tends to be more associated with the intensification of 'monopolistic' industry and services especially via public sector investment in nationalised industries, defence-based activities, infrastructure and industrial services, and decentralised state offices. The ambivalent role of the state in the economy is thus reflected in the spatial impact of the public sector; the 'effective demand' effect may tend to some extent to redress the imbalances associated with modern development, yet the 'production' effect may tend to intensify them, but this is a contingent matter. It would be dogmatic to identify the demand effect solely with redistribution and the production effect solely with restructuring, a priori.

a) Impact on Consumption

Public expenditure per capita is greater in Wales than in the U.K. on all counts except Housing and Law and Order. Average household expenditure is made up by social security benefits to a far higher extent in Wales (12.8 per cent) than in the U.K. (10 per cent) and this effet is more pronounced in the more deprived areas. In addition the public sector employs proportionately more people in rural areas than does the private sector, thus 7 per cent of public sector establishments employing over 25 persons are in mid-Wales compared with only 3 per cent of private sector establishments (Tomkins and Lovering, 1973). This is because the public sector, including local authorities and nationalised industries, provides most of those services which are needs-related and cannot be centralised so easily. The inflow from the state permits this provision to rise to a higher level than would otherwise be the case, thus raising employment, incomes and demand.

The impact is greater than is suggested by aggregate figures due to the effect of a high multiplier. The Anglesey study, for example, found that an increase of 1,000 in local authority spending generated a final increase in demand of 1,570, significantly higher than that produced by engineering or financial services (Sadler, et.al., 1974). In the long run, this may have a major effect of inhibiting decline by sustaining local activity.

b) Impact on Productive Apparatus

The restructuring effects of the state are more than simply the sum of interventionist policies, for the state in the second half of the twentieth century plays a fundamental role at a deeper level. Decisions reached within the state affect the ranking of economic priorities, and so structure patterns of demand and supply. This effect is now so pervasive that it is no longer possible to regard the state as solely concerned with ameliorating or controlling the consequences of economic activity, it also partly guides that activity. The state, is, of course, constrained in arriving at these decisions, and considerable debate has taken place over the degree and form of its 'autonomy' (Jessop : 1982). However, an interactive process is at work here; if economic interests constrain state policy, state policy in turn constrains economic developments. It becomes impossible to map this process in terms of a simple base'superstructure model, and the relationship might be seen instread as one in which state action is largely constitutive of the economic structure, particularly at a regional level (Poulantzas, 1975). For example, it determines, within limits, the size of particular labour and product markets. These limits, however, may be set by factors beyond the states immediate influence, such as international competetion.

The terms of reference of state actors are, moreover, political rather than economic, in that their concern is with the 'national interest' as requiring the defence of the existing social roder against internal challenge, and any commercial, military or ideological challenge from other states (Miliband, 1983). Their ability to preserve order is greater than their ability to influence economic activity since the latter is partly controlled via private transnational institutions. As a result, the nation-state tends to assume the function of maintaining order rather than maximising the whole set of conditions for accumulation. Internationally this reads out in global demand, and in the politically sustained recession of the 1970s and 1980s, but it has less impact on global capacity since that is mainly in the hands of private capital, which may respond contrarily to market shortage by redoubling its efforts to increase productivity. The concern with 'national interest' does, however, lead to direct productive effects where this is deemed necessary. The most outstanding example is perhaps that of defence; the state has a monopoly of the legitimate use of armed force. It aims to maintain the effectiveness of that monopoly against both internal and external threats, and this commits it to intervention in productive industries in the defence sectors. Here too, however, political and ideological considerations intervene, by defining what is a suitable defence strategy and appropriate defence industry. The adoption of a heavy defence role, first for Imperial and then for NATO goals, committed the British state to supporting a cluster of leading firms and industries. This had immediate results on spatial development. In the 1930s, it brought about stable employment in Bristol while south Wales was deep in unemployment, since the war it has consolidated the south east of England's lead in technological innovation (Karldor, 1982).

After the war the compromise in favour of working class interests was embodied in a number of industrial and social policies. The explicit regional element was a minor part. Far more important in terms of employment and industrial development in Wales was the commitment to nationalised industries. This grew out of the alliance between organised labour and industrial capital and reflected the immediate interests of both. The nationalisation of coal, for example, met the demands both of the miners and the Labour party and the demand for cheaper organised output voiced by industrial capital. This policy resulted in consolidating the existing spatial pattern of coal production. The post-war development of the steel industry also reflected the political pressure of the trades unions to consolidate the existing centres of steel employment, and the locational inertia of the entrenched private monopolies which owned the industry. In both cases, policy was limited to these conservative demands, and no attempt was made to modernise the industries coherently, to develop associated industries as part of a powerful integrated bloc, or to link sectoral expansion to regional questions:

> . . . . it has been no part of the policy of the Iron and Steel Board, or for that matter of the steel industry while under temporary public ownership, to consider regional economic development (Morgan, 1979 : 9).

These industries consequently developed on lines similar to those of 'monopolistic' sector firms.

Government office development led to the emergence of major employment at Swansea, Newport and on a 'regional state machine' in Cardiff (Cooke, 1982a). This was also partly a consequence of the regional form given to class interests, as embodied in the Welsh pressure groups in the Labour movement. It did not result in the creation of a regionally integrated economy but, on the contrary, intensified the disarticulation of activities within the same territory. Regional policy is a relatively minor dimension of the state's productive impact. Nevertheless it had an impact in increasing employment in Wales, especially from the early 1960s to the early 1970s. On one estimate some 70,000 jobs were created in the 1960s, (Moore and Rhodes, 1975) on another it accounted for one third of manufacturing jobs (MacKay, 1979). Any estimate of this kind involves assumptins about what would otherwise have happened, and begs difficult economic and political questions (Massey, 1979). In our perspective it was but one element of a paticular state orientation and cohered with other components, but this is not to dismiss the variations due to different policies.

Overall, it seems probable that the role of the U.K. state was an ambivalent one. On the one hand it exacerbated the development of separate economic layers within Wales by directing the British economy as a whole along a path characterised by increasing internationalisation, increasing industrial concentration and the consolidation of existing large firms. On the other hand its sectoral and regional measures ensured for many workers in Wales a relatively advantaged place in the consequent division of labour. In terms of our model, it probably expanded employment in both the 'monopolistic' and 'localised' sectors. The result was to generate a number of effects both in the realm of production and of distribution or consumption. These together intensified the 'disintegration' of the economic apparatus situated in Wales while redistributing income in a broadly compensatory manner.

Here is the major feature differentiating the development of Wales from that of independent small nations through the agency of the unitary state: the development of territorial consumption was detached from that of the territorial pattern of production, while the development of production was itself modified and expanded.

Class Formation

The argument here suggests that 'general' state functions may read-out spatially in quite uneven and important ways. The Welsh example can be visualised - very simplistically - in terms of 'shifts' in the local boundaries of economic sectors. (Figure 4:2).

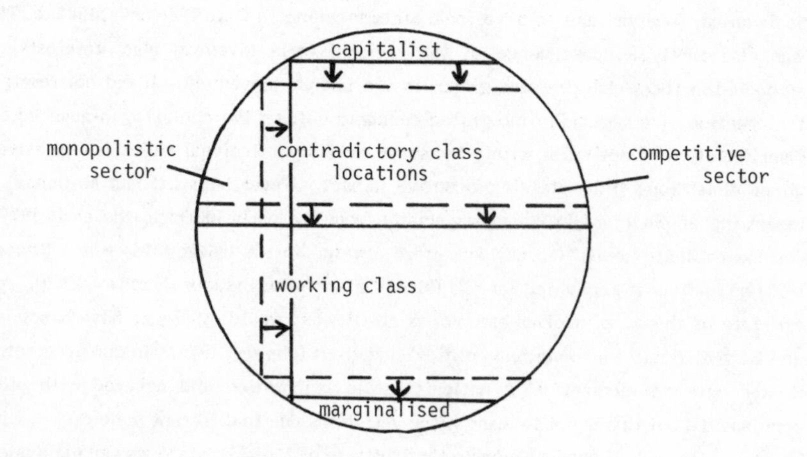

Figure 4:2 EFFECTS OF AN OVERARCHING STATE
(Effects represented by the arrows showing : expansion of the 'contradictory locations' and 'marginalised').

If this interpretation is correct then one result of state measures has been to expand the ranks of those occuyping 'contradictory class locations'. This is partly through expanding the 'monopolistic' private sector and so creating more niches for managers, technicians, supervisors, and advantaged workers, but it is more a result of public sector expansion, particularly in central and local state office employment. To some extent it is also a consequence of the new lease of life the state has given to the competetive 'localised' sector, insofar as this has generated a cadre of owner-managers who have risen to become small capitals. So whereas the early development pattern dramatically hindered the growth of a bourgeoisie in Wales the current pattern has generated several new 'quasi-bourgeois' niches. This social pattern has had a profound impact on cultural and political developments in Wales. It is widely recognised, for example, that the emergence of this 'middle class' cluster has been associated with the political growth of nationalism. Khlief, for example, refers to the social background of Welsh nationalism in 'the new intelligentsia' which has 'used ethnicity as a tool for recreating a sense of distinctiveness, a rallying point for unity . . . . a symbol of a quest for economic advancement' (1978 : 116).

Khlief's argument, may now be re-situated: the Welsh economy has been re-structured in a manner that created a large group of workers who experience an ambivalent relation to class categories. In this contradictory milieu, it has often been argued that the prime source of ideological development tends to lie outside the domain of work (Poulantzas, 1975; Williams, 1981) and to be centred in the family. Various studies have suggested that that the family, closely bound up with religion and notions of community, is the main sphere in which traditional institutions are reproduced; more specifically, the family and informal domains tend to be those in which the Welsh language is predominant (Clayton, 1958; Williams, In press). It is perhaps not surprising, therefore, that in its heyday the new development pattern resulted in a new emphasis on the Welsh language. The new class locations provided a new material basis for 'ethnicity'.

This effect has been confined to those areas where the new pattern overlaid communities which already 'lived in Welsh'. Inevitably the same process of class formation in other areas would produce different effects, indeed it may elsewhere have been the material basis for quite different forms of familistic ideology, such as Thatcherism. Thus the fragmentation of the economy, the decomposition of the working class, and the 'over-development' of ambiguous class positions has resulted in the emergence of an ambivalent nationalist movement, particular to Wales. Yet at the same time it has resulted in the emergence of quite different political patterns which closely echo developments in England. The growth of nationalism has, after all, been matched by the growth of conservatism, and a rising Toryand SDP share of Welsh elected seats (Williams, 1982).

Conclusion

The particular political alliance, and combination of global market conditions which characterised the post-war pattern of accumulation began to decay rapidly from the mid-1960s. The well established British firm could once "hardly help making money" (Turner, 1971 : 55) but foreign competition re-emerged, and the familiar pattern of relative economic decline set in. A number of attempts from the early 1960s to the mid 1970s failed to restructure the institutions of the British state and of private capital to generate a thorough-going modernisation which might have restored international competetiveness. The result was accelerating de-industrialisation and even more rapid internationalisation. Major firms increased their investment abroad and abandoned traditional products without replacing them with alternatives that had the same employment content. Meanwhile, the post-war political consensus had institutionalised working class demands for rising general living standards. The compromise became unworkable, and the political balance of forces became unstable (Nairn, 1981).

Throughout the 1970s orthodox economists argued that a resolution of this tenstion could only come through a radical shift to the left or the right (Bacon and Eltis, 1978) and both conservative and marxist historians anticipated a restructuring of the policies, the institutions, and the ethos of the state (Middlemas, 1981; Nairn, 1981). From 1979 a solution of a sort emerged in the form of the Thatcher government. For the first period in office it concentrated on re-assembling the apparatus of policies oriented towards industry in an effort to break with inherited patterns by 'crashing the economy' (Harrison, 1982). It was highly successful, in forcing up unemployment beyond what had been thought unacceptable levels, in substantially subverting the autonomy of local government and trades unions, and in accelerating militarism, thereby shattering several icons of received political wisdom. At the time of writing it is poised to apply equally drastic surgery to the welfare state via further public spending cuts and the privatisation of education and health (Lee, 1982). The foreseeable future, therfore, is one in which the economic and social apparatus are drastically re-modelled along lines that differ fundamentally from those of the long post-war era. The role of the state, after two generations or more of stability, is changing radically.

The consequences have already manifested themselves dramatically in Wales. Steel was targeted for rapid sectoral restructuring and this was achieved through a burst of redundancies, reducing employment in metal manufacturing in Wales by 34,000 in three years. Meanwhile, regional policies were redesigned. In addition to a decline in overt regional assistance a covert shift appears to have taken place towards encouraging new development in English areas which have never had 'regional problems' at all - the 'Western Corridor' along the M4 or the 'Sunbelt' from Bristol to Cambridge - and the funding and autonomy of local government is apparently, being restructured in line (Thomas, 1983).

In the terms of the model the consequences may be visualised, comfortingly, as merely shifts in lines and a reversal of arrows, a tendency for all categories to contract except that of the marginalised. Of course, it is just possible that a general decline in wages and work conditions sustain the 'localised' sector by creating some new openings for small local capitals while some small consumer service markets may survive around the fortunate few employed in high productivity activities in the 'monopolistic' sector. The heightened salience of government policy, the 'shift to dominance of the political', means that it is hard to predict the rate of change. However, there seems little doubt that a fundamental change in patterns of consumption is under way both in terms of consumption through markets and consumption of collectively-provided goods and services, together with a long term restructuring of productive activity.

As the state abandons the ameliorative and adaptive role it has played for nearly two generations, the disjuncture of production and consumption in its spatial sub-regions is likely to diminish. In Wales in particular, the effect of allowing consumption patterns to be governed more closely by production patterns, means that the polarising tendencies of contemporary development are certain to become more starkly apparent.

CHAPTER 5

THE REGIONAL DIVISION OF LABOUR

Philip Cooke

The post war development of the Welsh economy has been marked by three large scale tendencies each of which has had a profound effect on the class composition of the different areas within Wales. The first and most obvious change has involved the massive reduction in employment in the male dominated heavy industries of mining, quarrying and steelmaking. These industries were mainly responsible for the proletarian character of quite large areas of the country as Wales developed and retained its position as the major export resource base of imperial Britain until at least the inter-war years. Despite apparent attempts at diversification of the Welsh economy after the war, coal and especially steel retained an important presence until the reconstruction effort of Harold Wilson's white-hot technological revolution "modernised" the Welsh coal industry into relative insignificance in the 1960s. Then, after a false dawn of employment growth and security following re-nationalisation of the steel industry in 1967, the 1970s saw the reversal of the upward employment trend as the over optimism of the British Steel Corporation management in estimating market expansion and U.K. competetiveness was reflected in rationalisations and closure threats to smaller Welsh works. Finally, of course, the 1980s have witnessed a decimation of steel employment in Wales quite unlike that experienced in any equivalent geographical area, as was recognised by the Welsh Select Committee in commenting upon the effect of monetarist government policy upon the steel industry (Committee on Welsh Affairs, 1980).

The second tendency visible in the Welsh economy has been the fairly belated growth of a secondary manufacturing sector to balance the traditional dependence upon a primary extractive and heavy industry structure, a factor which Hobsbawm (1968) has argued, rather obscurely, prevented Wales from experiencing a proper industrial revolution. As will be shown, an important growth in manufacturing industry employment took place in very diverse areas of Wales during the 1960s and early 1970s to build on the more localised implantation of manufacturing branch-plants during the 1940s. However, during the sustained recession of the 1970s and 1980s it is precisely this sector which has witnessed by far the largest absolute loss of employment in Wales, adding to the distress caused by the rapid "slimming down" of the steel industry and giving Wales the unenviable title of "U.K. region most affected by the recession" in terms of proportionate job-loss. Between 1976 and 1980, Wales lost 75,000 jobs, or 7.4 per cent of its employed population, the next worst affected regions being the west midlands and the north of England, which experienced a 6.5 per cent employment decline (Townsend, 1982).

This loss of employment has also affected the sector of the Welsh economy which, otherwise, has revealed a different general tendency to the other sectors during the post-war period, that is, the service industry. The recession in services has come later and has had a generally slighter effect than that witnessed in manufacturing. Until very recently there has been a long-run upward trend in employment in the service sector in Wales. It is this sector which, to a considerable extent, is responsible for revolutionising the occupational patterns of workers in the diverse areas of Wales. As will be shown below, there have been successive waves of employment growth in services in Wales, beginning in the early 1960s in the Cardiff-Newport area. This was the only area in Wales to be de-industrialising in net terms at the time. Services employment increased its dominance over manufacturing by 9 per cent from 62 per cent of the manufacturing and services total to 71 per cent of that total. Later this pattern spread to the older industrial and coalfield regions until they too began de-industrialising after 1975. The only areas in which there is any manufacturing employment growth at the same time as services employment continues to rise are the rural areas of central and south west Wales. In every case, the majority of workers in this broad setor are women, whose attachment to the labour force has grown massively as that of men has declined.

In what follows, I will seek to show three things. First of all I hope to convey the idea that a changing structure of employment is by no mans unique to Wales. Rather that it has been a general feature of advanced industrial capitalism since the middle of the 1960s and has accelerated through the 1970s. The essence of this idea will be that in order to maintain profitability firms have been splitting up the various stages of the process of production and relocating them where local conditions are most favourable to minimising overall costs. More recently, they have been finding it necessary to make workers redundant, either by introducing new technology, or making those still in employment work harder, while releasing the rest, or simply closing plants down as foreign competition has bitten deeply into traditional markets. Second, I want to examine the effects of this changing regional fragmentation of geographical space within Wales. I hope to demonstrate that in Wales different regions are developing different combinations of characteristics as new developments, often with state guidance, penetrate the distinctive labour markets which are found in different areas of Britain. Of particular importance during the recent past has been the existence of substantial pools of unskilled and unqualified labour in both rural and urban contexts. Third and finally, I hope to show that the variations in the geographical division of labour must be seen primarly as effects of the continuing struggle of firms to solve the constant problem of overcoming the barriers to efficient capital accumulation imposed by the defensive strength of labour. The most significant result of this process in contemporary Wales is the thoroughgoing recomposition of the social structure which it entails. In the latter part of this paper, attention will be devoted to the implications of this restructuring process for Welsh class structure and class relations.

The Concept of a Regional Division of Labour

In order to clarify the above argument, it is important that the concept of a regional division of labour is specified. To do this it will be convenient to define the notion of a "division of labour" first and then relate it to geographical space, justifying the use of the term "regional" at that point.

In a capitalist society the production of commodities is accomplished by members of a class of owners of capital purchasing the skill and strength of members of a class of wage-labourers, and setting them to work on the machinery and raw materials of the capitalist enterprise. The point of this exercise is not simply to produce the means of subsistence, which can be achieved without a class of capitalists, but to accumulate wealth. Continued accumulation depends on increased profits. Because of class resistance expressed through strikes or legal constraints against employers seeking to speed up or prolong the work process, more profits ultimately rely on increased labour productivity. There are two important forms of increasing productivity. The first involves reducing the heterogeneity of tasks for the individual worker by fragmenting the process of production into a series of tasks. The worker may then be assigned the function of repeating a single task rather than attending to the whole range of tasks involved in the production of a commodity. Thus, by dividing up the labour process, greater economic efficiency in terms of more output for the same input, and hence more profits, are achieved for the capitalist.

The second form of increasing productivity arises from the observation that a "primitive" division of labour as described above divides the labour process unevenly. That is, some tasks require a greater input of skill than others. As skill is a scarce resource, those workers in possession of a desired skill will be able to negotiate a higher than average wage for themselves. In order to reduce the knowledge base which enables the skilled worker to demand a higher wage, and thus offset the tendency towards reduced profits, it is in the interests of the employer to simplify the different tasks that go to make up the process of production. This is done by introducting machinery which both lowers the skill factor required and, more importantly, removes the knowledge of the whole production process from de-skilled worker to employer. Since unskilled labour is found everywhere, the capitalist is released from a major constraint on profitability, namely, the shortage and frequent geographical concentration of skilled labour. Thus labour costs may be markedly reduced even though de-skilling may be accompanied by limited re-skilling.

The crucial point here is that by releasing the pressure towards geographical concentration through diminishing the supply problems posed by the scarcity of skilled labour, firms can begin dividing up their labour forces across geographical space. The principal limitations upon this opportunity are, firstly, technical ones such as ease and cheapness of transportation or the degree to which these are offset by government aid. Secondly, a more important limitation is the degree of militancy of particular labour forces. This is often closely related to the degree of competition in regional and local labour markets, and the tradition of labour organisation in various areas of the country.

In Britain the regional division of labour has passed through three phases under capitalism and is now entering a fourth. In the first phase the familiar heavy industry and textile regions became dominant concentrations of production tied closely to imperial export markets. Strong craft unionism was associated with both relatively high regional wage rates and low rates of technical de-skilling. Because of their overwhelming concentration on production of means of production these may be termed Department 1 regions. In the inter-war period the supremacy of these regions began to give way to regions in which the production of consumer and luxury goods was predominant. A primitive regional division of labour between these newer Department 2/3 regions and the older Department 1 regions became evident as the latter increasingly took on the role of suppliers of raw and semi-processed materials to the former. We are talking here in terms of the new centres of light engineering, vehicles, aircraft and consumer durables production in the west midlands of England and the London periphery. These new regions depended heavily upon unskilled local, and de-skilled Department 1 labour, and repressive rules regarding unionisation within the new plants. Labour organisation remained poorly developed in some parts of these regions until as late as the 1960s. Unionism was gradually established during periods of wartime and post-war expansion, and militant opposition to speed-ups grew as general union membership of T.G.W.U. and N.U.G.M.W. also increased at the expense of the craft unions (Beynon, 1973; Massey, 1980; Cooke, 1978).

The tight labour markets and militant opposition to job-shedding productivity deals associated with increased labour organisation in Department 2/3 regions have been key factors in the relatively recent transformation of the regional division of labour. As Department 1 regions showed increasing signs of generating surplus labour to accompany traditionally low female participation rates, branch plants of the English midlands and London car factories, electrical engineering and plastics manufacturers began being located in south Wales and similiar regions from the mid-1960s. Later, these plants were to be found located in north Wales too, and eventually the same has happened in mid Wales.

Once industrialism came to dominate the everyday lives of the majority of Welsh people, quite large parts of the country developed a markedly cohesive working-class culture. Whether in the specialised slate, metal-working or coalmining regions, a familiar, male dominated framework of chapel and/or institute - trade union - Labour Party helped to sustain a strong, locally-created collectivism. Individualism, in the narrow economic sense of the word, failed to make a widespread appeal. Hence, such regions remained very largely working-class, with their few entrepreneurial, animal spirits seeking betterment elsewhere. The interesting, and often understated, feature of the political representation chosen throughout the industrial areas of Wales is how mild this brand of socialism has been. The mainstream of the British Labour Party could hardly have been better served by the Welsh working class.

Whether or not this factor was a hangover from the era of Britain's imperial supremacy, the specialisation in heavy industry in Wales was one aspect of the imperial division of labour on which Britain's world workshop reputation was built. Yet, as erly as 1945, as the high-tide of Labourism was flowing, that imperial division of labour was in substantial decline. In recent years, most obviously during the current slump, it has slid into virtual oblivion under the post-operative neglect of bureaucratic state management. Simultaneously, and also under state guidance, a new division of labour was already emerging. This came to be known as the "branch-plant economy", where industrial estates such as Treforest, and old ammunition sites such as Bridgend or Hirwaun became centres of semi-skilled assembly work in plants managed from the south east of England, the U.S.A. and elsewhere. For a time this process staved off really sharp increases in unemployment, especially in the late 1960s and early 1970s as the coal industry was run down. However, it is precisely in the branch-plant sector that some of the highest rates of unemployment, after those in the steel industry, have been recorded. This is shown in table 5:1, which summarises manufacturing employment change for Welsh regions during the years between 1951 and 1981.

Table 5:1: Employment in Manufacturing

Region	1959	1975	% 1959–1975	(estimated) 1981	% 1975–1981
Central & east Valleys	77,300	111,600	+44	85,000	-24
West south Wales	70,800	81,200	+15	69,000	-15
South Wales Coast	80,700	76,200	-6	60,000	-21
North east Wales	30,800	33,400	+8	25,000	-25
North Wales Coast	3,200	5,900	+84	5,400	-9
North west Wales	7,800	11,900	+53	10,000	-17
Central Wales	1,500	6,200	+313	9,200	+48
South west Wales	2,600	6,00	+131	8,000	+33

Sources: Department of Employment, Office of Population Censuses and Surveys

The remarkable employment switchback effect in manufacturing industry has been spread unevenly throughout the Welsh sub regions. However, there are three main features worth noting from the figures. First, even by 1975 de-industrialisation, in the sense of net manufacturing job loss, was evident in the most prosperous Welsh region centred on the Cardiff-Newport axis. This has speeded up substantially in the last few years. Second, the manufacturing "enclave" which built up rapidly throughout the 1960s and early 1970s in the eastern and central coalfield has suffered a serious employment cutback. Although steel redundancies account for some of these losses, it is clear that branch plants, while not necessarily closing down in large numbers, have shed a large proportion of their employees during this recession. Despite these plants being located in the coalfield, supposedly to employ redundant coalminers, it is well known that many of them only intended to employ women and younger males in the main, preferring these to older, unionised and industrially experienced former miners. Thus unemployment here affects both males and females, although the proportion experiencing redundancy has generally been higher among males, a reflection of the lower cost of female labour. The third feature is that, to some extent, the growth of an "archipelego" of manufacturing industry in parts of rural Wales, which was a feature of the 1960s, has continued, though at a much reduced rate and from what remains a small manufacturing base. This phenomenon of rural industrialisation is also found in parts of rural England and Scotland and may represent a new location strategy by medium-sized firms to escape high costs, union militancy and poor urban environments in more traditional industrial locations.

A New Form of Regional Division of Labour in Wales

It is clear therefore, that by 1975, Wales seemed to have developed a threefold spatial division of labour at a time when changes in manufacturing employment were related to the older Department 1 regionalisation. First of all, there was a single "de-industrialising" region around Cardiff, then an intensive branch plant region in the coalfield area of south Wales and, to a much lesser extent, in the north east Wales. Thirdly, there emerged what appears to be a diffused, rurally based archipelago of branch plants mixed with the traditional agricultural activities of north west and mid Wales. In the two latter subdivisions we would argue that managerial control from within Wales is absolutely minimised but that the archipelago firms are overwhelmingly British owned, whereas the coalfield branch plants have a higher incidence of foreign owned plants.

However, we have to map onto this pattern another more complex one, the clue to the character of which is suggested by the de-industrialising feature of the Cardiff-Newport region. This area has not been losing jobs during the period 1959-

1981, on the contrary, there was a net increase in total employment of 44,000 jobs, more than off-setting the 21,000 jobs lost in manufacturing. The difference was made up by service employment, to which we now turn to consider its effects upon the regional division of labour in Wales.

This process which has continued in the regions of Wales, although to varying degrees, is what might be called the "tertiarisation" of the economy. The primary sector involving coal, quarrying and agriculture has declined massively in employment; the secondary sector of manufacturing industry in Wales has declined after a bried peak in the mid-1970s; but everywhere in Wales, employment in services such as office and shop work, teaching, nursing, maintenance of appliances, and so on, has continued to grow. This is shown in Table 5:2, which indicates the local variations in services employment, until recently the fastest growing general employment sector in Wales. It can be seen that although the rate of increase in tertiary sector employment has slowed, employment growth has been sufficient in numerical terms almost to offset the loss of manufacturing jobs throughout Wales as a whole during the 1976-1981 period.

Table 5:2: Employment in Services

Region	1959	1976	% 1959-1976	(estimated) 1981	% 1976-1981
Central and east Valleys	61,300	95,560	+57	104,000	+7
West south Wales	67,200	88,120	+31	105,000	+19
South Wales Coast	132,00o	180,730	+37	197,000	+9
North east Wales	22,600	36,740	+61	39,000	+5
North Wales Coast	23,500	30,500	+30	31,100	+2
North west Wales	33,000	43,560	+33	46,000	+6
Central Wales	14,600	16,250	+13	19,450	+20
South west Wales	34,100	45,380	+33	54,000	+20

Sources: Department of Employment, Office of Population Censuses and Surveys

If we look at the areas where significant changes have occurred, we find that, first of all, the oldest de-industrialising region, centred on the south Wales coast, has continued to develop as the major concentration of services employment. More surprisingly, if we leave aside parts of rural Wales, it was the industrialised coalfield and metal-working fringe stretching from Swansea to eastern Gwent which registered the largest percentage increases up to the mid 1970s. This process was also evident in north east Wales up to the last few years. In rural Wales growth was slower, especially in mid Wales, although some catching up has been occurring there lately. The north west and south west of Wales were fuelled by growth in tourism and government employment, factors which seem to have diminished more rapidly in north Wales.

Interpreting the New Division of Labour : the Class Dimension

The most striking feature of the changing occupation structure which has been described so far is the distinctiveness of local, or, more accurately, regional patterns. We have been able to identify four groupings:

(a) The Cardiff region which is intensively service orientated, having developed what might be termed a primarily "vocational" services base in the 1960s with the growth of public sector employment. During the 1970s this base has substantially broadened as private sector employment has expanded, especially in miscellaneous commercial sectors. Manufacturing employment is in substantial decline in this area.

(b) There are, next, the urbanised regions in the coalfields and older industrial towns, but also increasingly the administrative/market centres in non industrial regions where there has been a substantial growth in the vocational public services in the 1970s. This development has overlain a temporary growth of manufacturing employment where women are well represented. Women have been even more predominant in the new service occupations.

(c) There are what may be termed the "leisure reserves" of north and west Wales which divide evenly between diffused vocational service growth inland, and concentrated tourism employment nearer to the coast.

(d) There is a large region covering mid Wales which is undergoing "reconversion" from being a primarily agricultural area back to being a service employment although service industries traditionally linked to an agricultural economy are well established. Growth is stronger in manufacturing employment under close state supervision through the Development Board for Rural Wales.

The south Wales coast region is, in parts, notably in south Glamorgan, overwhelmingly tertiarised. Even before the closure of its steelworks with the loss of 4,000 mainly manufacturing jobs, Cardiff in 1976 had 73 per cent of its employment in services, a statistic which has subsequently probably settled closer to the Penarth level of 84 per cent. However, this is the region in which are located the regional headquarters of state productive activity, such as the nationalised industries and government departments which allocate financial assistance to industry, as well as non capitalist state activity such as education and health facilities at all levels of importance. As such, there is a markedly higher representation of higher order state employment, the productive part of which constitutes a fraction of the capitalist class, since it acts directly to further the interests of that class. In addition, since the region offers the widest range of consumption amenities such as high quality housing, environmental and retailing goods, it is likely tht state managers whose workplace is outside the region are nevertheless resident within it, some of these too will be responsible for state productive activity. This is consistent with the evidence that south Glamorgan is the only Welsh county to display higher gross and disposable earnings for men in non manual occupations than the Great Britain average in recent years. Women in non-manual occupations do not earn such high wages in the region (Welsh Economic Trends, 1979).

Having devoted some attention to the state sector in Wales, it is necessary finally to turn to the activities and class effects of the private sector of the economy. It seems likely that there is a greater diversity, in both spatial and class terms, of occupational affiliations here. To return to the basic fourfold regional division identified above, it will be recalled that while the Cardiff area was becoming heavily services orientated, recent growth here was in miscellaneous services such as hotel, entertainment and motor related employment rather than state sector employment. More importantly, parts of the region at a distance from Cardiff, between Bridgend in the west and Cwmbran in the east, have been recipients of new manufacturing jobs, mainly in branch plants. Llantrisant, for example, experienced a 29 per cent increase in employment between 1971 and 1976, mainly in manufacturing, and while growth was more evenly spread between manufacturing and service employment in Caerphilly, Bridgend, Cwmbran and Risca, nevertheless these are developing as notable counter-magnets to the de-industrialising cities of Cardiff and Newport.

In this region, therefore, it seems likely tht during the 1970s, there was an overall increase in low order manual and non manual employment, even though the large centres of employment showed declining trends. These losses were more than compensated for by increases, especially in manufacturing jobs, in the smaller outlying towns. The crucial social distinction to be made about the increases in employment which have been made in these smaller centres is that although they may be new jobs, they are more homogeneous in terms of the low skill level required of their recipients than those manufacturing jobs which have been lost in the cities of Newport and Cardiff.

Associated with the changing division of labour is de-skilling, an associated proletarianisation of the labour force, and the increased involvement of women rather than men in the new employment. The proletarianisation effect is supplemented by growing levels of female employment in low order service occupations in both the public and the private sector. Substantially more women in these jobs in Wales work part time than is the case in other parts of Britain (Cooke, 1982b), a reflection of high male unemployment and a willingness on the part of females to accept poor wages and conditions of work in the context of over supply in the labour market. Proletarianisation of the kind discussed is occurring in the relatively prosperous south Wales coast region to a greater extent than in most regions of Wales, but unlike elsewhere it is accompanied by the growth of a state bourgeoisie and a class of middle order managers of decentralised productive and non productive (e.g. banks, finance houses) private enterprises. Together these latter enterprises supply a distinctive and spatially concentrated flavour to the regional bourgeoisie.

The second distinctive kind of region is that focussed upon the older industrialised regions such as the coalfield and metal manufacturing centres in the central and east Valleys, west south Wales and north east Wales. Each of these has certain common features but is also quite distinctive in terms of the developing regional division of labour.

Each of these gained in manufacturing employment throughout the 1960s and early 1970s, but subsequently de-industrialisation has taken its toll, less so in west south Wales than in the other two regions. These coalfield regions were developing as exemplars of the branch plant economy during this period as government incentives attracted expanding British, and some overseas, firms to a location which offered abundant supplies of labour for the unskilled and semi-skilled stages of the manufacturing production process. It has by now become a well established observation that it was not the former coalminers, made redundant by opportunistic changes in state energy policy, who were being re-employed in great numbers, but their wives and daughters. The latter, often new to non domestic work, constituted a prime source of non militant low wage workers vital to the routine assembly work which is typical of the branch plant in the Valleys. The result of this transformation has been contradictory in terms of the local class structure. Clearly, the process described is one which has augmented the proportion of the regional population having experience of a proletarian class position, since the new workers are selling their only asset, which is their labour power, to private enterprise. At the same time, however, experienced male workers have been driven out of the labour force to occupy a marginalised position of long term unemployment, thus constituting, or rather augmenting, a permanent labour reserve.

Despite these characteristics, which relate to manufacturing employment, it remains the case that service sector employment is becoming predominant in the central and east Valleys, especially since the early 1970s. The most rapid growth has been in the vocational, distributive and miscellaneous service industries and these jobs have overwhelmingly been taken by women. It is also of considerable importance to note that there is an exceptionally high incidence of part time working in these feminised occupations, and that such employment is normally associated with poor working conditins, a lack of any serious career structure, and exclusion from many rights statutorily available to full time employees. There seems to be some basis for the argument that this latter group comprises a burgeoning secondary segment of the labour market in Wales (McNabb, 1980).

Finally, it should also be noted that there is a small and relatively unimportant group of self employed workers in this region, marginally less in proportion than that found in other regions of industrial south Wales. This group, insofar as it is composed of individuals who own capital and employ labour in exchange for wages, belong to the same broad class grouping as the state bourgeoisie and regional managers of capitalist enterprise.

West south Wales shares many of the features described above, except, outstandingly, for the part occupied by Swansea. In that city, there has been substantial concentration of regional service sector growth. Employment in services in Swansea is proportionately quite close to that of Cardiff and much higher than that of Newport. Most of this growth has been in state service sector employment in both decentralised central government as well as expanded local government tertiary activity. The work which is available in these growth sectors seems unlikely to be substantially different in terms of skill or qualification requirements from much of the new state employment elsewhere in Wales. North east Wales too has been recipient of new branch plant employment but at a much lower level and at a slower rate of increase than has been the case in industrial south Wales. Also, the impact of employment growth in the steel industry in the 1960s, and to a lesser extent throughout the the 1970s, made a significant contribution to a manufacturing workforce whch remained heavily male dominated. In this respect, the region has until recently retained a more traditional employment structure than those in the industrial south. Tertiarisation has nonetheless taken place, though at a more evenly accelerting pace than elsewhere in Wales with feminised vocational and miscellaneous occupations predominating. The proportion of self employed workers is almost as low as in the south, and it seems likely that this region, like the south, remains overwhelmingly proletarianised.

Before discussing the north west Wales, south west Wales, and central Wales regions, it is important to consider the interesting outlier regions focussed upon the north Wales coast. For here is an area with very different development patterns from those in its neighbouring regions. Unlike north east Wales, it has demonstrated substantially greater percentage increase in manufacturing employment, albeit from a low base, than in its tradtionally large service sector. Unlike north west Wales, it still remais a sharply increasing level of tertiary activity as well as a higher rate of manufacturing employment growth. Employment in tourism is plainly the dominant economic activity although this is beig supplemented by some growth in vocational and miscellaneous services. In the centres where service activity predominates, female activity rates are higher as in Rhyl, Colwyn Bay and Llandudno. However, female wage rates in precisely these areas are amongst the lowest to be found anywhere in Wales, averaging 6 per cent less than the Welsh average and 11 per cent less than that for Great Britain. Male earnings are also low, though not so depressed in relative terms as those of women. This region is characterised by an exploited class of service employees concentrated in the seasonal tourist trade, augmented by a smaller element of lower order local state service workers and a small but growing manufacturing workforce. Only the latter groups are likely to be in a position, through their comparative advantage with regard to unionisation, to improve wages and working conditions discernibly; the former group is likely to be a disorganised secondary segment in the labour market united only by a shared objective class position. The dominance of the self employed in tertiary activity in this region is suggestive of a substantial petty bourgeoisie of owners of productive service sector capital, employing wage labour under conditions markedly favourable to the interests of the former class.

Next, it is important to comment upon changes occurring in the large "leisure reserves" of north west Wales and south west Wales, in which some tendencies are shared with the region just described, notably an increasing level of penetration by industrial capital in industries such as textiles, light engineering and food processing, though still at a relatively low absolute level of employment. In addition there has been service sector growth, mainly in professional services, notably in education and health. The rate of such growth has climbed sharply in south west Wales while falling back somewhat in north west Wales. Nonetheless, between two thirds and three quarters of workers in these regions are neither owners of capital nor employers of labour and to that extent should rightly be considered working class, this should also include most of the state employees in these regions, including the substantial numbers of military operatives, few of whom are engaged in either productive or unproductive capitaist state activity. It seems likely that the development of tourism in these regions will tend to reproduce elements of the north Wales coast class structure over an extended area.

The latter process has remained least developed in the last region to be considered, which is central Wales. Here the level of service employment approaches half of the civilian labour force and yet, unlike the position elsewhere, there has been relatively low growth in the tertiarisation of the economy in the 1970s to compensate for the lowest growth in the period up to 1959. Manufacturing employment has grown threefold from a minute base in 1959 as mid Wales has become a state managed branch plant outpost of the midlands and south of England.

Conclusion

There are three important conclusions that can be drawn from the preceding evidence. First of all, the old, relatively cohesive, class structures of the Welsh regions have been radically recomposed by economic forces. One key to this recomposition lies in juxtaposing the massively increased levels of unemployment - increasing from 8 per cent in north east Wales, 7 per cent to 16 per cent in west south Wales, 6 per cent to 14 per cent on the south Wales coast, 8 per cent to 17 per cent in central and east Valleys, between 1976 and 1981, for instance - with the fact that taken together, employment has only declined slightly in manufacturing and services, even during the height of the present recession.

Basically, unemployment has affected males in manufacturing industry most severely with between 5 per cent and 10 per cent of jobs in this sector having been lost in most regions. By contrast, the level of unemployment among women has risen by between 5 per cent and 10 per cent in the same areas, quite striking increases in part time working having occurred. So the typical worker in the old foalfield will now be a woman, probably married, possibly with grown-up children, who may work part-time in a shop or office. The old class structures of industrial Wales have thus fragmented into an underclass of long-term unemployed older males and young people, a male and female working-class including small remnants of the imperial division of labour, larger remnants of the branch plant economy, and a growing army of women service workers, many of whom are non unionised and in receipt of low wages and poor working conditions. In rural Wales, the old social structure of petty-bourgeoisie (farmers, auctioneers, solicitors, etc.) and agricultural workers has been invaded by a small, but growing, industrial working class and the ubiquitous service workers. In the service dominated centres of the south Wales and north Wales coasts, there is a diminishing industrial working class and a growing managerial middle class, on the one hand, and a white collar proletariat on the other.

The second point, is that it cannot be assumed that the disappearance of heavy industry and, to an increasing extent, light industry, and the growth of female and white collar work means that Wales is becoming objectively more middle-class. There has been of late, a grieving disinclination to return socialist candidates at elections. But, as we have seen, many of the new jobs, especially for women, are in poorly paid occupations with poor working conditions, whether in branch plants or the service industries. While households, in which both husband and wife are working, may enjoy a reasonable level of living by comparison with many, their work experience will remain proletarian and so may their political outlook. The key sector may be the large group which works for the state in one of its many guises. Most of the state jobs in Wales do not involve either higher managerial functions or profit making, but are middle to lower order educational, health or administration jobs whose occupants may be politically undecided, and hence look to the S.D.P. or

Liberal Party.

Despite the financial assistance from the State, there has been a large decline in manufacturing employment and a continuing increase in service sector employment which is less strongly supported by government assistance. This points to the inadequacy of central government efforts to aid the regions of Wales. Such efforts seem to be diminishing in relevance, given three important tendencies which are emerging from recent social and economic transformations. The first is a growth in "localism"; that is, a greater attempt by local communities to come to terms with their economic problems (Urry, 1981). This is reflected in the growth of the "self-service" economy involving more do-it-yourself activity or the exchanging of local skills, leading into the black economy, and so on. This will be likely to develop further to the extent that long term unemployment is consolidated. Secondly, there is the continuing growth of the formal services sector, which is often labour intensive, feminised, and offers poor pay for long hours, especially in the private sector. This sector may well keep growing, especially where fast food and fast fixing services are concerned. Lastly there are visible signs of efforts by some local councils to develop integrated local development, local manpower planning, and local funding and infrastructural provisions for local ventures. Efforts in this direction in Wales have been pitiful when compared to, for example, Sheffield's establishment of a new local authority department of employment, or the local enterprise boards in London and Birmingham. While these efforts may make only a limited impact upon present unemployment levels, the collective experiences and confidence which people, who in the past were merely employed "hands", may gain through the rediscovery of localism in their now more broadly skilled communities, may enable them to make out if local politicians and bureaucracies also begin to recognise that a familiar world has been unmade and an unfamiliear one is already upon us.

CHAPTER 6

POPULATION TRENDS IN MID-WALES: SOME POLICY IMPLICATIONS[1]

Richard H. Morgan

The two pieces of research reported in this paper are part of wider studies of patterns of migration out of, and into, mid-Wales. The origins of the research are explained in brief and, in so doing, an attempt is made to relate the specific findings of these pieces of research to a wider body of research findings. The first study is a survey of out-migrants who left the Tregaron area of mid-Wales during the period 1965-1970. The second set of results is drawn from a study of recent patterns in the movement of population to Newtown, mid-Wales' major growth centre. Finally the research results provide a framework for an examination of some of the policy issues relevant in mid-Wales at the present time.

Out-Migration

Several research workers have examined the flows of migrants between areas by using census data. Such studies have looked at migration between standard metropolitan areas in the U.S.A. (Lowry, 1966; Rogers, 1966; Greenwood, 1969), and between standard regions in the U.K. (Hart, 1970; Masser, 1970). The premise of all this research has been that differences in the volume of inter-regional migration can be explained by inter regional economic differences. Hypotheses related to differences in unemployment rates, in regional incomes and so on have been tested in these analyses. One of the main conclusions to emerge from these inquiries has been that, in spite of reasonably high levels of statistical explanation, the variables measuring differences in economic opportunity seem to play an insignificant role. Cordey-Hayes and Gleave (1973) found a strong direct correlation between the per capita rates of in-migration in their analysis of city-region data for England and Wales. Declining regions with low wages and high unemployment were observed to have the lowest per capita rates of out-migration and minimal in-migration. They suggest that regional decline should be associated with a lack of a compensating flow of in-migrants rather than with high out-migration. Rogers (1976) challenged their interpretation of the results and has demonstrated that the empirical results do not necessarily contradict the economic push-pull hypothesis of migration which states that migrants will tend to move from regions with either high unemployment rates or low wages to regions with low unemployment rates or high wages.

Williams (1978) has suggested that the long-term solution to this debate lies in the acquisition of disaggregated data on migration. Any general model of migration should ideally include only those variables which have a fairly uniform impact upon all potential migrants. It is likely, however, that any aggregate migration flow may conceal innumerable, and perhaps divergent characteristics. In any one migration stream there are likely to be considerable variations of age, occupation, aspirations, motivation and so on. Consequently, differences in economic opportunity may be significant for some migrants but not for others. Recognition of this point has led some researchers to disaggregate migration flows. One of the best examples is the analysis undertaken by Rogers (1966). He examined the flows of migrants between administrative areas in California to determine how far the models of economic opportunity could be applied to seventeen age-specific flows. He found that the models most closely explained the behaviour of the young adults, those aged between twenty and thirty four.

Migrants who form part of the aggregate flows reported by the census have, at the very least, only two characteristics in common. One is that they all migrate from a particular administrative area; the other is that they all migrate to a particular administrative area. It is in fact location which has been used as the criterion for aggregation. If we wish to derive models which more accurately reflect the characteristics of migrants it is necessary to form alternative aggregations based on individual migrant data. In this way it becomes possible to identify groups of migrants with similar characteristics.

The hypothesis that these models of economic opportunity explain the behaviour of some groups of migrants better than of others was tested using data from the Tregaron out-migration stream during the period 1965-70 (Morgan, 1974). A first scan of the data had suggested that there were significant differences in the distances moved, while the independent variables described the characteristics of migrants and of the areas to which those migrants moved.

When all out-migrants were considered, the model was only able to account for about fifty one per cent of the variation in migration distances. However, the most significant conclusions were that most of the variation could be accounted for by the variables relating to the destinations of migrants, and that the model was able to explain the pattern of migration of some groups better than others. The results for age are shown in Table 6:1. The model provides the best fit for the twenty three to twenty seven age group, although the figures for the last two quintiles are also surprisingly high. Separating the migration stream into people who had, and people who had not retired shows that the model was able to explain fifty six per cent of the variation in distances moved by those who were moving to retire, and forty nine per cent of the variation for those who were not.

Table 6:1 Per cent explanation provided by the model for age quintile groups

Group	Age	Per cent Explanation
1	19-22	53
2	23-27	84
3	28-37	39
4	38-56	52
5	58 & over	63
All Migrants		51

Many of the retirement moves are probably long-distance moves to areas of better economic opportunity, although these people may move for non-economic reasons. Non-economic reasons include not only retirement but also a desire to live nearer to, or with, relatives. When the stream is analysed according to whether people moved for economic or non-economic reasons, the model explains fifty three per cent of the variation for the economically motivated and fifty eight per cent for the non-economically motivated. In other words, people who move in order to be nearer their relatives and those who move for economic reasons tend to go to the same places. Where their relatives live may well have been determined by earlier differences in economic opportunity, so that people who move to be closer to relatives following retirement, perhaps, may well end up in areas of lower relative unemployment, higher relative income, and so on, than those areas from which they came. That is, children may well have moved to areas where economic opportunities are relatively good and their parents, on retirement, may well follow them to those areas, although their reasons for doing so are very different.

These examples show how a body of data about individuals can be used to derive aggregate formulations. They also demonstrate that the model explains the behaviour of some groups of migrants better than others. Our analysis has not so far succeeded in taking account of a number of characteristics which together comprise the different migration components which make up one migration stream. The question which is being posed is this: "what are the characteristics of those migrants, who, during the period of 1965-70, left the Tregaron area of mid Wales?" To provide a satisfatory answer, a grouping procedure needs to be used, so that groups of migrants with characteristics in common can be identified. In order to derive mutually exclusive groups, a divisive classification was used (Taylor and Spence, 1969). To use a divisive approach entails a considerable loss of detail, but this was considered acceptable, in order to obtain a mutually exclusive set of groups.

A number of groups was identified, which fell into two broad categories: those migrants moving long distances and those moving short distances. This separation into short and long distance movement is broadly the same as that which is usually made between intra-regional and inter-regional migration (Williams, 1978). Each of these two groups must be considered in turn.

There were several kinds of short distance movers. Firstly, there was a group of young family movers, all under thirty years of age and all with dependent children. All the men were employed in skilled or semi-skilled manual jobs. All the moves were economically motivated, one half moving as a result of a change of employment, the other half moving on being promoted within the present firm or organisation. All the moves were made to rented accommodation, although all the migrants regarded this as a temporary state of affairs. There was also a second group of young family movers who were somewhat younger than the first group, being all aged less than twenty four. They were all skilled or semi-skilled workers. All the moves were made to rented accommodation from their previous accommodation with parents or parents-in-law and they moved in order to be more independent and to improve their job opportunities. Thirdly, there was a group of children of farming families who had married and moved to farms of their own. A fourth group consisted mainly of retired people whose age, marital status and occupational background varied.

Of those migrating long distances, there were three distinctive groups. First, there was a group of family movers, all younger than thirty four years of age, all in professional occupations and without children. They moved mainly for economic reasons. A large proportion of the families in this group moved because of their relatively high income and occupational aspirations, which were being satisfied by moving in order to get promotion. There was also a second group of appreciably younger families of mainly skilled and semi-skilled manual workers. Dissatisfaction with employment prospects was the dominant reason for their moving. The third and last group was made up of married couples and single persons from non-farming backgrounds who were moving because of retirement. Their motivation was non-economic since they wanted to spend their retirement with children who lived considerable distances away. This group's motive for leaving the area was generally the same as that of the other people who were retiring, but the factors determining their choice of destination were quite different.

Given what we have now established that a migration stream may be made up of a large number of distinct groups, it is little wonder that aggregate models provide rather poor explanations of migration flow. Several interesting findings emerge from the identification of these groups of migrants. The first concerns the selective nature of out-migration, the results of which are often used as justification for policy intervention in depresssed areas (Holding, 1972). The precise form of the relationship between selective out-migration and regional problems needs elaboration, and this has recently been done in relation to rural depopulation (Treasury Department, 1976). Only a brief account of the extent of selectivity will be made here.

The Tregaron out-migration stream was very age-selective; sixty one per cent of the migrants were under forty years of age, compared with thirty two per cent in the population of the area as a whole. The stream was also selective at the other age extreme, so that the age group forty to sixty was markedly under-represented. Age selectivity is well-established empirically, particularly at the younger end of the age continuum (Thomas, 1938, 1958; Claeson, 1968). Fairly familiar patterns of motivation and of aspirations are closely related to the age factor, perhaps best described by Keown's (1971) concept of the 'career transient'. A quarter of the out-migrants were found in the professional groups compared with eighteen per cent in the population at large. Semi-skilled and unskilled manual workers are under-represented in the out-migration stream (Benewitz, 1956; Tarver, 1964).

Statements about the selectivity of out-migration cannot, of course, be divorced from patterns of in-migration since in-migration may well be compensating for losses brought about by out-migration. For the Tregaron area, higher proportions of young people leave than enter, especially in the twenty one to thirty nine age group; while, conversely, a much higher proportion of in-migrants are aged forty five to fifty nine and many are people who move on retirement. The general trend is that the more productive groups are lost and those with few, if any, years of working life left are gained.

This pattern is replicated in much of mid Wales as is shown in Table 6:2. Between 1951 and 1961 mid Wales experienced net outward migration of around 6,000. The only age group to show a net increase during this period was the retired age group. Net outward migration between 1961 and 1971 declined to around 2,500 with net increases in the forty five to sixty four retired age groups. Net losses in the fifteen to forty four age group continued at about the same level during both decades. The change in the fortunes of the forty five to sixty four age group must, in part, be the result of the industrial developments which have taken place in the region. This change does suggest that many of the workers who have moved to mid-Wales tend to be found in the post family-formation stages of life. Reference will be made to this point when we analyse the motivations of those migrants who have moved recently to Newtown.

The analysis of net migration trends for the individual counties shows the western counties of Cardiganshire and Meirioneth as the main receiving areas for retired persons. Comparison of the 1951 to 1961 trends with those for 1961 to 1971 shows considerable changes in the fortunes of all the county areas, but particularly Montgomery and Meirioneth. In the case of Montgomeryshire a net migration loss of around 3,500 in the first period has been transformed into a loss of less than 500 in the second. Towards the latter end of the second period Montgomeryshire was beginning to experience a net migration gain. A fall in the losses experienced in the younger age groups has been far more dramatic here than elsewhere. Such a conclusion is hardly surprising given that many of the job opportunities which have been created in mid Wales have been allocated to Newtown and Welshpool.

Changes for Montgomeryshire are associated with the growth of Newtown, designated as the major growth centre for the mid Wales region and I will now go on to consider recent trends in the movement of population to Newtown. In the same way that it has not proved possible to generalise about out-migration from mid Wales as a whole on the basis of a study of out-migration from one area, so it is also impossible to generalise about patterns of in-migration from one study based on the

Table 6:2 Mid Wales: net migration by age groups 1961-66 and 1966-71.

Area Age in years

1961-66

	0-14	15-44	45-64	+65	Total
Brecon	-40	-530	+100	+140	-330
Cardigan	+100	-590	+560	+360	+430
Meirioneth	-120	-1280	+10	+50	-1340
Montgomery	-170	-660	+30	+120	-680
Radnor	+150	-190	-130	+20	-250
Mid-Wales	-180	-3250	+510	+690	-2170

1966-71

	0-14	15-44	45-64	+65	Total
Brecon	+90	-240	+310	+150	+310
Cardigan	+80	-870	+590	+310	+110
Meirioneth	-300	-890	+270	+230	-690
Montgomery	+170	-90	+130	+20	+230
Radnor	+20	-300	+30	-10	-260
Mid-Wales	+60	2390	+1330	+700	-300

experience of in-migration into Newtown. It will become apparent that the Newtown pattern is in fact significatly different from that of much of the rest of mid Wales. The crucial factor is that Newtown is a growth centre. There is already a hint of

Newtown's distinctiveness in the data provided for 1966-71 in Table 6:2; Montgomeryshire is the area of mid-Wales which shows the clearest changes in patterns of net migration.

In-Migration

In September 1976 a survey was undertaken to determine the characteristics of persons who had taken up residence on the Trehafren and Treowen housing estates put up by the Mid Wales Development Corporation in Newtown. Seventy three interviews were completed, a response rate of eighty one per cent. However, as no private estates were included in the survey, the results presented below cannot be taken as representative of all migrants who have come to Newtown.

The framework for the analysis which follows is derived from similar work undertaken by Jones (1974, 1976). He suggested that in deciding to move to Newtown, householders passed through a series of stages. This is a model of decision-making which is both sequential and cyclical. Each of the stages will be examined here. Jones (1976) has also suggested that his study can be placed in the framework of a more general feature of migration which has been taking place in the United Kingdom during the last twenty to thirty years; the planned migration of thousands of people to new towns. Newtown is very small in relation to most new town development schemes, but the experience of new town and town expansion schemes elsewhere in Britain could well provide useful comparative material.

The first consideration is the mobility potential of a given household. It is well-known that migrants tend to have quite distinctive demographic and socio-economic characteristics. They are, for example, more likely to be young people than old. Furthermore, mobility tends to be correlated directly with social class. The selective nature of migration was noted earlier in our discussions of out-migration. Where a population has characteristics such as those which are closely related to mobility, it is said to have a high mobility potential. The dominance of young, married persons and children of primary school age is a well-known characteristic of the population structures of new and expanded towns. Our data confirm this point. Comparing the age distribution of the Newtown respondents with that of the population of the United Kingdom as a whole (Table 6:3), seventy two per cent of the former as compared with only thirty six per cent of the latter were under forty years of age while the corresponding proportions of people aged over fifty were eleven and forty five per cent. Furthermore, sixty nine per cent of the migrant households had dependent children and seventy three per cent of the children were of primary school age.

Table 6:3 Age distribution of respondents compared with that of the population of the United Kingdom (1971)

Age Group	Newtown (%)	United Kingdom (%)
19-25	21.9	9.2
26-40	47.9	26.7
41-50	19.2	18.9
51-64	9.6	26.7
65+	1.4	18.6

Mobility potential is also related to the social and economic characteristics of the migrants. Once again, migration theory is helpful in suggesting that migration is directly corelated with status. Information on socio-economic groups was reclassified into five social class groups, and the distribution for the respondents compared with the distribution for the county as a whole. Differences between the two distributions were not statistically significant. This is probably explained by the fact that the development of Newtown has depended almost exclusively upon manufacturing. The slight over-representation of social classes IV and V, though not statistically significant, suggests that Newtown may be attracting more unskilled and semi-skilled workers than is usually the case in the development of new towns.

Jones (1974, 1976) hypothesised that in-migrants to Newtown would include a significant proportion of Welshmen returning from England, so that the presence in England of persons with a Welsh background could be a significant aspect of migration potential. Our data, however, does not support this expectation. Certainly a good proportion of our sample had Welsh connections, but they were mostly already living in Wales before they moved. Thus, in forty seven per cent of the households which were interviewed, the husband or the wife, and sometimes both of them, had been born in Wales and in a quarter of them specifically in mid Wales, while forty two per cent had moved to Newtown from other parts of Wales and twenty three per cent from elsewhere in mid-Wales. The reasons provided by respondents for choosing to come to Newtown indicated that only seven families actually wished to return to Wales and only two of these families considered this to be the most important factor in their decision to move.

Even where there is a high mobility potential, people will not consider moving, still less will they actually move unless they experience stress of some kind where they are. Respondents were asked what led them to think about moving away from where they lived before actually deciding to move to Newtown. Dissatisfaction with employment was mentioned by forty five per cent of the sample; it was also mentioned by a further sixteen per cent, but this time, in combination with dissatisfaction with housing conditions and opportunities. Dissatisfaction with employment was the most important source of stress, but the exact form which it takes is not clear until the results of the rankings of important reasons are examined. Eighteen per cent had been unemployed and a further forty one per cent had not had a secure job. Poor environmental conditions and factors associated with urban stress was mentioned by sixty three per cent of the sample while fifty one per cent referred to inadequate housing conditions, a factor which thirty per cent valued highest in their list of reasons.

It is well-known that inadequately housed families figure prominently in movement to new and expanded towns (Wilmott, 1967; MHLG, 1967), but housing factors were certainly less important than employment considerations for most of the respondents. There are some difficulties in separating these two factors, however, and the possibility of a new house was certainly a significant attraction for some families.

The effects of stress together with a relatively high mobility potential may not be enough to cause migration. Where these forces are strong enough migration studies are again useful in suggesting that potential migrants engage in some type of space-search procedure. Though this is a kind of space-sampling process, it cannot be said to be random sampling. The places that are considered are mainly determined by the kinds of information which a potential migrant gets. He/she will no doubt get information from many different sources about many possible destinations, but it is his/her interpretation of that information and his/her assessment of its reliability which will influence his/her decision about where he/she will move to.

Table 6:4: Reasons for leaving: number of times 'conditions' ranked and number of times 'conditions' ranked first (total number of respondents = 73)

Conditions	Times Ranked	Times Ranked First
Previously unemployed	13	10
Lack of job security	30	18
Inadequate housing	37	22
Environmental conditions	29	16
Urban Stress	17	4
Other	15	3

The survey data confirmed the existence of this process. Thirty per cent of households indicated that they had considered other places before finally deciding to move to Newtown. It is also likely that a number of households 'sampled' Newtown in one way or another before eventually deciding to move there. Forty-four per cent obtained information about Newtown from friends or relatives or both. A number of larger-scale investigations have indicated that in explaining migration from one area to another, personal contacts play a significant role (Greenwood, 1969, 1970). Clearly, the search-space of a potential migrant must be influenced strongly by his/her spatial networks of friends and relatives.

Once the move has been made the same network of friends and relatives help the new arrivals to settle down in their new living and working environments. Once again, although other sources of assistance are important, for example the Development Corporation and works organisations, friends and relatives were the most frequently mentioned sources of assistance. Among the reasons for people wanting to move to Newtown, the desire to live near friends or relatives was not very important. This is all the more surprising because of the seemingly important roles for friends and relatives in providing information on migration opportunities. This does suggest that the role of friends and relatives in the migration process is more functional than emotional (Jones, 1976). This is not to suggest that friends and relatives cannot play this emotional role in the migration process, since when our informants were asked about the characteristics of those families who had left

Newtown after a relatively short stay, eighty three per cent of informants stated that they knew of families who had left after a stay of less than two years; fifty four per cent of informants knew of families who had left after a stay of less than one year, fifteen per cent thought that the main reason they left Newtown was that they were missing old friends in the towns which they had left.

Among the obstacles or deterrents to migration, Jones suggests that physical distance is of considerable significance. Indeed, it has frequently been demonstrated that, in countries like Britain, most moves are over quite short distances. This reflects the effect of factors such as people's limited awareness of opportunities, access to information, removal costs and the costs of severing personal and community ties. So important are these factors that Lee (1966) considers that people must overcome a natural inertia if migration is to take place at all. Of the families interviewed, twenty three per cent came to Newtown from other parts of mid-Wales, nineteen per cent from the rest of Wales, and a quarter from the west-midlands of England.

Having made the move to Newtown people begin to evaluate its effects upon their lives and if the evaluation is unfavourable this constitutes a new source of stress which may induce another sequence of searching out an alternative. One possibility will be a return from whence they came in the first place. Of course, evaluation is not easily separable from stress, and in any such evaluation factors relating to mobility potential clearly come into play. For even though people may be dissatisfied with the move, changes in mobility potential, such as the fact that the family and especially its main breadwinner is getting older, may make it more difficult for them to consider yet another move. Our informants for the most part evaluated their move to Newtown very favourably. Eighty per cent of respondents felt that the change of work represented an improvement, while a quarter indicated that they found their present jobs more satisfying than their previous ones, even though they did not appear to be very different one from the other. This may be the result of the complex pattern of factors which focus on the job and the place of work but which are underlain by a more general sense of satisfaction of living in Newtown.

The move to Newtown was also evaluated favourably in terms of incomes and standard of living. Sixty-one per cent indicated that their income had risen in Newtown, with nineteen per cent indicating that it had not changed appreciably. Higher incomes were explained in terms of better paid jobs and more regular employment, as well as increased opportunities for overtime working, although a significant proportion, thirty per cent, considered that there had been a deterioration in opportunities for overtime. As compared with the sixty one per cent whose income had increased, only forty four per cent regarded their standard of living as having improved. A further thirty seven per cent of respondents thought that it had not changed in any significant way. This interesting discrepancy between results for incomes and standard of living may arise because the additional income gained from better paid and more regular employment is being spent on goods and services which are generally more expensive in Newtown than where the respondents lived before.

About one half of respondents thought that they had to pay more for furnishings and accommodation and as many as three-quarters thought food was more expensive. Travel and recreation, on the other hand, were not so widely regarded as being more expensive. This could be the result of the relatively limited range of recreational opportunities in Newtown and the fact that most people live near their place of work and are employed in the town. This reflects the policy of the Development Corporation which seeks to balance the in-flow of emloyment and labour to Newtown, so that normally only those households who have obtained jobs in Newtown would be considered for the allocation of a tenancy.

Thirty eight per cent of respondents were very pleased with the move, while a further forty two per cent indiciated that while they had some reservations they were generally pleased with the move. Only fifteen per cent were unhappy or would prefer to move away. Housing is beyond doubt a source of general satisfaction, eighty two per cent of informants stating that housing was certainly better in Newtown than in their previous place of residence.

There are, however, two major causes of dissatisfaction in regard to job opportunities and recreation. Forty-six per cent of respondents indicated that, with the movement to Newtown, there had been a deterioration in the range of jobs available. Of the families who made this point, many had relatively high aspirations for their children. These parents recognised that such aspirations were not likely to be satisfied in Newtown, and they complained about the relative shortage of jobs outside the field of manufacturing industry. Sixty-one per cent of respondents reported that Newtown compared very unfavourably with where they had lived previously for recreational facilities. In particular, attention was drawn to the relatively narrow range of such facilities in Newtown.

Some families found these deficiencies so serious that they finally decided to leave the town altogether. All of the families interviewed were aware of at least two families who had already moved from Newtown. These were families which had usually remained in the town for only a relatively short period of time. Thus fifty four per cent of respondents knew of families which had been resident in the town for less than one year; eighty three per cent knew of families which had been resident in Newtown for less than two years. The men in these families were generally skilled and semi-skilled workers who had left because of redundancy in Newtown, but also because they had wanted to return to their previous place of residence, largely because they had missed their relatives and old friends. In some cases, they had come into conflict with their neighbours while in others the fact that they had experienced some animosity from residents who had lived there longer than themselves appears to have contributed to their desire to get away. More generally, however, our informants considered that the people who had left Newtown after a relatively short stay were people who had high aspirations, particularly for their children, which could not be satisfied locally. The implications of this conclusion will be explored in the final section of this paper.

Conclusions: policy implications

The findings of both the research projects outlined in this paper can be related to two policy issues which are of critical importance for mid Wales. This concluding section does little more than to raise these issues. The first has to do with what is the most appropriate type of development for an area such as mid-Wales. The second issue has to do with how best to organise and locate that development. Answers to this second question are surprisingly few in number and thin in substance (Moseley, 1974).

Both studies show evidence of selective out-migraton, as does the aggregated analysis of inter-regional migration. The two studies also pinpoint the fact that absence of suitable employment is a major factor causing people to think of leaving the area. Therefore, a broader range of employment opportunities needs to be provided, particularly to satisfy people who want relatively high incomes and employment opportunities. During the 1970s central government has widened the scope of its regional policy measures so as to give support for offices, while it has itself been actively concerned to decentralise some of its own offices. The experience of mid Wales, and specifically of Newtown, suggest that these measures may not go far enough. Such a conclusion does, of course, depend upon normative judgements as to the acceptability of certain levels of selective out-migration.

The Mid-Wales Development Corporation recognised that a broader range of employment opportunities would be very desirable. With this point in mind the Corporation built an office block, Ladywell House, in Newtown. Unfortunately it has remained under used since it was built because it proved impossible to attract this kind of employment to the town. If this was so difficult in a town so favourably sited and as relatively well developed as Newtown, it could well be still more difficult, if not impossible elsewhere.

To accept the desirability of providing a better mix of jobs does carry certain implications for the spatial distribution of development in mid-Wales. The policy is now well established with the bulk of the investment being committed to Newtown as the major growth centre (Welsh Council, 1971) and over sixty per cent of the money available to the recently formed Development Board for Rural Wales has been allocated to the development of Newtown. A policy which aims to concentrate investment in Newtown and in six other centres can be criticised as implying 'planning for decline' in the remoter areas of the region. On the other hand, considering mid-Wales as a whole, this same strategy is an example of 'planning for growth' of the region. The debate here revolves around the scale of the analysis. However, the benefits of the 'spread' or 'trickle-down' effects (Myrdal, 1957; Hirschmann, 1958), as well as economies of scale, upon which faith in a growth centre strategy is supposedly based, are unlikely to materialise unless a more concentrated strategy is followed. By adopting such a strategy, the income and employment aspirations of at least some potential migrants are more likely to be <u>within</u> the mid-Wales region to a great extent that would otherwise be possible.

CHAPTER 7

MIGRATION, INDUSTRIAL RESTRUCTURING AND CLASS RELATIONS: AN ANALYSIS OF SOUTH WALES[1]

Gareth Rees and Teresa L. Rees

We set out to achieve two objectives in this paper. The first of these is straighforwardly empirical. Perhaps more than any other region of Britain, the character of south Wales society has been shaped during the past two hundred years or so by the ebb and flow of population. In what follows, we attempt to identify the major trends in this process of population change, highlighting the ways in which divergent patterns of migration have characterised different historical eras. In doing this, we focus particular attention on the post-war period, which until now has been relatively neglected.

Secondly, however, our concerns are theoretical. Research into population migration has been carried out, for the most part, within the framework of quite specific assumptions as to the nature of the phenomena to be explained and as to the form of appropriate explanation. Certainly, the quite extensive analysis that has been carried out on the Welsh experience of demographic change falls squarely within this conventional wisdom.[2] It is our view that this research has yielded only a very partial understanding of the migration process and, more particularly, of the latter's functions within the wider context of regional development. Accordingly, we try to set our empirical review within an alternative, and more coherent, theoretical analysis.

Migration analysis: toward a reformulation

A great deal has been written about the nature of population migration - its volume, direction, distance and so forth - and about why people of particular kinds undertake this sort of movement. Those who have contributed to this literature would, perhaps, themselves stress its diversity and the conflict between the various theoretical positions that have been adopted within it. In contrast, we want to emphasise what is common to this body of research.[3]

Conventionally, the migration process is analysed as if it took place in a world whose crucial characteristics are predetermined and, hence, unproblematic. The inequalities between locations in terms of such factors as unemployment, or wage levels, to which migration is, in some sense, a response, are deemed to be given a priori, a feature which betrays the roots of much migration analysis in marginalist economic theory. The origins of these inequalities are never examined, and therefore, the role of migration itself in generating them is considered only in the most partial ways.

Given this assumption of a priori distribution of spatial inequalities, the sort of 'explanation' of migration frequently given in economic analyses, in terms of the 'net benefits' of moving to a new area and the 'costs' of living there, becomes tautological. Such 'explanations' cannot tell us anything that we do not already know. As Amin (1974 : 90) states: 'It is evident that the migrants, being rational, would be heading towards areas where they have a better chance of success'. Moreover, this point holds irrespective of the complexities introduced to take account of, for example, imperfect knowledge (Garbett and Kapferer, 1970), diverse 'social constructions of reality' (Mitchell, 1971) or the 'normative context' in which migration takes place (Taylor, 1969). All that changes here is that 'net benefits', 'costs' and, indeed, 'rational' are defined rather more carefully and, most often, in terms which attempt to replicate those of the migrant him/herself.

It is also significant that migration analysis tends to be cast in terms of the atomistic behaviour of individuals. They are abstracted from the structured society of which they are a part. Indeed, society is itself considered to be merely an aggregate of individuals who are faced with the choice of moving or staying where they are. In consequence, of course, the systematic relationships between migration and changes in the structure of socio-economic organisation remain largely unexplored.

It is our contention that these limitations of conventional migration research have more than a narrowly scholastic interest. What is really significant is that once migration is conceptualised as an individual's response to patterns of inequality which are given, it is imbued with a degree if inevitability. It is viewed as a natural feature of social and economic life; attention is directed away from the context which sets the necessary pre-conditions for population movement.

Furthermore, clear practical or political consequences flow from such a perspective: namely, that the best that can be done in terms of policy is to try to ameliorate the problems that population migration poses: a syndrome which is all too familiar in many parts of Wales.

In contrast to the conventional wisdom which we have criticised, our starting point must be the historical processes by which the inequalities between areas have been generated. Moreover, these processes should be viewed both as the product of the actions of individuals, including, of course, migrations, and as constraints which limit the courses of action which individuals are able to pursue. More specifically, the focus of our analysis must be the relationships between population migration, on the one hand, and modes of economic organisation and their associated social relations, on the other. If we are to concern ourselves with the fairly recent past in Wales, this means coming to terms with the implications for population movement of the ways in which capitalist production is organised.

As Massey (1978, 1979) has argued, at any historical period there is an uneven distribution over space of the conditions for profitable and competitive that is, capitalist production. However, as changes in the nature of the production process, transport, communications and so forth occur, so different conditions, with different geographical distributions become necessary. Hence, capital is constantly in process of reorganising the way in which it uses space in order to sustain accumulation; that is, it is continually generating new spatial divisions of labour. In reality, of course, this process is massively complex in that different types of economic activity or different sectors of industry, use space in different ways, according to their specific requirements. Equally, for any given area, its economic structure is the product of its role within successive spatial divisions of labour, often in a number of varying types of economic activity. However, Massey (1978 : 106), puts the essential point most succinctly:

> The process of accumulation within capitalism continually engenders the desertion of some areas, and the creation there of new reserves of labour-power, the opening up of other areas to new branches of production, and the restructuring of the territorial division of labour and class relations overall.

The implications for migration flow quite directly from this context. On the one hand, it is frequently necessary for workers to move to new areas in order to be able to sell their labour-power for wages, although they may vary considerably in their actual ability to do so. Equally, it may be necessary for capital to offer relatively high real wages in order to generate sufficient labour-power of the kind required at the place where new production is located. However, this necessity is constrained in that, as a result of migration, there is always an 'active reserve army of labour' (Friedman, 1977) exerting a downward pressure on wage levels and undermining worker resistance to capital in general. On the other hand, the very fact that a region has a ready pool of labour-power may itself constitute a reason for certain types of capital moving there. In any event, it is certainly necessary to understand migration in terms of the systematic relations between regions which are structured out of the process of accumulation itself.

A number of these points may be illustrated by reference to the penetration of industrial capitalism from the late eighteenth century onwards into Wales, which was previously an area of non-capitalist forms of production and social relations (Hobsbawm, 1968). We refer here, of course, to the development of the iron and steel and, subsequenty, coal industries, predominantly in the south of the country. The potential for capital accumulation was so great here that the existing population was unable to reproduce anything like the labour-power necessary to support the exceptionally rapid expansion of production that was sought by the 'in Welsh terms' new class of industrial capitalists. In consequence, relatively high levels of wages, in spite of their precariousness in the face of trade depressions, individual injury and so forth, attracted an enormous in-migration to the coalfield. Thus, the Welsh coal-mining areas gained some 313,000 people through net migration between 1851 and 1911, the period of greatest expansion, and by the beginning of this century was absorbing in-migrants at a rate not much less than the United States of America during the same period: an annual rate of 4.5 per thousand population, as against 6.3 per thousand (Thomas, 1972).

There was, of course, a ready reserve of labour-power to supply the developing industries. Some migrants were drawn from areas in which metal-manufacture and coal-mining were unable to compete with south Wales, hence the movements from parts of the west midlands of England or from Somerset and the Forest of Dean in Gloucestershire. The majority, however, came from the vast pool of labour-power in the countryside. Rural Wales, for example, supplied thousands who had previously been subsistence farmers or were engaged in the collapsing woollen trade (Thomas, 1930; Hodges, 1947; Friedlander and Roshier, 1965/6). In short, there was a classic reserve army of labour, which, through the mechanism of migration, provided a ready supply of labour-power and thereby acted to keep wages in the industrial enclave of the coalfield lower than they may otherwise have been (Laclau, 1971).[4]

Equally, dramatic changes can take place after the establishment of capitalist production in a region. Hence, the mushroom growth of industrial south Wales is to a degree mirrored by the economic collapse of the inter-war period. This collapse was one part of a much more wide-reaching restructuring of British capitalism largely as a result of international pressures; the other principal manifestation of which was the substantial growth of new, Department II industries in the south east and midlands of England (McCrone, 1969). Given these changes in the use of space by capital, it is not at all surprising that workers responded by migrating from south Wales to the new poles of industrial growth. Hence, the total population of the region actually fell by some 115,000 during the 1930s; whilst Freidlander and Roshier (1965/6) have calculated that the county of Glamorgan lost one hundred and thirty one people per thousand population due to net migration between 1911 and 1931 and one hundred and nine per thousand between 1931 and 1951. It is also clear that most of these migrants did go to the areas of new industry. Brinley Thomas (1937, 1938) estimates that over ten per cent of the average insured population in Wales had found its way to the south east or the midlands of England by 1937, a figure over twice that for the next area, the south west of England.[5] There is also evidence to suggest that these migrants acted very much as a reserve army in their willingness to sell their labour-power at a rate which undercut the prevailing wage levels in the new industries (Francis and Smith, 1980 : 103).

However, it is important to guard against the presumption that this response to capital's reorganisation was in some sense automatic. It is significant that many workers did not take the road to Slough or Coventry. In part, of course, this simply reflected individuals' differing social constraints on moving. Many were tied by the responsibilities of families and house-ownership, for example (Thomas, 1931; Francis and Smith, 1980), but it was also the product of active organisation on the part of workers themselves. At one level, this is shown in the way in which labour organisations, such as the South Wales Miners' Federation, organised the reproduction of an at least tolerable existence in some areas of the coalfield during the hardest years (Francis and Smith, 1980). At another, it is reflected in the concerted 'and ultimately successful' opposition that was mounted against those policies of the state which were intended to encourage emigration from regions like south Wales and, in particular, against the Industrial Transference Scheme (Page, 1977).[5] It should not be forgotten that the state was finally moved to provide some relief for the depressed areas, thereby removing some of the pressure to migrate, precisely because of its concern over the disruptive consequences of this organised opposition (Page, 1977).[7]

What we are arguing is that the major changes in the pattern of migration flows which we have identified as part of the development of south Wales were not in any simple sense the product of individual motivations. They have to be located within a complex of capital restructuring and of labour organisation and worker opposition. Moreover, and this is a crucial point, migration is itself an integral element in the determination of both the strategy adopted by capital in respect of restructuring and the nature of workers' responses to it.

Patterns of migration in the post-war restructuring of south Wales

At first sight, the post-war period in south Wales is characterised by a much less dramatic experience of population change than the earlier periods we have sketched. The total population of the region has climbed only rather slowly from some 1.74 million in 1951 to just over 1.8 million by the late 1970s. However, it would be quite mistaken to infer from these aggregate statistics that the flows of population between areas have been less significant in shaping the character of south Wales than previously.

This is so for at least two reasons. Firstly, although the net balance of migration streams has been smaller than during other eras, it is clearly necessary to examine the <u>composition</u> of the two streams before drawing conclusions as to the effects of population movement. This is something that we shall return to later. Secondly, there has been a major redistribution of population <u>within</u> the region. This can be gauged very simply be looking at the changes in the total populations of the various sub-regions of south Wales (Table 7:1). What is most striking here is that the central and eastern valleys, comprising a substantial part of the coalfield itself, have been displaced from their dominance in terms of the population of the region as a whole by the coastal belt.

Clearly, this redistribution is the product of two sets of forces: natural change, that is, the difference between the number of births and deaths and migration. Table 7:2 shows the relative contribution of each. Although the detail of the figures shown here should be treated with some caution, the contrasting profiles of the sub-regions emerge quite distinctly.[8] Hence, the predominantly coalfield areas of the central and eastern valleys are marked by a massive and persistent net out-migration. Moreover, falling birth rates toward the end of the period were eroding the 'cushion' provided by positive natural change and accentuating overall

Table 7:1: Distribution of population, by sub-region, 1951-1971 (thousands)

	1951	1961	1971
Industrial South Wales	1742	1791	1834
West South Wales	449	457	461
Central & Eastern Valleys	680	653	633
Coastal Belt	613	681	740

Source: Welsh Office (1979)

population decline. Indeed, by the early 1970s, a number of these areas were actually experiencing natural decrease, that is more deaths than births, for the first time. In west south Wales, dominated industrially by metal manufacture and associated activities, after an early transfusion of net in-migration, the story is again one of a slow bleeding away of population, although on a scale much less than for the central and eastern valleys. In addition, at least until the end of the 1960s, natural increase was large enough to ensure a growth in total population. Without doubt, however, the primary focus of growth has been the coastal belt. Here, a combination of very high levels of net in-migration and closely associated rates of natural increase has produced a considerable expansion of total population, which appeared to falter only after the mid 1960s.

Unfortunately, it is not possible to bring the picture up to date with the experience of the 1970s, as the basis upon which these statistics are prepared was changed with the reorganisation of local government in 1974. However, Table 7:3 gives the analysis for the new counties of south Wales. Initially, the figures may appear rather surprising. However, as we shall show in a more detailed analysis they do in fact confirm the broad trends of earlier decades.

Table 7:2: Components of population change, by sub-region, 1951-1971 (thousands)

	1951 - 1956			1956 - 1961			1961 - 1966			1966 - 1971		
	Total Change	Natural Change	Net Migration	Total Change	Natural Change	Net Migration	Total Change	Natural Change	Net Migration	Total Change	Natural Change	Net Migration
Industrial South Wales	22.4	31.4	-9.1	27.9	38.4	-10.4	43.1	47.4	-4.3	-0.5	33.2	-33.7
West South Wales	6.4	5.4	1.1	1.9	6.3	-4.5	7.1	6.5	0.6	-3.5	2.7	-6.2
Central & Eastern Valleys	-7.4	11.4	-18.7	-19.8	10.7	-30.6	-3.8	13.5	-17.3	-16.2	9.5	-25.7
Coastal Belt	23.3	14.6	8.7	45.9	21.3	24.6	39.8	27.3	12.5	19.2	21.1	-1.9

Source: Welsh Office (1979)

Table 7:3: Components of population change, by county, 1961-1978 (thousands)

	1961 - 1971			1971 - 1978		
	Total Change	Natural Change	Net Migration	Total Change	Natural Change	Net Migration
Gwent	18.4	25.0	-6.6	-3.4	2.9	-6.3
Mid Glamorgan	12.9	22.4	-9.5	7.5	4.1	3.4
South Glamorgan	8.2	23.2	-15.0	-3.8	3.2	-7.0
West Glamorgan	6.4	10.6	-4.2	-4.0	-1.2	-2.8

Source: Welsh Office (1980)

Moreover, these trends of population change that we have described should be understood as the expression of the particular form of industrial restructuring that has been taking place in south Wales during the post-war period. This is clearly not the place to give a detailed analysis of this process (for preliminary accounts, see Lovering, 1978; Morgan, 1979; Rees, 1980; Cooke, 1981b). However, it is necessary to identify its key features in order to understand the essential context of demographic change.

The essential notion of the restructuring process has been that of modernisation, the creation of an economic structure attuned to the needs of the twentieth century. To this end, there has been a major 'rationalisation' of the older industries of coal and steel, whilst the economic structure of the region has been 'diversified' by the introduction of the 'new' manufacturing and service industries. In short, a new economic base has been developed through a new combination of 'spatial divisions of labour'. In all this, of course, the state has played a key role, mediating the conflicts which have arisen over the course of development. Nowhere is this better illustrated than in the nationalised coal industry.

In 1945, over 110,000 people were employed in the south Wales coalfield, producing 21 million tonnes of saleable output. By 1978, only some 27,000 were employed and a mere 7.5 million tonnes of coal were produced. Most of this decline took place during the 1960s, with eighty-six collieries closing between 1959 and 1970. The reasons for this massive programme of closures have yet to be fully articulated. However, in general terms, the closures have to be located in the context of, on the one hand, state direction of the coal industry to ensure rationalisation and pricing policies which would guarantee cheap coal to private industrial capital and, on the other, state fuel policies to transform the British economy from one based on coal to one which used a diversity of cheaper energy sources (Carney and Lewis, 1978; Morgan, 1979).[9]

Confronted with these massive changes in the structure of the coalfield, miners and their families were left with very few options for their future lives. Many accepted transference either to other 'cost-effective' pits within south Wales or to other coalfields, where their skilled and experienced labour-power could be put to good use. Clearly, these transferees constitute a significant element in the migration streams out of and within the region. However, especially for younger miners and even more particularly for those entering the labour market after the pits in their area closed, a major alternative was to enter employment in the 'new' industries which were developing, for the most part, off the coalfield and on the prime sites at the mouths of the valleys and on the coastal plain itself (Sewel, 1975; Town, 1978). For others again, such opportunities were unavailable locally, or even within the region, and migration in the footsteps of an earlier generation to the more prosperous parts of Britain followed with a degree of inevitability; the south east and south west of England appear to have been especially important (Welsh Office, 1979).

It is arguable, however, that the major element of the restructuring process was the drastic reorganisation of the south Wales steel industry. Not only did the reconstructed industry provide high-wage jobs, during the 1950s and 1960s, it also provided the basis for a sizeable metal goods industry. Moreover, it was the steel industry's demand for coking coal that ensured the survival of the rump of the coal industry. Indeed, it is only now, faced with the consequences of the run-down of the major south Wales plants following closely upon the ending of steel-making at Ebbw Vale and the closure of the East Moors plant in Cardiff, that the centrality of the industry to the economy in south Wales is being fully recognised. As yet, it is still too early to specify the effects on immigration of this decline.

This reorganisation warrants a specialist study in itself (Warren, 1970), but again what is clear is the intensely political nature of the investment decisions. In the immediate post-war period, the state's policies reflected pressures from both labour and the private steel capitals; on the one hand, to retain employment in a traditional metal-making area and, on the other, to minimise the dislocation to production by preserving the spatial <u>status quo</u>, whilst gaining new, efficient plants (Morgan, 1979). Whatever the explanations, new integrated steel plants were located at Port Talbot (The Abbey Works opened in 1951) and at Llanwern (the Spencer Works opened in 1963), while at the same time, tin-plate production was concentrated at Ebbw Vale and the new plants at Trostre, near Llanelli (opened in 1953) and Felindre, north of Swansea, (opened in 1956). What this meant, in turn, was a considerable rise in the total number of jobs, but a much more dramatic relocation of the demand for labour-power. Hence, the siting of the new plants at coastal locations and the consequent closure of many of the old, largely obsolete inland plants meant, after an initial period of daily commuting, a permanent movement of steel workers and their families from the traditional Llanelli-Swansea area, further east to Port Talbot and beyond. A similiar movement took place from the Pontypool-Risca area to Newport with the opening of the works at Llanwern. In addition, of course, the new steel works attracted considerable influxes of workers from outside of the industry and from outside of the traditional steel-making areas. This is reflected, at least in part, in the net in-migration to west south Wales during the early part of the 1950s, whilst the use of 'green labour' at Llanwern is well-known.

However, steel was only the forerunner of the creation of an enclave of modern, manufacturing industry in south east Wales. Hence, for example, there has been a considerable expansion in sectors such as electrical goods, vehicles and chemicals, particularly during the 1960s and early 1970s. The essential point about this 'diversification' is that there has been a high degree of locational specificity in the development of these enterprises. With certain well-known exceptions such as the Hoover factories at Merthyr Tydfil, these incoming industries have been concentrated in valley mouth and coastal belt locations. For example, Davies and Thomas (1976) report that some seventy per cent of overseas-owned establishments, a major element within the enclave, located within ten miles of the motorway route which cuts across the mouths of the valleys (the M4).

This is, of course, precisely the distributional pattern that has been encouraged by the state in its decisions about infrastructural investments (Rees and Lambert, 1981). Also, at a more general level the state has been active in persuading new firms to locate in the region by means of its regional policy incentives. It is not clear, however, as is sometimes suggested, that the expansion of these 'new' sectors is any simple result of regional policy. It needs to be re-emphasised, of course, that different types of capital use space in different ways. Hence, it has been argued most cogently that for certain sectors, the prime case of which is electronics, the hierarchisation of production results in regions such as south Wales becoming focuses of the 'bottom rung' of assembly work. Moreover, reserves of labour power, especially female labour power, that is available for low-wages and without trade union organisation, become the principal criterion in determining locational choices, rather than regional policy incentives. Here then, is an example of particular capitals which are prepared to move themselves in order to capitalise upon the availability of a particular reserve army of labour, which is itself unlikely to be inter-regionally mobile. In other sectors, of course, it may be that cost pressures or, indeed, regional policy are major considerations in bringing about relocation to an area like south Wales (Massey, 1978, 1979).

In the case of service industries, the situation is likely to be different again. The growth of this type of activity has been by far the most striking aspect of change. Thus, by 1976, some 370,000 were employed in services in south Wales, compared with 340,000 in index of production industries. Moreover, by the mid-1970s, some forty to fifty per cent of those in employment in the region were working in this type of sector. However, this growth has been concentrated in activities such as professional and scientific services, distributive trades and public administration. Within these sectors, the jobs which tend to have been created have been concentrated in the lower-skill and routine categories, rather than in high level functions; and, again, many have been filled by women (McNabb, 1980). In part, of course, this growth reflects simply the entirely general trends of development in services, in terms of the general importance of these activities and the way in which they are organised (Mandel, 1975). However, south Wales has been affected by particular factors too. For example, central government has relocated a number of its operations to the region, while there has also been a sizeable expansion of local government. Moreover, the process of restructuring has created auspicious conditions for the expansion of certain types of retail businesses. This expansion has coincided with a marked decline in smaller retail outlets, which were dispersed much more widely over the region than the new ones are. Indeed, it is generally true that service activity is focused on the major urban centres of the coast - Cardiff, Swansea and, to a lesser extent, Newport - which have been extensively redeveloped with this very objective in mind (Cooke, 1980a).

Again, whatever the distinctions to be drawn between different types of economic activity, the implications of the spatial patterning of industrial restructuring for the movement of population are fairly clear. Capital's, and indeed, the state's strategy of concentration of these 'new' manufacturing and service activities at the mouths of the valleys and on the coastal plain has yielded the essential context within which the distribution of population has been shaped. It is here, of course, that we should seek the basic explantion of the growth of population in the coastal belt area (see Tables 7:1 and 7:2). However, it is significant that this growth is itself not wholly undifferentiated; there have been both ebb and flow of people within the sub-region.

Hence, Herbert (1972 : 328) reports of the decade 1951-1961:

> Areas of (population) gain included the larger towns - Cardiff, Swansea and Newport - new growth centres of employment, such as Port Talbot, and a number of coastal areas and residential districts which began to increase their roles as residential dormitories.

However, what is striking about the following ten years is that some of the older urban centres, in parallel with many of the much larger cities of England (Hall et.al, 1973), actually began to lose population through net out-migration. Cardiff provides the best example here, with a loss of some 22,000 people over the decade, but other towns, such as Newport and Llanelli, display similar features. The areas experiencing growth and net in-migration became much more clearly focussed. They comprised, on the one hand, rural and coastal areas, serving clear dormitory functions for the major urban settlements - for example, Gower RD and Llwchwr UD around Swansea; Caerleon UD and Chepstow RD around Newport; and Cardiff RD, Penarth UD and Cowbridge RD around the capital city itself. On the other hand, there were certain of the valley mouth localities, which functioned not only as dormitories, but also received population from the declining coalfield areas to the north - examples included Penybont RD, Caerphilly UD, Llantrisant RD and, in rather special circumstances because of the New Town, Cwmbran UD.

Much the same local patterns have been mainatained, it would appear, during the 1970s, although it is much more difficult to make sense of them on the basis of the new local authority districts. Hence, Cardiff and Newport have continued to lose population; whilst one suspects that the small positive balance shown by Swansea is attributable to in-migration to the Gower, rather than the city itself. Conversely, the valley mouth and other dormitory areas have continued to grow rapidly, as the statistics for districts such as the Vale of Glamorgan, Taff-Ely,

Ogwr, Monmouth and the Lliw Valley demonstrate (Bracken and Hume, 1979).

The general configuration of these local movements is confirmed by two studies based upon the data about migration between 1966 and 1971 that was collected as part of the 1971 Census of Population. Hence, Rees (1976) reports evidence of a step-by-step pattern of movement down the valleys of the coalfield to their mouths, whilst a Welsh Office study (1979 : 10) comments: 'Cardiff's hinterland is heavily influenced by the net outward flow from Cardiff itself and also downwards from the Valleys'. This evidence is of some significance in that it is a direct record of migration flows, unlike much of the data that we have used earlier.[10]

In considering short-distance migrations such as these, it is important to bear in mind that it is not only the sphere of production, that is industrial restructuring *per se* that has a major influence upon population flows. Hence, Rees (1978) argues on the basis of a questionnaire survey of migrants from one particular former mining area that whilst employment considerations were uppermost in people's minds in their decision to move, housing and the sphere of reproduction generally were also given considerable weight. Our essential argument so far has been that industrial restructuring has provided the basic framework shaping the pattern of population change. However, this is not simply a question of creating new demands for labour-power; it should be acknowledged that there are important effects upon the urban environment as well, and that these have acted significantly and independently upon migration. Hence, for example, the failure to invest adequately in the social infrastructure of the coalfield areas and the concentration of this type of investment elsewhere in the region cannot be disassociated either from the spatial form of the industrial restructuring or from the nature of people's geographical movement. Similarly, we have already mentioned the significance of the redevelopment of the major urban centres for the growth of service industry. Equally, of course, such redevelopment has almost certainly had a profound impact upon the population losses experienced by these centres.

Considerations such as these also serve to remind us that migrants very often *benefit* substantially from their move. Rees (1978) reports for her sample significant improvements after moving not only in employment and income, but also in housing standards, educational facilities, social amenities and a number of other counts. However, this is not to deny the central argument of this paper: that population migration is a key mechanism enabling capital accumulation to proceed; and that it is the accumulation process which sets the primary context for demographic movement. Indeed, some migrants themselves experience the constraints imposed upon their actions by these objective, structural conditions. Thus, for example, Rees (1978) shows that some fifty per cent of her respondents felt their moves to have been forced upon them by 'external circumstances beyond their control'. Rather, it is to reassert our earlier point that migration itself constitutes a significant determinant of the course of restructuring in the spheres of production and reproduction. It is to this point that we return in our concluding remarks.

Concluding Remarks

We argued earlier that migration has to be understood in the context of both industrial restructuring and labour organisation and struggle. What is striking, perhaps about our discussion of the post-war period in south Wales is the absence of reference to labour as an active force in the developments we have sketched. Certainly, it would appear that workers' opposition to the changes that have taken place have been muted and ineffective, in spite of the costs that have been, and are being, imposed by them (Francis and Smith, 1980; Rees, 1980). Indeed it has been argued that, on the contrary, certain elements of organised labour have co-operated in the facilitation of the restructuring process (Rees and Lambert, 1981). Obviously, we cannot account for this quiescence here. However, we want to conclude by outlining certain effects on class relations in south Wales, generated in part through migration, which seem to us at least to contribute toward an explanation; and, thereby, to establish migration's determining role on restructuring itself. We should emphasise, however, that as yet our argument is somewhat tentative.[11]

The keypoint in this argument is that the established balance of classes in south Wales and the powerful labour and political organisations which emerged from this class configuration, have been transformed by the economic changes that have engulfed the region during the post-war period. This transformation, in turn, has set one of the pre-conditions for further industrial restructuring by weakening the basis of potential worker opposition. Finally, migration has played a not insignificant part in all this.

Firstly, let us consider the effects of the development of the 'new' types of manufacturing and service activities. This has resulted in the introduction of new types of work into the region. Most clearly, there has been an increase in the significance of low-skill and routinised jobs, and this has occurred, albeit in somewhat different ways, across a diversity of industrial sectors. The consequences of this sort of change have been considerable; most significantly, the absorption of many married women into capitalist wage-relations. It seems likely that this shift has weakened trade union organisation in south Wales overall, given the difficulties which face women in participating in such activity. However, the role of migration in this context has been limited to population shifts within the region, given that the availability of a reserve of appropriate labour-power was itself a significant condition of the growth of much of the advanced enclave.

These developments have also resulted in the creation in south Wales of a sizeable grouping of middle managers and state functionaries, strata which have been largely absent from the traditional class configuration of the region. Here, it seems likely that population movement has played a much more decisive part. On the one hand, it can be argued that such people have actually moved into south Wales from other parts of Britain, although the detailed patterns are by no means clear.[12] Within the region, however, it is clear that these groups have concentrated into precisely those areas of the coastal belt which have experienced rapid population growth. This movement, allied with the sort of urban environment which has been reproduced for them, has led to the 'embourgeoisement' of such areas, with predictable consequences in terms of their political complexion (Rees and Lambert, 1981).

The importance of these trends is heightened, however, when they are taken together with the changes that have taken place within the traditional working class. We refer here principally to the decline in the significance of the coal miners as a class grouping, although, the run-down that has taken place in steel during the 1970s and, much more markedly, the butchery the industry during the 1980s may make it appropriate to consider the steel-workers as well. Most obviously, there has been an absolute fall in the number of workers of this type; and we know that emigration to other regions has contributed heavily to this fall. Hence, although the net balance of migration flows for south Wales has been much smaller since the War than in earlier periods, it is likely that this population movement has had a disproportionate effect upon the class structures of the region because of the differing composition of the in-migration and out-migration streams.

However, perhaps of even greater significance have been the changes which have occurred wholly within the region. The industrial reorganisations which we have outlined have generated new structures of demand for labour-power. It is apparent that for reasons of their age, frequent ill health, political and trade union militance and so forth, many of those men who have been discarded by the traditional industries are most unlikely to be offered employment in the 'new' sectors or, indeed, in other parts of Britain. It would appear, then, that long-term unemployment is their only future. It is no coincidence, for example, that of the men who have been out of work for more than six months in mid-Glamorgan, some forty-four per cent are over fifty years of age. Indeed, there are close parallels here with the process of 'marginalisation' described, in a very different context, by Quijano Obregon (1974); a residual stratum of the working class is being created which is not even important as a reserve army of labour, but is simply an 'excluded labour force'. As the experience of the 1930s shows, such a stratum is enormously difficult to organise precisely because of its excluded satus.

However, this is only one side of the coin. As we have seen, others within the working class are able to respond in a very direct way to the changes in the organisation of the economic and urban structure that are going on around them. They are able to sell their labour power in the growing sectors of industry, and, as we have seen, they very often capitalise upon the superior conditions of the valley mouth and coastal plain settlements by migrating, albeit perhaps step-by-step, to these locations. Not surprisingly, these migrants are marked off from those who do not move by virtue of their relative youth, economic activity, superior level of education and qualifications and higher socio-economic grouping (Rees, 1976; Rees, 1980). What is happening is that those working class people who are able to 'make out' in the changing world of post-war south Wales are distancing themselves from the less fortunate members of working class communities, not only in terms of the material conditions of their lives, but also in a literal, spatial sense. What this means is that migration is compounding the break-up of the 'resonant' communities (Friedman, 1977) in which the close integration of work and the social relations of the locality once provided the bed-rock of working-class organisation in south Wales. Population movement constitutes an important mechanism through which workers become divided and disorganised amongst themselves. They are thereby less able to exert an influence upon capital's strategy of restructuring and are made increasingly vulnerable to the costs imposed by the imperatives of the accumulation process.

CHAPTER 8

POWER IN A WELSH TOWN : THE DOUBLE HELIX OF ITS INDUSTRY AND SOCIAL LIFE

Colin Fletcher

> There was a background of guns and bombs. Bullies maintained their power for a season. Cash had its say still in the disposal of seats, titles . . . . (Thomas, 1972 : 25)

In 1974, the British Steel Corporation sponsored an unusual research project. The proposal was to study power in one of its plants in relation to power in the host community. The location was a works of 2,000 employees in a Welsh town of 28,000 people. Why the project was funded partly explains the roundabout nature of the fieldwork.

The year 1974 was a turning point in the Steel Corporation during its second period of nationalisation. There had been seven years of comparative plenty during which plans had been made to completely resructure the industry. Originally steel towns had grown because of the availability of iron ore, coal and water. As all iron ore is now imported the plans favoured the creation of huge steelmaking works on the coast. Medium grade steel made in great quantity would then be supplied to the Corporation's own works to shape into sheets or bars. The latter would be put next to the customer's manufacturing plants wherever they happened to be. The Corporation planned to close inland steel making plants and create new steel towns on the coast. Steel towns are always company towns and the plans projected social collapse in some areas and a bonanza of social development in others.

There was no love of steel towns amongst the majority of the Corporation's Head Office management. They found the works difficult to understand and even more difficult to control. There was a camaraderie between managers and men in these older works. Resistance to Head Office was equally widespread throughout the works and the town. The social connection and solidarity of the towns was undermining the Head Office's authority. In London, management and unions were invariably and implacably on opposite sides. In steel towns, however, it looked as if they stood together against Head Office management.

That was their problem, then, the defection of local management. Yet, when Head Office personnel visited their steel works they did not find corporate solidarity but class conflict. They found what they regarded as finely tuned status divisions transformed into chasm-like divides. The works' hierarchies appeared to fuel or even to form the intense class politics of the towns.

These observations were not, in themselves, startling. Domestic disputes are often patched over when faced with the threat of an external enemy, but the Head Office question was how real were the supposed local solidarity and the apparent local struggles? They sought answers to such questions without triggering off a blaze of embarassing publicity?

The Corporation was also interested in a study of community power because it had a 'social responsibility' clause written into its Charter. This clause stated a requirement to consider the wider effects of steel towns being Company towns. The economic effects were obvious; and involved the rates paid, purchases made, sub-contracts given and the wages and salaries bill. The social effects were, in comparison, a mystery.

The research proposal aimed to kill two birds with one stone. Voluntary service and charitable activity held clues about connections within the works and between the works and the town. Such a study would also provide data about social effects. The proposal was to study an "infrastructure" and supply the results of a "social audit".

"Good works" in voluntary organisations were to be the starting point for study. It was proposed to follow this lead and continue to others until the principles of connection became at least as clear as the connections actually established. The sociological goal was a unitary account of community power.

Remember too, that the town was in west Wales. One Head Office Executive remarked ruefully that the works in focus was "their only foreign language plant". In the space of some six years with two years of intensive fieldwork, one works and one town were closely studied. They were not studied from afar; I lived in the area and, because of the study's subject, it was assumed that I was 'trying to find my way in'.

Charity

Charity, wrote Veblen, (1971) is the work of the leisure class and the leisure of the working class. The idea of beginning with charity was, therefore, to explore the way in which the strata in the works became publicly affirmed in the town.

Three findings upon Voluntary Service illustrate the proposition. First, a charitable contribution was made from the shop floor by a deduction of two-pence per week from their pay. The charities which they elected to support were charities of which their Works' Manager was a Trustee. The second feature was the patronage of Departmental Managers. They supported the Works Club. They were Presidents or Vice-Presidents of the Town's Choir, Sports Clubs and Rugby Clubs. No manager was without a social position. Their patronage was important because they would tolerate absences of workers or help with changes of shift to accommodate practices and performances. This particularly applied to coaches, trainers and those with specialised interests. On the other side of the relationship, as it were, the voluntary contributions or voluntary work of the manual workers enabled their managers to become influential patrons outside the works.

The Works was also involved in larger charity rituals. Each year there was the Mayor's christmas Appeal and in 1977 there was the Jubilee Appeal. Local newspaper listings could be read as sociological news; for those who gave first and gave most were the more prestigious and were then followed each week by firms and individuals wishing to be included on the list. The works and the works' manager appeared in the first week's list.

Charity meant more that 'good-works' it meant raising money and supplementing the social, welfare, medical and educational services with donations. Controversial charity, on the other hand, occurred when people banded together as a movement for personal and social change. The latter happened when an independent youth club was being formed, or a pressure group, Shelter, was seeking support. Controversial charity was not 'welcome' because it did not reinforce existing class positions, the action was coming from the bottom rather than the top.

In contrast, non-controversial charity reached its peak when there was a presentation of 'the cheque', when social honour was due to all those whose photograph subsequently appeared in the local newspaper. The cheque presentation was a ceremony at which contact was made with the receiver. Whoever received the donation would be prestigious in that particular charity. They were not weakened by having to receive charity, rather, their social position was enhanced.

Non-controversial charity had indeed provided a good initial lead because it focussed upon an alignment of identity which was publicly acclaimed. The works functioned as one organic entity in this respect and the process by which the function operated was that of patronage. Charity had also led to a more general understanding of voluntary service because it was thought of as an act of civic duty rather than an act of general social good.

Civic Duty

The Works' Manager appeared at most public functions. He attended the annual dinners of the Chamber of Commerce, the Board of Governors of the Technical College and the Regional Institute of Bankers. The Bankers' Dinner was the most important event because the assembled works' managers and bank managers had as honoured guests titled people with some breeding and substantial business interests. Such people would hold yet more senior ranks on the National Savings Committee and the Welsh committee for the Cancer Research Campaign. Later in the year these guests would be invited to an Open Day at the works or to address meetings of the Works' Discussion Society upon their charities' most recent endeavours. The manual grades would listen and ask questions. The Departmental Managers would meet and entertain the guest afterwards. Civic duty did not always elide with non-controversial charity. There were eighteen councillors in a works; that is, the Company actively supported political voluntary service.

All of the councillors were interviewed and asked about their commitments. No councillor was a member of every type of neighbourhood interest group. They ranged from a man who went to a gardening club and a chapel to a man who was a member of four out of five types of group. (table 8:1)

Table 8:1 Neighbourhood Memberships of Councillors

Community Centres	(2)
Vocational Clubs, e.g. Gardening, Working Men's Clubs	(6)
Church or Chapel	(12)
Sports and Social Club	(14)

Welsh male social life separates into clubs and pubs - pubs are marginal. Sports and Social Clubs have an almost totemic significance for neighbourhoods, they are the inner sanctum of Welsh neighbourhoods. In the clubs, drinks cost less, a committee position carries status and Club membership is a badge of respectability. Membership of a church or chapel can also be considered in a similar light. Chapels comprise one or more extended families, they are the meeting places of Welsh clans. Most of the councillors, over two thirds, could claim such established connections, that is, with a family in its chapel in its ancestral neighbourhood or area.

A further finding was that the greater the number of local group memberships, the greater the probability of further memberships in the district and the region beyond. The distributions of these were as follows:

District		Region	
Co-operative Society	(2)	County Charity	(2)
Service Club	(4)	Masonic Order	(4)
Union Executive	(6)	Area Administration	(8)
Party Executive	(10)		

The key factor in the 'escalation' of involvement was being a patron or leader of a neighbourhood group or groups. In effect, such honorary positions constituted a gateway to 'broader' responsibilities. In this respect locality groups both recognise the achievements of one of their own and promote their own to the next level of achievement. In so doing, they accord the highest honour and make the councillor a link man to other groups. He then appears as one of the chief guests within the locality and as a guest in other localities.

Councillors with regional responsiblities have a host of connections through their county council. The county councillor with the least extensive list had the following duties:

1. Member of County Council

2. Committees of County Council:

   a) Policy and Resources Committee
   b) Personnel committee
   c) Joint Consultative Committees: Manual, Ancillary and Administrative

d) Public Protection Committee, which includes Fire Brigade, Consumer Protection, Civil and Emergency Defence
e) Education Committee
f) Further and Technical Education Committee

3. Police Authority

4. Court of Governors, University College

5. Valuation Court

6. Governor of the Technical College

7. Governor of the Grammar School

Most of the senior councillors were Governors of the Technical College as was the Works Manager. The patronage of the works was vital to these new professional politicians.

Professional local politicians could not pursue a political career without independent means or patronage. It was up to the 'good nature' of employers to grant paid leave. This boon placed an obligation upon 'professionals' "to serve two masters" - to advise and inform their management as well as their constituency of matters which might affect them. This dualism was the hinge of some tension. There was a feeling amongst managers that 'we lose them more than we use them'.

Such disgruntlement points to a distinct confusion over constituency. Councillors represented all their connections as well as their designated geographical area; from the 'boys in the club' to the chapel congregation; from the 'shop floor' to the management. When asked to describe their constituency many councillors spoke of "the boys at work" and "the lads in the club". Quite often, of course, they were actually referring to the same men. There was ample evidence of 'shop floor surgery' particularly in matters of squabbles between neighbours and housing problems.

It was usually an occupational advantage to be a councillor. Almost all of the hourly paid councillor/employees worked 'days regular' or were on '90 per cent mornings'. There was also a tendency towards less demanding or less visible jobs. The 'near professionals' had staff jobs. The work's patronage of allowing a day or exceptionally two days, a week to these men for civic duties enabled them to 'rise up' and meet their heavy responsiblities; for it must be remembered that those with regional duties also had district and neighbourhood duties.

Councillors were called for interview by asking the time office to put a note in their cards. At the appointed time one cheerful sort tapped lightly on the door, put his head round and said 'I know what it's about : it's the phones, isn't it? Well alright - I'll use them less. Okay?', and off he went back up the corridor. It was not pleasant to be interviewed at work as a councillor because me acting as 'management' and they as 'workers' was not a proper representation of their connections.

Yet again, the exceptions were most illuminating. Not all councillors were Club, Chapel and Charity men with the benefit of convenient times and conditions of work. Independent Labour councillors for one large council estate whose only Club was on the estate and who had other connections worked on the production line and on a full continental shift basis.

The processes which propelled civic duty were many. First there was the advocacy and defence of territory; neighbourhoods had their watering holes and private meeting places where respectable members could share their concerns. No councillor was independent of these groups. In himself, however, was the meeting point of interest groups and political groups. In this way, neighbourhoods were represented to each other, by their councillors. Collectively, too, they represented one strata. All the councillors were manual or clerical grade workers. Being a councillor was like being a node or cluster on the very edge of a class divide.

Or was it really so simple? Four councillors straddled the strata with a foot in each. The regional councillors included connections with country charities and the Masonic Order. The common cause aspect of charitable involvement has been touched upon already. Its path now led to a doorway into secret societies.

Secret Societies

The connections of club men can go well beyond the social importance of the choir and the local rugby team. For there is a whole menagerie of secret ad semi-secret organisations whose nerve fibres are regional, national and international in their own right. For clerical and lower order managerial grades there were the Moose, the Elk and the Buffalo. For the first generation white collar workers there was the Lions International. For towns people, in a second or third generation of profession or business, the carpeted steps from Round Table to Rotary. At the risk of being trite, the lower orders model themselves on herds of endangered species whilst the upper echelons describe themselves in terms of discreet circles.

The organisations mentioned so far are semi-secret; they do not welcome close enquiry nor publish lists of members, nor openly recruit. Neither, of course, do the strictly secret organisations such as the Masonic Order. But the importance of the Masonic Order cannot be too heavily stressed, it is probably the link both within and between works and town.[1]

There were five Lodges in the town, which, as one Mason observed, "that's Divisions 1, 2, 3, 4 and 5". The Works Manager, eleven of his middle managers and four councillors all said that they were members of Masonic Orders. The most senior, regional base, councillors were thereby members of the most 'junior' Lodge whist the Works Manager belonged to the most 'senior'; (the Lodge with a Royalist name). At this critical point, therefore, the strata connected whilst some degree of distance was preserved.

There are yet more secret societies and closed clubs about whom even less is known. For example, during the period of the Rebecca riots, the landowners combined to form an organisation nown as 'The Society of Sea Serjeants'. This Society raised money in order to hire a private army, paid for informants, and organised "atrocities" in order to discredit the "rioters". As far as is known the Society of Sea-Serjeants was not disbanded and exists to this day as one of the highest order secret societies in south Wales. The Works Manager had "heard" of it.

The point of Secret Societies is that they provide for influential people in different strata to meet as members of one extensive group.

The Process of Connection

The account so far has been somewhat static. The lead which began with charity was followed to the more complex clusters of voluntary service, of civic duty and secret society. Charity conveyed an image of unity or common identity. Civic duty pointed to interest groups as competing constituencies. Secret societies, in particular the Masonic Order, identified their members as having the potential for influence beyond their immediate strata - a unity of inluentials so to speak.

However, it would be a mistake to confuse influence with power. The latter, according to Weber (1948), is the ability to make things happen, to be able to override the wishes and claims of others if need be. Some suggestions about how this might happen have already been made. Patronage and promotion within vountary organisations have seemed particuarly significant. All the same, power is difficult to prove because the objective has to be clear. This was the problem with the starting point, what was the point of the charitable contributions beyond the benign exercise of financial muscle? Civic duty, in contrast, showed the web of tissue which holds together the solidarity of the manual workers' stratum. By them power was called 'pull', it meant the ability to get jobs for close relatives.

Amongst manual workers in the works there were three distinct 'careers' in manufacturing, in finishing and in 'craft' or trade. It was found that, as a rule, families of shop floor workers held one of the three career paths as dynasties and took their status from generation to generation by successful "recruitment". It was not unknown for money to change hands, to buy the support of supervisors or shop stewards, though it was much less frequent if the relative was adult than if he was a teenager. Of those workers over 45, three quarters were second generation and they and an average of three uncles, one cousin and one in-law 'in the works'. For those under 45, half were third generation and they had fewer uncles, cousins and in-laws. The bonds may be less pervasive but they are still there. It is this quality which makes the works a 'family firm' and the term also applies to how office staff and management are recruited. 'Pull' actually makes job advertising unnecessary and an undesirable stimulus for open competition. It is said of this works that, when it opened, if you did not have a relative 'inside' then the next best thing was to join the Personnel Manager's chapel.

'Pull' is part of a family's mutual protection and once inside the works all manner of mutual protection links can be made. One such connection was the Burial Fund. This fund was run voluntarily by a wages clerk to help the family of a man who dies 'in service'. The sum has gradually risen from £100 to £130 "which just covers the cost of a hearse, two cars and some clothes for the children". Members of the Fund pay 5p in advance; after a death there is an immediate collection which raises the fund for the next occasion. In all, 228 payments have been made. The contributors to this fund also make exceptional collections; they gave ¢119.08 for the Aberfan Disaster and have provided six televisions for local hosptials. Mutual protection lends itself to charity.

Civic duty, and the career of the councillors, gave sight of personal objectives for power. The process of rising up the stratum, achieving the edge and also becoming established in the next stratum was not a straightforward step by step progression. It was crabwise, backwards and forwards, edging upwards. Rising one point up in voluntary service then another notch of greater comfort and reward at work. The movement was like a pendelum-swing back and forth but each time a little higher. It was just this motion which the embedded manual workers criticised when they said "it's not what you know but who" and "they'r only in it for themselves". They said this even of those who had been denied, or who had denied themselves, promotion.

This pendulation of promotion, rising up the works and voluntary organisations with a compounding complementarity, was clearly recognisable within those who had been appointed to the Bench. The Works Manager was a JP as were three other managers. All three had been promoted both immediately before and soon after they had become JPs. The combined effect of two rapid promotions in the works had been to change their status from the clerical grade to that of middle management. By virtue of their knot of connections consisting of club, chapel, court and works' management, they were invariably referred to by manual and clerical workers as "Mr Fixits". Surely, though you might think the works' JPs could not "fix" the law? Most certainly not. How some cases avoided prosecution was a deep source of concern to at least one JP. He hinted at the fact that moral blackmail could be a reason. Moral blackmail is more than scandal or gossip, it is knowledge used for the purposes of pacification. The process, very roughly is something like this:

(a) Thefts from work and traffic offences are common crimes.

(b) If you commit a crime and others know, it will always count against you.

(c) If you confess the crime and ask for justice to pass over you then you create an obligation and that indebtedness then rests in private hands.

(d) From that moment on you can commit more crimes and deepen the debt; providing you pay something off the account. Those who are caught in moral blackmail are therefore useful as listening devices, messengers, or as the townspeople would say the "cat's paw".

Those high up who are party to the private knowledge will not, necessarily wish to use it, other than to prevent you "rocking the boat" which means to:

a) prevent you from gaining control over them,

b) prevent you revealing everything about them and

c) make you aware of the fragility of your position by using a shorthand reference to the crime and obligation in question.

The objectives of power therefore reveal the complicity between strata; the parade of patronage, the periodic 'pull' to gain work for relatives, the promotion to dual strata status for the politically and personally ambitious and pacification potential of minor crimes which fail to reach the public attention - a unity, its divisions and its secret, strong links.

In the region beyond the town

In 1977 the Lord Lieutenant died. As the Bishop said to the mourners, "the wide cross section of the congregation was an indication of his broad interests". The local newspaper carried a full account:

> "A GRAND HEARTED, noble gentleman who had a profound sense of duty and a tremendous desire to serve"
>
> That was the description of the late Lord Lieutenant given by the Bishop - last week.
>
> The Bishop was giving the address in a memorial service for the Lord Lieutenant at - Church. Colonel - died on January 2nd, aged 66.
>
> "It is the weaker members of society who will miss him most, for they were his greatest concern", said the Bishop. He regarded the wide cross-section of the congregation as an indication of Col. - broad interests.
>
> Among those present were members of the family, his widow - ; two sons - ; sister - and other relatives.
>
> The Queen was represented by Mr - , Deputy Lieutenant for - .
>
> Among those present were the Mayor - and the Lord Lieutenants of - , - , and - . The Lord Lieutenant of - was represented by Lady - .

Others guest included Mr - High Sherriff of - and several past High Sherriffs; Mr - M.P. for - ; Councillor - Chairman of - County Council; Town Clerk Mr - ; Mayor of - Ald. - ; - Town Clerk Mr - ; and Mayor of - Mr - .

There were also representatives of the police, - U.D.C., - U.D.C., - R.D.C., - R.D.C., - R.D.C., - R.D.C., and - U.D.C.

- Parish Council, the Crown Court, the magistracy, Income Tax Commissioners; representative of G.O.C. Wales, the Colonel of the Royal Regiment of Wales; - Army Cadet Force, - Squadron R.C.T., the Experimental Establishment; No. - Welsh Wing A.T.C., the R.A.F. Association and representatives from - Rotary Club, - Round Table, - Rotary Club, - Antiquarian Society, Coombe Cheshire Home, the Community Council, the United Counties.

- Federation of Young Farmers' Clubs, - red Cross, South West Wales Hospital Management Committee, the National Library of Wales, National Farmers' Union, - Branch of the Farmers' Union of Wales, County Scout Council, Girls Guides Association, - R.F.C., R.N.L.I., the National Eisteddfod, West Wales Association for the Arts, N.S.P.C.C., South West Wales Trustee Savings Bank, - O.A.P. Branch, - Federation of Womens' Institutes, W.R.V.S., Chamber of Trade, Burma Star Association and Sea Cadets CCorps.

A large number of representatives from - Co.Ltd., were also present.

Ministers attended from - ; - ; - ; - ; and - ;

The Service was conducted by Canon - , Vicar of - .

Lessons were read by Mr -, and the Rt.Rev. - Catholic Bishop of - .

The blessing was read by the Bishop.

The funeral was virtually a full turn out of all the Lord Lieutenant's connections - though most individuals could have given at least one other body which they were representing. The funeral was thus a kind of rite de passage for all the list groups attending the funeral put them in the presence of the next Lord Lieutenant. A few of those present would expect to be upon the list of eligibles laid before the Queen. The works' manager would not expect her silver bodkin to pinpoint his name. He was there at the funeral, though not representing B.S.C. but a voluntary organisation. The works' manager on this occasion was in the company of country and county superiors as well as council executives and their chairmen.

The Double Helix

The evidence put together does convey an impression of a town and its works as being both divided into strata and linked up either through the voluntary positions which some people held or through the extensive membership of secret societies. B.S.C. Head Office's impression of a divided unity was confirmed.

The fieldwork, and especially the pattern of promotion, suggested an image by which the principles and process of power might be described. Occupational status and voluntary service status rose up together as if twisted round each other. The actual structure resembled something like two bed springs which had been pushed into each other. So that there were levels, that is strata, which became gradual slopes until the next levelling off. On the gradient's slope there were points of connection like paths intended to weave between growing apart and coming together again. Sometimes the respective levels were prominent. At other times attention was drawn to their fleeting but almost electric points of connnection. The image was similar to a double helix, to the structure of DNA molecule (Watson, 1968).

The fit of image and findings was not quite exact because the work's spiral stopped short at the limit of the works' manager's power. The voluntary organisation spiral continued upwards and outwards beyond, as the Lord Lieutenant's funeral showed. However, within the confines of the town the image did X-ray the bones of its struggles, its solidarity and its secret sharing. A complexity which included class conflict, cohesion through charity and collaboration between those with careers had been revealed.

Above the Works' Manager in the occupational status spiral were the migrant English factory owners. Higher still were the English educated landowners with military rank and bearing who demured from discussing their business interests. At the top of both spirals there was an essential Englishness.

Conclusion

There are, then, two sets of findings which really need to be brought together. First the strata pointed towards the possibility of further correlations. Languge and politics, in particular, seemed to follow the broad bands of:

Language	Politics	Position
English	Conservative	Landowner
Anglo-Welsh	Liberal	Manager
Welsh	Labour	Worker

The region's new Lord Lieutenant was indistinguishable from Lord Lieutenants in any English county, for the uppermost echelon were English educated and who had served as Majors or Colonels in the Army. Some six or seven of them would regularly meet; as Inland Revenue commissioners, or as antiquarians, or on the Board of the Brewery or at a Conservative Party Function.[2] The English owner-managers, the relatively recent arrivals, would also support their political party. The latter were incorporated by membership of political and sporting groups but excluded by not being members or religious organisations and secret societies. All the same the emphasis at the top of the region's spiral was distinctly upon Englishness as a qualification for position and connection.

Secondly, within the town the findings were as much about linkages as they were about strata - apart from controversial charities and Independent Labour councillors having to fend for themselves. The links between the works and the town went from top to bottom and side to side. The point is that this very emphasis upon linkage rather than division could depend upon the fact that the town is in Wales. Again, B.S.C. Head Office had been right. The two intertwined spirals within the town were indeed in plain recognition of the need for a pooling of power between the local, essentially subordinate, Welsh people.

CHAPTER 9

ON CLASS AND STATUS GROUPS IN WELSH RURAL SOCIETY

Glyn Williams

A recent critical reassessment of Dafydd Jenkins' (1951, 1960, 1971) work on rural Wales by Day and Fitton (1975) contains several points which cannot go unchallenged. The analyses of social inequality presented by the two parties presents two different styles of thought in the social sciences. Furthermore, they pose and answer questions which are not only different in particulars, but are also different in kind.

The central issue concerns Jenkin's emphasis upon the importance of status groups as a basis for social organization within Welsh rural communities. The status groups derive from conformity or lack of conformity with a life style which depends upon values associated with protestant religion, and which were recognized to cut across class position in their significance for social division. Although at least part of his work consists of a synchronic community study, an understanding of his argument cannot be fully achieved without reference to social change in nineteenth century Wales, a point that is underlined in Jenkins' (1971) more recent work. The nature of the social organization which he discusses derives from a specific historical process. Yet it would appear that Day and Fitton's critique derives in part from a lack of understanding of the historical context and it might therefore be useful to begin by considering the customary picture of rural society in nineteenth century Wales.

Historical Context

The introduction of industrial capitalism had as profound an impact upon rural society in Wales as it did on other parts of Europe. Even prior to the advent of the industrial revolution the position of the gentry in Wales had changed in the sense that their actions tended not to be defined by reference to Welsh culture and society but rather with reference to the position which they occupied as adjuncts of English society. During the industrial revolution the actions of the gentry became comprehensible only in terms of the stratification of the wider capitalist system, they were integrated into the English aristocratic and ruling class. As rural Wales became incorporated into the expanding capitalist system the position of the gentry became defined not in terms of local interests but rather in terms of the wider economic system. In a spatial context the self-definition of the class to which the gentry became articulated was expanded and in many cases they retained an interest in rural Wales only insofar as the area provided them with an income. The focus of their lives revolved around the metropolitan centres where they had a status to uphold among those whom were held to be of a similar class position. It is often claimed that the symbolic context of this position focused upon the Church of England, the English language and the Conservative Party (Williams, 1950 : 246).

This by no means implies that the gentry did not exert their influence locally. The absentee landlords did so through their agents who generally were not Welsh, either by birth or culture. The landlord owned virtually all of the means of production on his estate, and whether the resources permitted occupational pluralism or merely agricultural exploitation, the only relationship between the gentry and the masses consisted of the relations of production. Since the local proletariat was dependant on the gentry's resources in order to meet household maintenance his/her position relative to the stratification system was structured through the relationships which he/she held with the gentry or their brokers.

However, while the diversification within the stratification of rural Wales was narrow it was not restricted to the simplistic division outlined above. The peripheral nature of the economy, together with the gentry's control over the means of production tended to restrict the breadth of the stratification whereas the integration with the capitalist economy guaranteed a diversification of class positions. The persistence of a high level of surplus appropriation by the gentry limited internally generated diversification whereas articulation with the wider society counteracted this tendency. The intermediary positions were assumed by a certain number of independent farmers, large tenants who employed a labour force, the factors and other officials of estate management, the clergy, schoolteachers and some traders and merchants.

It is claimed that some members of this intermediate group aligned themselves in oppostion to the gentry and struggled to gain support of the proletariat. The vehicle through which this was achieved was Welsh ethnicity in general and non-conformism in particular. It is claimed that during the first half of the nineteenth century the non-conformist chapels were predominantly working class institutions with a part-time, often lay ministry which was often parapatetic. By the second half of the century, and especially after the revivals of 1840 and 1859, it was claimed that ninety per cent of the working class in Wales were non-conformists (Davies, 1965 : 38) and the Chapels had full-time resident ministers. There was a considerable difference in the spatial distribution of the four main denominations which had different world views and organisational structures. Yet, as a generalization, it is correct to say that during the second half of the nineteenth century the various denominations united to express an opposition to the gentry and their interests, an opposition which focussed upon the gentry's control of local government and their hegemony in the world of ideas and social institutions. The opposition between the two interest groups had a strong ethnic content with the non-conformist leaders stressing the Welsh language, the protestant chapels and , in time, the Liberal party. As several commentators have implied, there was a strong element of both cultural and political nationalism in their ideological orientation, with the growth of the Liberal party after disestablishment representing an opposition in terms which were as cultural as they were political (Butt Phillip, 1974). The intermediate chapel leadership tended to define itself in terms of an intermediate class position and low ethnic status while recognizing the congruence of the proletariat's low class position and ethnic status. A redressing of the low ethnic status was seen as an altruistic rather than an egotistical orientation since it aimed at the collective upward mobility of the ethnic group. It was manifested in terms of action on behalf of the Welsh 'gwerin' (folk) which was imputed with many of the romantic connotations of nineteenth century folk movements in Europe.

The institutional basis of the articulation of the altruism and collective ethnic identity was the non-conformist chapels which extended a number of support functions which did not carry the customary stigmatic connotations of welfare associated with the parish since they were expressed in terms of community membership and humanitarian assistance for the worthy and needy members of the flock. Such facilities were open to all members of the congregation, the poorer members of which were linked to the institution by a series of patron-client relationships with those of the deaconate who, as a result of their economic standing, were in a position to extend essential credit and other facilities in return for support of the chapels. Thus, many of the economically marginal of the proletariat or small tenant farmers were tied into bound-dependent reciprocal relationships with the larger tenant farmers involving the exchange of labour for resources. These relationships constituted strategies for reducing risk and maximising security in economic marginality while also serving as a means of enterprise expansion. For example a form of rotating credit system was employed to finance life transitions (Owen, 1976). Similarly, both religious and secular voluntary associations were deployed as support facilities in crisis situations. The ability to participate in such institutions depended upon one's good name and the general social credit rating of the individual which resulted from potential access to the support mechanisms and could become the basis for upward social mobility. One's social credit rating in turn depended upon conformity to the life style based upon the normative context of the religious ideology. There is little need to underline the potential power of the institutions and their leaders. The power of the deaconate derived from their ability to suspend members and thereby deny them of the chapel facilities, or the support which the chapel community could offer as a pressure group for reinstatement in cases of wrongful dismissal, or even to offer alternative employment for members.

The chapel leadership played a primary role in the formation of aims as spokesmen or brokers striving to achieve cultural mobilization through the development of a Welsh language press. The proletariat was taught to read in its native language in the Sunday schools and both the political propaganda and the religious ideology reached them in a syncretinized form through the Welsh language press which was largely written and edited by members of the religious leadership. Several authors (Davies, 1965, Williams, 1950) have commented upon the function of the chapels as educational centres in terms of both literacy and democratic participation. The latter claim stemmed from the availability of office to all members regardless of economic standing. It is hardly surprising therefore that the themes of cultural mobilization and individual social mobility were integrated in the religious ideology by reference to a protestant ethic thesis which stressed the essential need for religious values in order to achieve economic mobility (see Chapter 11). These values were encapsulated in what was regarded as a lifestyle which everyone should strive to achieve, this being seen as a meaningful sociocultural order which symbolized the 'good society' and constituted a social order and collective goal. It was referred to as 'buchedd'. Thus the sacred or pure 'buchedd' had its contradiction in an unsaved 'buchedd' and it was the duty of the saved to recruit new members to their 'buchedd'. Thus one source (Rowlands, n.d.) states:

> It is hardly necessary to add that it is of extreme importance for you on behalf of your 'buchedd' to extend the teachings of God our Saviour in everything.

while adding:

> May God give you grace, dear brothers, to live in such a way that your pure 'buchedd' is a glory to His sacred name (Rowlands, n.d.).

It is claimed that recruitment to the lifestyle was associated with the numerous religious revivals which swept Wales during the eighteenth and nineteenth century.

Membership of the superior 'buchedd' relied not only upon religious values but also upon social values which were given a religious connotation. Among these values were knowledge, education, brotherly love, cooperation, unselfishness, humility, frugality, forgiveness, perseverance, honesty and concern for the less fortunate. These were seen as the converse of such values as jealousy, selfishness, dishonesty, etc. Several of the values argued against conspicious consumption with the display of wealth being seen as evidence of selfishness and arrogance which resulted in:

> . . . . the temptation of success (being) much more dangerous than the temptation of failure and poverty (Rowlands, n.d.).

Thus the ideology tended to diffuse any differences between members which were based upon materialism by stressing spiritual goals and corporate belonging. The shared concept of honour and dishonour was the basis for the status groups which were held to have a distinctive Welsh quality although they were based upon religious premises which held a much wider cultural and geographical relevance. Indeed conformity with the requisite values was seen as an essential ingredient of Welshness with members of the secular 'buchedd' being regarded as less worthy of being defined as Welsh.

Individuals came to interact with one another as members of religious, ethnic and living communities with communal membership being given an elaborate cultural rationale. In a sense an awareness of similar life circumstances came to be responsible for the fusion of religious and ethnic elements which was translated into ethnic, religious and political opposition. As a result the potential internal tensions which were based upon economic differences were diffused. This process involved the development within the social, cultural and political order of common reference points which served as the basis for strata awareness in ethnic terms. Thus the status groups became ethnically based and served as reference points for one another while developing common orientations by which they could compare one another. Interdependence among the various sub-units was maintained and loyalty to the system was insured.

This rather lengthy introduction should serve to clarify some of the issues in the Day-Fitton/Jenkins debate by presenting the historical data in a more complete and relevant framework. While not conforming entirely to Jenkins' work it does serve to highlight the basic elements of his argument and thereby allows us to proceed to a discussion of Day and Fitton's criticism of that argument.

The Debate

The focus of Day and Fitton's disagreement with Jenkins' thesis surrounds the discussion of inequality. Jenkins places considerable emphasis upon 'buchedd' as a status group associated with behaviour relating to religious values which served to 'differentiate' as opposed to stratifying the local community. While he is not clear as one would have wished with reference to 'buchedd' being a matter of showing common patterns of behaviour he does indicate that the differences between 'bucheddau' A and B derives from 'differences of group values and codes of behaviour' (Jenkins, 1960 : 15). This difference between 'values' and 'patterns', between 'behaviour' and 'codes of behaviour' clearly demonstrates that he views culture as generative of behaviour rather than as behaviour itself. While culture is not treated in an analytically precise sense there is no doubt that he is dealing with observable social relations and not an abstract superorganic culture.

Beyond the distinctions of 'bucheddau' is that of socio-economic ranking. Jenkins does recognize the stratification implicit in the individual's position in the process of economic production. In his earlier work he discusses the status allocated locally to those working in different occupations, an approach which Day and Fitton describe as:

> . . . . very like the conventional notion of occupational ranking, with basically non-manual/white collar group being placed above the manual . . . . when one takes account of all the reward and power characteristics of these two sets of occupations, this type of prestige rating has a reasonably sound connection with objective inequalities of class situation . . . . (Day and Fitton, 1975 : 877)

In his more recent work Jenkins (1971) focuses attention upon the division of labour associated with the relations of agricultural production. He maintains that the ecological basis of economic organization served to determine the precise nature of social relationships between community members of different economic standing. An argument is presented to the effect that bound-dependent reciprocal relationships between the working-class and the tenant farmers serves to counter marginality while also substantiating the stratification. Within the farm economy economic roles hold considerable autonomy but only within a highly stratified set of occupational roles in both status and economic terms.

The point of disagreement involves the nature of the relationship between the status groups and social classes. Day and Fitton (1975 : 873) paraphrase Jenkins' position as follows:

> The claim for a basis of stratification independent of economic factors is however precisely the claim made for the 'buchedd' system - that its foundations are not economic, but cultural, lodged in religious values, and that the social patterns to which it gave rise decisively cut across those engendered by relationships of production. In the extreme form, the economic order, is held to be irrelevant because the situation is one of a fundamentally classless society.

Here they appear to introduce into Jenkins' discussion of 'buchedd' an element which is not apparent in the relevant sources, that of stratification. Nowhere does Jenkins claim that 'buchedd' is a 'basis of stratification', independent of economic factors or otherwise. Indeed Day and Fitton (1975 : 883) elsewhere state:

> . . . . nowhere in this or any of the other Welsh (sic) studies do we find a single quotation in which the word 'buchedd' itself appears and can be seen in use as a term of stratification.

It would appear that an overriding commitment to class analysis has resulted in establishing this system of stratification by fiat.

More important perhaps are the statements by Day and Fitton to the effect that: '. . . . all non-religious criteria of stratification' (1975 : 867), that 'stratification in Wales is essentially independent of economic foundations' (1975 : 867), that the acceptance of status groups deriving from religious involvement or non-involvement implies i) the existence of a classless society (1975 : 867) and ii) the existence of a stratification that is independent of economic foundations

(1975 : 813) or that the economic order is irrelevant because it (Welsh society) is a classless society (1975 : 873). Such a reaction to Jenkins' work in unwarranted and one suspects that it relates to the claims which others have made for his work.

Nowhere does Jenkins deny the existence of an economically based stratification. On the contrary, in his discussion of status allocation he maintains that the economic order did spill over into the religious sphere of activity with leadership roles in the chapels generally being allocated to those of high economic standing, often in deference to their wealth. Not only does he indicate that status relates to the general division of labour (1971 : 180) but that an awareness of economically derived strata generated tension in non-economic spheres of activity (1971 : 186) and that the religious leadership supported the economical hierarchy (1971 : 180). However this tendency was never complete and there was:

> . . . . a possibility of an incompatability between the person's status and duties in one field of relations as contrasted with his status and duties in other fields of relations (my emphasis) (Jenkins, 1971 : 190).

Thus congruence was not absolute and there were wealthy farmers who were not leaders and poor cottagers who were leaders. The problem as Jenkins sees it is one of resolving the possible incompatability between status and duties in one field of activity as contrasted with status and duties in another field of activity. While Day and Fitton might expect to find such a tendency they do not appear to be at odds with Jenkins, whose concern lies rather with the deviant cases of status inconsistency.

To state that several dimensions of stratification are independent of one another, both theoretically and empirically, does not mean that they are not also interdependent. That is that they affect one another to some extent and yet retain a measure of autonomy with, for example, occupational prestige, power, income and education being to some extent independent so that occupational prestige might be respected regardless of the amount of power or income implied, or that power or income can achieve respect regardless of the low occupational prestige. Weber (Gerth and Mills, 1970 : 193) argued that although the original source of prestige may have been economic, a situation was conceivable in which a status system, once in existence, could operate independently of the class system and even seek to negate its value with, for example, the acquisition of wealth being viewed as 'vulgar materialism'. It is only on empirical grounds that the several dimensions of multi dimensional stratification models are justified. On theoretical grounds each of the dimensions has to be, and can be, justified in terms of the special and independent functions that the specific dimensions plays in society. Thus one of the important tasks for a multi dimensional theory is to conduct research that leads to more and more precise statements, preferably in empirical terms, of the various measures of independence and interdependence that the several dimensions of stratification have with reference to one another.

It seems to me that, if I understand him correctly, Jenkins does not claim empirical independence but rather consistently infers an interdependence while treating them in theoretical terms as independent categories of differentiation. Independence is substantiated by referring to the role of religious values and conformity with these values. A claim is made for the incompatability of the values of the religious and economic spheres. Thus one assumes that the values of frugality, cooperation and humility were the converse of those in the economic sphere and served as checks on consumptive aspects of economic behaviour. Similarly what has been stated above about the economic functions of the chapels which served as alternative support systems and whose ideology involved an emphasis upon the need for adherence to the religious values as a basis for upward social mobility is relevant. The power of the religious sphere was considerable, sufficient to grant a degree of security which could compensate for loss of employment and even to give a strong guarantee against the occurrence of such an event. Furthermore, as has been suggested, the status group distinction involved an ethnic cleavage which would magnify the tendency for class distinctions to be blurred.

Even if we do not assume the independence of economic leadership and prestige hierarchies and focus upon the nature and degree of interdependence it does not mean than they cannot, for analytic purposes, be seen as independent of one another as Lenski (1954) does in his discussion of status crystalization where he looks at the comparison of the ranks of the statuses concurrently occupied by the individual in a number of '. . . . parallel vertical hierarchies which are usually imperfectly correlated with one another'. This is close to Jenkins' position in positing the existence of '. . . . not one unitary social field but two fields, necessarily related because both concern the same individuals but with independent bases' (Jenkins, 1971:193). It is conceivable that the prevailing basis would be determined by the context of the situation with, for example, economic rank prevailing in economic relationship and religious position in a different relationship, although one would expect to see avoidance or compromise being resorted to in order to resolve an inconsistency.

It is useful here to recognize that within the Weberian perspective which Jenkins and Day and Fitton assume classes are not communities but that status groups are usually communities if only of an amorphous kind. (Gerth and Mills, 1970:181,186). Distinctions based upon prestige or status honour reflect an awareness that aspects of rank systems are traditionally ranked as ends in themselves and that some sense of community exists among rank groups in complex societies. Thus such distinctions of status honour could serve to predict behaviour which could be picked up in community studies. It is precisely this which Day and Fitton (1975:872) appear to refute in stating,

> . . . . our general expectation would be that other dimensions and criteria of social ranking will tend to be pulled back towards this basic order; for our general understanding of society is that class, and the occupational order it econompasses, is the most crucial determinent of a wide array of social phenomenon.

In pursuing their argument Day and Fitton appear to conclude that Jenkins' affirmation of the status group equates with an irrational attachment to the idea of Welsh culture, that Welsh culture is relatively unimportant in the social life of rural Wales and that any claim to the contrary is a result of the lack of objectivity in the native sociologists analysis. While this is an interesting twist in the recent debate on subjectivity-objectivity and intellectual colonialism their own position as presented in the above statement appears to be even more dogmatic and would suggest the complete irrelevance of the status group concept. While on the one hand they appear to accept the existence of status groups in asserting a simple deterministic view of class they imply that the status group is no more than a manifestation of class behaviour in miniature. Neither Marx nor Weber claimed that class was the sine qua non of society. Marx (Evans, 1975:142-143) referred to religious beliefs and ethnic loyalty as the '. . . . fragmentation of interest and rank' which cut across any proletarian class consciousness while Weber (Gerth and Mills, 1970:189) claimed that '. . . . status honour need not necessarily be linked with a class situation' but '. . . . normally stands in sharp opposition to the pretensions of sheer property'. Jenkins seeks to explain the lack of correlation between low economic ranking and membership of a superior status group by clearly demonstrating that those of high economic rank were of high status. The fact that the status variables are functionally inter-related does not imply that they are strongly inter-correlated statistically. What Jenkins suggests is that one's status, and the associated roles as a member of a status group which exists on the basis of conformity to religiously based values rather than the status that accrues from his economic rank, might determine how a person behaves in a given situation. The 'poor but deserving' ethos of the religious ideology was merely part of a tendency to countervene economic rank.

This does not of course alter the power relationship implicit in a division of labour but it is conceivable that such relationships could be profoundly influenced by the tenets of such an ideology to such an extent that in some contexts it can negate the power aspects of the interaction, with all members of the interactional group operating upon the basic principles of the ideology. Thus if an actor is to desire the status which conforms to his economic standing and power he can only achieve it by conforming to the rules of the game as dictated by the religious code. Thus a person who does not pay allegiance to this code is denied prestige credit. In a sense what is being argued is that while ranking in terms of power is inevitable, ranking in terms of reward is not, individuals can be rewarded with absolute equality. In the case in question this was assisted by the equation of the religious code with ethnicity, Welshness being defined in terms of the cohesion of the status group and the integrity of allegiance to the moral code which served to define the status group. Thus the argument maintains that ethnic allegiance cuts across class consciousness and serves to channel the conflict implicit in economic relationships to the more obvious wealthy, the gentry, who were labelled as an ethnic out-group. Those of the proletariat who aligned themselves with the gentry were similarly denied ethnic or in-group affinity. Such an explanation has the advantage of integrating the interests of both parties with an ethnic movement enhancing the interests of the leaders while also being aimed at improving the lot of the economically poorer ethnic cohorts. Day and Fitton's argument (1975:887) that it is a means by which those in superior economic positions subordinate their economic inferiors is also possible but as Eistenstadt (1971:84) remarks:

> Sociological knowledge is not yet adequate to know how it is possible for a collectivity to impose a collective goal on all, or most, of its individual members.

Certainly their suggestion concerning the imposition of social order on egotistical grounds is no more satisfactory than an explanation based on altruism, it merely places conflict in a different context.

While Day and Fitton bring no new data to bear on the issue they do attempt a re-analysis of Jenkins' original data. In so doing they exercise an interesting twist in the argument. They proceed to substitute Jenkins' argument about parallel but distinct occupational and religious status systems which is found in the historical study published in 1971 for the original 'buchedd' argument so that 'buchedd' becomes primarily a ranking system. In the 1971 study Jenkins (1971:193) observes that the nature of Welsh non-conformity at the turn of the century was such that discrepancies could arise between an individual's occupational status and his religious status and states:

> . . . . people went part of the way to resolving the incongruity by being readier to elect to the highest chapel offices those who were of high standing in everyday life.

Having recast 'buchedd' in stratification terms, and bearing in mind that the incongruency argument is advanced in the 1971 study, Day and Fitton (1975:876) proceed to claim that '. . . . the incongruence thesis is again advanced in the study of Aberporth (the earlier study)' and conclude by quoting from Jenkins (1951) M.A. dissertation written twenty years before the 'incongruency argument' was formalized. Whatever the chronological inelegancies of Day and Fitton's critique the point remains that what is originally discussed by Jenkins as an aspect of 'buchedd' is taken by Day and Fitton to be 'buchedd'. The deisgn of their refutation of Jenkins thus becomes a simple matter of showing that religious and occupational status correlate statistically. They assert that if Jenkins' position were to be upheld:

> The most convincing evidence would be to show a clear-cut incongruence between the two orders of class and status ranking, such that knowledge of position in the occupational order did not increase the accuracy of predictions about status position (Day and Fitton, 1975:874).

However Jenkins himself indicates that there is indeed a statistical correlation between occupational and religious status, he merely denies that there is a necessary correlation between them, which is a different matter altogether. The claim that the validity of Jenkins' analysis rests on the total incongruence of status systems has no foundation in Jenkins' own work since it is nowhere claimed that these are 'systematically unrelated'. Jenkins states that knowledge of occupational rank enhances the analysts ability to predict religious status and vice versa but this directly concerns individual actors and the actual social relations in which they participate. It does not lead directly to the 'orders' or 'systems' of occupational class or religious status as Day and Fitton apparently believe since it is difficult in small communities to statistically (inductively) derive two 'orders' of 'systems' of behaviour from actual behaviour in which the two are typically present simultaneously. Clearly it is tautologically true that two of anything which are 'systematically unrelated' are 'independent', although there is no reason to assume that if orders are systematically unrelated it makes them independent systems.

It would appear therefore that Day and Fitton's 're-analysis' of Jenkins' data succeeds only in showing that, as Jenkins (1960:102) himself stated, '. . . . class and buchedd groups overlap to a considerable extent'. Yet this is heralded as a significant finding. Day and Fitton (1975:880) also conclude from their analysis of the associational matrix that: '. . . . most interaction occurs within 'buchedd' groups' which is scarcely surprising when one considers that they are status groups based on common life styles. Indeed Day and Fitton's demonstration that the complete autonomy of the occupational and religious orders is not supported by Jenkins' data, is completely unremarkable and does not constitute a refutation of 'buchedd' which survives what appears to be a highly motivated critique in quite good form.

If we follow Weber and recognize classes and status groups as complementary bases of group formation in complex societies the question that should be asked does not involve overall predominance of one over the other but rather what determines the respective strength of the different principles of group formation and stratification and under what circumstances. While Jenkins does fail to adequately develop the 'buchedd' argument and while Day and Fitton do succeed in uncovering some inelegancies in Jenkins' argument, their own attempt to fit the data into their own conceptual scheme hardly serves to resolve the issue.

CHAPTER 10

MODERNIZATION AND LANGUAGE MAINTENANCE

E. Glyn Lewis

Introduction

Language maintenance issues reflect, and may be regarded in some countries even as arising from, profound changes in the structure of society as well as in the norms by which the behaviours of groups within society are guided. On this view, bilingual education is the institutionalization of social change. In considering language maintenance in the context of such economic, demographic and broadly interpreted cultural change, two contrasting attitudes have to be taken into account. According to the pronouncements of those who belong to the humanist tradition, expressed usually in highly emotive if not poetic language, as in the case of Saunders Lewis and a century earlier Thomas Davies of Ireland, attitude to the national language is governed by metaphysical arguments concerning the general nature and function of language:

> . . . . the language which has grown up with a people . . . . is fitted beyond any other to express their prevalent thoughts in the most natural and efficient way. To impose another language on such people . . . .is to cut off the entail of feeling and separate a people from their forefathers by a deep grief - 'tis to corrupt their very organs and abridge their power of expression (Davies, 1914 : 172-3).

Such a view implies that a particular language is central not only to aspects of the national culture but to self identity and total well being.

This view had little support prior to the eighteenth century when the philosophy of Herder and von Humboldt gave prominence to "folk" norms as the authentic foundations of a national way of life, and stressed the uniqueness and the equality of all languages. The opposite view has by far the longest history and up to the eighteenth century had guided educationists as well as writers in their concept of the relationship of languages to each other as well as to other aspects of social life. This view has been expressed in the following way:

> Of the various ties that bind human beings together that of a common language appears to possess no great strength. Other bonds protect it rather than it them. Where in the same city different languages are spoken in different quarters the quarters are not isolated because the inhabitants speak different languages but they speak different languages because they are isolated (Margoliouth, 1953).

There is little support for the humanist evaluation of the role of language as a determining factor in national habits of thought, and what evidence has been proferred, by Whorf for instance, has to be reinterpreted to such an extent as to make its implications ambiguous. There has not been very much hard evidence of the second view, either, though it conforms more nearly to the common sense view.

For these reasons, an analysis of the effect of social change upon the fate of the languages of Wales and on attitudes to them may help to dissipate a little of the obscurity which surrounds the subject. Modernization is the term we employ to encapsulate the changes which have affected developed societies since the seventeenth century and are now engulfing less developed and largely peasant societies in all parts of the world. That only very spasmodic and partial attempts have been made in Wales to identify the variables associated with languge maintenance or to formulate hypotheses concerning the inter correlation of these variables is a reflection of the conservative influence of the humanist way of thinking and the inertia which is inherent in the traditional humanist culture. Yet over a century ago Mathew Arnold who had a lively interest in the culture of Wales and its literature, at the mid-point of the process of modernization in Britain, drew attention to the malaise of humanist inertia and proposed a remedy which was supported in Wales by very few prominent among whom was Dr. Lewis Edwards who was severely attacked for his pains. Arnold (1853) pointed to

> . . . . one irresistible force which is gradually making its way everywhere, removing old conditions and imposing new, altering long fixed habits, undermining vererable institutions, even modifying national character – the modern spirit.

He goes on to claim that though any response to the modernizing process is likely to be imperfect

> . . . . yet to recognise a period of transformation when it comes and to adapt honestly and rationally to its laws is perhaps the nearest approach to perfection to which men and women are capable.

The present condition of the Welsh language is due partly to the failure of its intellectual elite, preachers and teachers at all levels of education, to recognise the modern spirit, or to consider its likely consequences; and partly to the fact that those Welshmen who were aware did not belong to the traditional intellectual elite and were associated with an extrinsic establishment.

Wales experienced the traumas of a social transformation which was externally motivated and which in the main Wales was almost powerless to control, and which it was inhibited therefore from adapting to in any positive way. The changes which occurred replaced or radically modified the infra-structure of Welsh social life - at the economic, demographic, legal and political level. The superstructure however, has remained firmly embedded in tradition. The problems associated with language maintenance are part of the erosion of the foundations of the superstructure, and those problems are urgent not because of the processes of modernization per se but because of the historical refusal of the Welsh elite to take account of it positively. The pressures of modernization need not have led to the present predicament : a language which had been shaped by contact with other languages on the continent and in these islands, and by the coming of new peoples into areas where it was spoken - Romans, English and the Norman French - was unable to meet the emergence of a new spirit. Modernization, or rather the attitude to it, produced a disabling withdrawal from reality. The net result was a 'sanctification' of the language not only in terms of its association with the pulpit and religious literature but in terms of attitudes, it was apotheosised.

The Use of a Modernization Model

The current discussion of modernization theory gives considerable prominence to differences which exist between patterns of modernization in developed Western countries and in developing countries, as well as differences between patterns in West and East European countries. With reference to a discussion of modernization in Britain we do not need to have regard for such differences. Wales was not simply within the Western European system but to a considerable extend led the development of British modernization. Nevertheless the position of Wales did not conform to the general norm of modernization. Prior to the development of modernized societies the European socio-political order was characterised by a high degree of congruence between cultural and political identities, a high level of affective and symbolic comittment to the political and cultural centres as well as a close relationship between those centres and the more primordial dimensions of life; an emphasis on politically defined collective goals for all members and a relatively autonomous access of broad strata to symbolic activities at the centre (Eiesenstadt, 1975: 64).

These conditions, prevalent in most European countries did not characterise Welsh society, any more than they did Spain which, like Wales, was culturally and linguistically heterogenous. In Wales there was no identity between cultural and political life; there was no committment to the centre, which in any case, was not indigenous; the relations between the centre and the primordial levels of life involving kinship and community patterns, were tenuous to say the least; there was no consensus on politically defined goals and there was no autonomous access for the Welsh people to the symbols of the centre. The base from which modernization in largely or entirely homogenous countries developed is not the base in those societies which were not simply peripheral to, but linguistically and culturally disparate from, the nation state. At various points in the progress of modernization Wales was prevented from determining the direction of the processes from within. It has been said

> .... that man lives from choice within the framework of his own experiences, trapped in his former achievements for generations to come (Braudel, 1973 : 25).

The Welsh during the initial stages of modernization had no choice but to remain trapped. For those at the centre modernization meant the appearance of new choices and options in human development, psychological, intellectual, political, social, cultural and economic. Where a minority, especially a linguistic minority, is concerned the options are never open ended, they are circumscribed by the requirements of the centre. A prior condition of modernization is that innovation is used if it maximises the advantage of the policy as a whole irrespective of the adverse consequences to any of its components. Modernization in Wales contributed greatly to the growth of the British state and to that of Europe but at a disproportionately heavy cost to the culture and language of the Principality itself.

Nevertheless, though Wales was modernized by the pressure of external forces and its modern spirit came to be discontinuous with traditional developments, the process of modernization as such was the same in Wales as in the rest of Europe. For that reason we are able to see what happened here in a very broad and general European context. Therefore, the use of the modernization model in considering the relation of social change to language maintenance offers several advantages. One is that cross cultural comparisons are facilitated and our understanding of our present position as well as our ability to plan for the future are clarified. Second, since modernization is the same in every country the convergence of cultures and policies, at first gradual and then accelerating, has been a marked feature of social life; and since the problems of language maintenance arise because of intensified convergence, this aspect of modernization is crucial to the students of language.

> Mankind only shows a tendency to become one with the development of modernized societies. Until then, and more and more as we go back further and further it was divided between different planets each sheltering an individual civilization or culture with its original features and ancient choices. However close to each other, their solutions were never able to intermingle (Braudel, 1973 : 443)

In so far as aspects of language maintenance reflect social change there are both deep and surface regularities which have to be taken into account. The deep structural regularities, involving economic, demographic, political and psychological variables, tend to be the same in all modernizing plurilingual societies. They are the universal laws of social change. For that reason the modernization of Wales is inextricably bound up with the history of the modernization of Western Europe from the eighteenth century onwards and with others parts of the world more recently. They must be explained in that very general context. Surface regularities reflect the different circumstances of the different countries as they affect particular responses to the deep structural changes. Therefore, while the causes of language maintenance problems tend to be the same in all modernizing countries, the manner in which the issues arise and the intensity with which they are experienced vary. These surface regularities have their own transformation rules, however so that in considering the problems of language maintenance which is an aspect of the transformation of the surface structure of society, we are able to institute cross national comparisons at the deep and surface levels and describe also the correlation of the changes on the two levels.

We cannot expect the modernization model to be unequivocal in its operation, it is not mechanistic and because it is a model of change which is inherently as well as extrinsically determined there are important contradictions within the model which help to facilitate inherently motivated change and modify change which is imposed from outside. Even at the level of the deep structure regularities the process between the fifteenth and seventeenth centuries the world

> . . . . constituted one vast peasantry where between 80 per cent and 95 per cent of people lived from the land and nothing else. The rhythm, quality and deficiency of harvests ordered all material life (Braudel, 1973 : 18-19).

In spite therefore of its being divided into 'separate planets' the world prior to modernization was fundamentally uniform in its economic organisation. The nature of this uniformity was radically changed but the changes tended everywhere in the same direction. What was produced by modernization, therefore, was a new uniformity to replace the old industrial rather than the agricultural order. However, whereas the former uniform system based on agriculture could co-exist with cultures which, because of the absence of a complex communications network which an agricultural economy is slow in encouraging, did not intermingle, the new economy, industrial and technological, depending absolutely on a complicated network of communications, has led to the rapid convergence of those different planets each sheltering an individual civilization or culture, while creating new disparate units, namely the nation states.

The Nature of Modernization

Modernization has been described from different standpoints. Pye and Rostow (1965) emphasise modernization as the establishment of national identities; for Solvert (1964), it is the rationalization and secularization of authority; Deutsch (1966), regards modernization as the process of social mobilization and differentiation of roles; political participation is the core of the process for Almond and Verba (1965); and the development of political capacity, a more general interpretation of participation is its main aspect in Eisenstadt's (1975) view; while for Rokkan (1968) and Bendix (1964) and Moore (1964), modernization is synonomous with "centre formation". All these approaches are equally relevant since they reflect necessary aspects of the global phenomenon; but all features are not present from the beginning. At certain stages of modernization some features, like political participation, may not have emerged, while other aspects such as the creation of nation states may need to be regarded as the precondition for effective modernization.

From the Welsh point of view it is tempting to look at these aspects as reflecting successive stages of process, and if we adopt this approach we can consider language maintenance in its relation to each aspect or stage rather than to modernization as a global concept. Lerner (1968) adopted a four stage model for his study of Turkey: first urbanization and then successively the development of literacy, the spread of mass media and finally increased political participation. It will be apparent that this is a highly simplified model and some aspects usually associated with modernization like psychological or attitudinal change are not specified directly. The articulation of the succession of stages is important from the point of view of language maintenance since, as it is hoped will become clear at a later point in the argument, the rationales for maintenance change with each stage, there is a paradigmatic shift corresponding to each stage of modernization. In Britain the first stage saw the thrust towards estabishing territorial control, including the territories of the Celtic peripheries, the creation of a beauracracy to manage those territories and the centralization of that beauracracy outside the areas of the linguistic minorities. This took place before the full monetization of the economy which was a precondition for the financial support of modernization, well before mass literacy and before the lower classes could participate politically. The centre, alien so far as the Celtic peripheries are concerned, had been formed before modernization as we know it got under way.

This fact had a profound influence on language maintenance since it meant the spearation of qualitative from quantitative controls of the development of the Welsh language. The territorial limits of the Welsh language had been set before the end of the thirteenth century and in terms of the demographic incidence of the language there was little change during the next six centuries. At the end of the eighteenth century Wales was still a very predominantly Welsh speaking country. Qualitatively however, the limits on the use of the language were constricted more and more. Apart from the Elizabethan inhibition on the use of the language for official purposes the language failed to establish itself in each area of social activity as it was modernized. Demographically the language was stabilised; functionally, it was destabilised, and structurally it remained very much as it had been three or four centuries before, with few if any concessions to the needs of a modern system of communication. The rhythms of economic, political, industrial and social change on the one hand and linguistic development, in functional and structural terms, became uncoordinated. Transition to a modern society gave increasing importance to core values associated with the centre from which the language was isolated. Being isolated, its maintenance came to be regarded as an end in itself, the language ceased to be simply or even mainly the medium and was itself regarded as the message. To this day it has remained so, part of a ritual rather than a tool.

If it were necessary to identify the one single factor which made modernization possible and which has coloured individual response to it we would have to point to the vast expansion of knowledge during the sixteenth and seventeenth centuries, together with changes of attitude towards the relevance of types or forms of knowledge. The new knowledge which was thought valuable tended to be that which could be validated or invalidated. It was also a kind of knowledge which, far from being an extension of elaboration of normal personal experience was on a different plane, discontinuous with normal experience, abstract in both nature ad expression, best exemplified by mathematics and physics. Its elaboration or extension did not depend on personal virtuosity but rather on the efficient use of instruments and tools. It was a method

> . . . . which left little to the acuteness and strength of wit and indeed tended rather to level wit and intellect. For as in the drawing of a straight line or accurate circle by the hand much depends on its steadiness and practice but if a ruler or compass be employed there is little occasion for either (Bacon, 1879 : Bk. I LXI).

The massive accumulation and the acceleration of that accumulation; its discontinuity, both in substance and expression with normal experience; together with its identification with successful technique made it necessary that even young children, limited though their requirements might be in terms of such knowledge, could not be expected to have the necessary grounding without formal instruction in school. In such formal scholastic situations their customary language, adequate though it might be for everyday affairs, would have to be adapted to the nature of what they were taught or to be replaced by a more flexible language. Even if the language used in school was the native language, Welsh or English, the requirements of the new curricula made it necessary that the language should be taught formally so that it might be adapted to a new range of experiences. If the school language was not the native tongue formal instruction in it was even more necessary. Modernization meant the differentiation of education as an independent, autonomous and specialised function no longer adequately fulfilled by the home with its diffused responsibilities. Thus the ground was prepared for the disassociation of the language of the school from that of the home. Functions which hitherto had been part of the general unarticulated role of the home were not taken over by the school simply because the pressure of new knowledge, its massiveness and abstractness, as well as changed attitudes to knowledge which reinforced the discontinuity of the new knowledge with personal experience, made the home as an educational institution outmoded. (Bruner, 1968 : 26, 31). An individual's place in society came to depend upon achievement in school: even sound psychological development, irrespective of social mobility, required the support of sound instruction in the context of a modern society. All these considerations meant that so far as modern society was concerned the language of the school, in principle, was of greater significance than that of the home. The new system of achievement carrying a new system of social and personal rewards led to a restructuring or a new stratification of society. The successful individual had his/her eyes on an environment, inside or outside Wales, which was served by the English language.

The knowledge which science made available was different not only in kind and amount, it came to be looked at in a different light from that in which knowledge and experience had hitherto been regarded. Rationality, rather than continuity with tradition became the criterion of relevance; and the efficiency of its deployment became the norm. This change and its implications were indicated by Bacon who argued that the accumulation of knowledge should be governed by considerations of utility. He regarded it as a considerable

> . . . . evil that men in their system and contemplation bestow their labour upon the investigation and discussion of the princples of things . . . . although all utility and means of action consist 'in intermediate objects (Bacon, 1879 : Bk. I LXVI).

The second aim of producing knowledge was to produce change,

> . . . . to generate and superinduce a new nature or new natures upon a given body is the labour and aim of human powers (Bacon, 1879 : Bk. II,I).

Change was no longer something to be experienced or simply endured, it was a goal to be achieved and sought. Language was valuable, live, technique only if it was useful in producing change so that its association with "intense meditation and a continued exercise and perpetual agitation of the mind" was discouraged. Apart from its usefulness as a tool for producing change language was regarded sceptically as tending to

> .... throw everything into confusion and lead mankind into vain and innumerable controversies and fallacies (Bacon, 1879 : Bk. I XLII)

Associated with the emphasis on the 'rational' use of language, a regard for it as an efficient instrument rather than as a hallowed institution, there were two other aspects of the modernizing spirit in the form of a scientific scepticism and a thrust towards a demystification of hitherto sanctified institutions, among which language came first, together with a tough mindedness: "Indeed, distrust of the intangible behind which one looked for tangible matters on which one relied for understanding" (Polany, 1958 : 12). Legitimacy was transferred from tradition and humanistic values to these new guidelines. The capacity of institutions, including language, to engender and maintain a belief that they are the instruments which are most important and appropriate for that society, which is what is meant by legitimacy, was identified with the aptness to promote efficiency, a sceptical frame of mind, a willingness to reduce the status of tradition with other tangibles and a general propensity to tough mindedness.

Because of this shift from humanstic and traditional values to rational and technical norms the reference groups for all elements in society were displaced in all modernizing societies, and especially in Britain. In all such cases, there was a decisive movement to assimilate to the new reference groups. However, it did not happen in Wales. There, reference groups remained the same as they had for centuries. Consisting mainly of the humanist elite and those of the remaining aristocracy who suckered and supported them. What shift occurred was away from Wales altogether and involved an identification with the centre. While within Wales, the traditional stratification remained by far the most significant stratification, especially so far as concerns the Welsh language, involved a distinction between the Welsh elite and the rising middle classes with reference to England, to which the modernizing Welsh gravitated. Early industries were expanding, professions were being shaped and the only means which the achievement oriented Welshman had to exploit these opportunities was the English language and an English oriented school. The choice of English was only partly due to the earlier prohibition of Welsh, it was due much more to the unwillingness of the Welsh traditionalists to be contaminated. Instead, they withdrew. The fundamental elitism of society prior to the eighteenth century was replaced in England, gradually it is true, by fundamental democratization (Mannheim, 1940). In Wales that elitism, humanist in essence, was confirmed and reinforced rather than modified by the processes of modernization.

Thus far, in discussing 'rationality' as an aspect of modernization in Wales, we have been concerned with its substantive aspects involving the use of critical powers and the development of a scientific mind as opposed to the acceptance of tradition and the ascribed status of such central institutions as the language. Modernization promoted other aspects of rationality, particularly a belief in the value and the need for planning. The democratization of the literary culture meant the advance of the vernacular, and in consequence most modernizing countries became interested in 'language planning'. In France the Academy was founded partly to undertake such planning. In England, the Royal Society was interested though not as intensely involved. The Univerities played their part. Wales, too, had its planners in the form of the early lexicographers and grammarians, but without a centre as in England and France, or a native university the efforts tended to be spasmodic, not cummulative or aggregative. Each lexicographer and grammarian directed his attention to the rediscovery of the wheel. The effect on the Welsh language as an instrument for a modernizing world was negligible. The language was stabilised in its written form very early except for the orthography which was permissive rather than prescriptive. The structural stabilisation was based on norms which, if not outmoded, were at least unrepresentative of the spoken language of the nineteenth century. This written standard was limited in its social usages and functions, which were mainly formal and rhetorical. The spoken language was not effectively stablised until the twentieth century and that degree of stabilisation was enforced by the demands of the mass media and the production of teaching materials to be used where Welsh was taught as a scond language (W.J.E.C.). The Morrises of Anglesey were interested in the elaboration, augmentation and enrichment of the lexicon but it was not until the University of Wales, jointly with the Welsh Department of the Ministry of Education, issued a series of specialist lexicons for scientific subjects taught in school and colleges that any planned attempt to bring the Welsh language into the modernizing world was attempted.

No criticism is implied by this account since the existence of a codified standard language as distinct from every day casual speech and a number of dialects, however authentic they may be, is a major linguistic correlate of an urban culture. In

Wales the planned development of the language was inhibited because urbanization was largely limited, almost exclusively to south Wales. Because of this geographical as well as cultural divide the tensions between the requirements of modernization and the demands of authenticity was critical. Authentication emphasises

> . . . . the sentimental uniformities and is constantly straining towards poorer and more genuine expression of the heritage of yesteryear (Fishman, 1972 : 17).

The issue was at the heart of the controversy which engaged Lewis Edwards in his contributions to the Traethodydd. He was aware and sympathetic to the claims of an authentic national culture and its associated language but there were more pressing claims:

> . . . . the nation and its language are lovely in our sight but lovelier still are knowledge and truth.

It was

> . . . . the nature's indifference towards the value of knowledge and its lack of understanding of the nature of instruction

that in his view was the

> . . . . greatest obstacle to the progress of Wales (Edwards, n.d.).

The effect of the upsurge of scientific knowledge and its associations with technology, especially in south Wales, could have enabled the Welsh language to operate within as wide a range of social functions and in turn could have ensured the continuous development of the language structurally as was the case with the English. But the will to be involved did not appear to have existed among the humanist elite. The early stages of modernization, especially the establishment and creation of a centre extrinsic to Wales, as a consequence of the emergence of a centralised beauracracy serving the new state limited the options open to those who used the language. Welsh was disassociated from the revolution of sensibility brought about by the new knowledge and by new attitudes to knowledge. As that revolution progressed and as modernization proceeded the language remained trapped within a consciousness of past achievements.

Industrialization and Urbanization

If the consolidation of control over the territory of Britain and the concomitant evolution of a centralised and alien beauracracy were the preconditions of modernization, and if the revolution of sensibility arising from the discovery of new dimensions of knowledge is the hallmark of the modern mind, the most salient aspects of modernization are rapid industrialization and urbanization. The pre-modern era in Wales as in Europe generally was characterised by small, dispersed communities of peasant agriculturalits and fishermen with few and only gradually increasing numbers of industrial workers congregating in large towns. Of the industries which became the foundations of Welsh development, coal was worked by small farmers for their own needs, while the forges and furnaces which heralded the contemporary vast steel complexes were scattered in the countryside employing only a few full-time workers and serviced by rudimentary communications systems. It was not until financial investment trickled and then flowed from England that these industries became significant features of social life beyond the clusters of peasant houses. For most of the people the economic life of the Principality centred on the local fairs and markets where the drovers provided a system of communication.

Soon the mining and metallurgical industries became organised as relatively large units employing large numbers requiring more investment. With this investment came a new and alien entrepreneurial elite like the Guests, Townsends, Homfrays and Protheroes. They were risk takers, achievement oriented, their criteria for action being efficiency and successful functioning. They were agents of change. By the end of the eighteenth century, though the geographical area of industrialisation was restricted, Wales had been set irrevocably on the path of industrial development and technological revolution. In the first half of the nineteenth century a movement away from the primary industries of coal and iron to include the secondary tin and copper industries was becoming wisespread, with still more investment from outside Wales and a resultant migration of English industrialists. By 1831 the proportion of families dependent on agricultural employment had declined in Wales as a whole from 53 per cent to 44 per cent in less than thirty years. In one of the areas which spearheaded modernization, Swansea, it had dropped from 51 per cent to 28 per cent. By 1871, the agricultural occupations accounted for only 5 per cent of Swansea males 20 years and over compared with 24 per cent for Wales and Monmouthshire; industrial occupations accounted for 54 per cent and commercial occupations 23 per cent.

Early industrialisation, drawing upon local and neighbourhood commuting labour, did not necessitate large scale urbanisation, but this condition did not last long. It is difficult to produce a satisfactory index of urbanization for Wales, partly because the counties have been too large and heterogenous to allow any one or at least all but two of them to be classified in one or other of the classes, urban or rural, unequivocally. Another reason is that the administrative classification, which is all we really have to go on, has been unreal for many decades: the rural districts are so in name only since though they may not be centres of industry they are closely related to such centres and accommodate their overspill. However, if we take a strictly defined area such as the Swansea region, which is less than a county and yet includes several districts designated either urban or rural, and which experienced rapid industrialization during the last century we find that in 1801 more than half the area had a population density of less that 25 per square kilometre and four fifths of the remainder had a density of less than 25 and 50 per square kilometer. In 1901, only a small and remote part of Gower and the north east mountainous areas bordering on Carmarthenshire had a density of under 25 per square kilometre, more than half the area had a density of between 100 and 250 per square kilometre, an eighth part had between 250 and 1000 per square kilometre and there were concentrated pockets of over 2,500 per square kilometre. In Wales as a whole, the percentage of urban population rose between 1861 and 1911 from 23.9 per cent to 62.6 per cent to 64.1 per cent in 1961, levelling off at approximately 63 per cent since then. According to Friedlander (1970) only Glamorgan and Monmouthshire in Wales belong to the group of urban counties in Britain, defined as having below 10 per cent of the population engaged in agriculture.

From the standpoint of the fate of the Welsh language the significant point is that these two counties were among the very first in Britain to become urban, next after London, Lancashire and Durham. In fact Glamorgan soon overtook Durham in the intensity and speed of urbanization. In 1871 the urbanization of the whole of Britain was still concentrated in only four areas, London, Durham and Lancashire in the north of England; Staffordshire and Warwickshire in the English midlands and the two Welsh counties. The economic pattern in Wales was dichotomised, ad this was achieved within less than half a century. One part, which was geographically much the largest, continued the traditional integration of the social and economic life with the national language; the other, accounting for two thirds of the population, experienced economic and social changes which drove a wedge between the customary language and the economic and social life of the community. Equally important, these changes were completed to all intents and purposes within a very small period of less than three generations, allowing of little opportunity to adjust naturally to the series of innovations.

The movements which account for the changes in population density and urbanization are centrifugal as well as centripetal. Populations concentrate on limited areas were industry is located, and this population may be drawn from the neighbourhood or imported from farther afield. Second, because neighbourhood populations are attracted, and later the same neighbourhoods take the overspills from the towns and cities, the rural areas come under very strong urban influences. The effect of centripetal movements and urban attraction from the rural areas was very strong initially and had a marked, though contradictory, influence on language maintenance, as we shall note. During the last few decades the centrifugal movement has become equally influential. Areas in west Wales, central and north west Wales which were outside the range of urbanization are now under intense urban influence. The initial centripetal movement dried up the resources of Welsh language maintenance by denuding the rural areas of numbers; the centrifugal movement diminishes the remaining resources by undermining the traditional economic and social foundations of the Welsh language locally.

Such then is the broad outline of the growth of urban populations in Wales during the last two centuries; but influential though that process was for its demographic and quantitative impact the psychological effects on those who spoke the language, and on their attitude to their ethnic heritage including language were equally pronounced.

> Towns are so many electric transformers. They increase tension, accelerate the rhythm of exchange and ceaslessly stir up men's lives (Braudel, 1973 : 373)

Towns and cities belong to a different dimension of existence from that which had shaped the Welsh language and whose social functions it had been accustomed to serve. Researchers in the Soviet Institute of Ethnography have conducted studies in depth of the effects of urbanization on the new industrial complexes in the areas of Central Asia to which heavy industries have been moved. They identify the following ethnic processes as rural populations move into new towns and cities : highly intense division of labour which cuts across ethnic divisions in the population; great diversity and activity of contacts between individuals and between entire groups; a high level of information exchange including the exchange of cultural values; bilingualism, and in some instances, considerable multilingualism; a high degree of saturation of high technology that tends to level any ethnic differences in ways of life; and types of urban layout that tend to reduce traditional ethnic individuality in housing (Pokshishevskiy, 1971). These changes have influenced the consciousness of the mobile populations so that the urban consciousness is vastly different from the consciousness of the rural poulation, and this difference gradually penetrates the surrounding rural areas. In this way, the role of the urban dwellers may actually be far greater than their quantitative share of the total population. In addition, urbanization, where it involves more than one ethnic and linguistic group, works in mutually opposed directions. In the first place it produces a new ethnic and linguistic mix and so tends to break down ethnic and linguistic boundaries and to restructure ethnic and linguistic groups. Urbanization also leads to an intensification of the separate ethnic consciousness, so that it is the cities rather than the small and traditional rural villages which become the centres of national-culture consciousness. The centre of gravity of the ethnos is transferred from the countryside to the town; it is here that we find educational institutions that train the best among the ethnic population. Towns are the centres of publishing and broadcasting in the national language. Above all the possibiity of constantly comparing one's own with other cultures within the matrix of an immensely complex network of cross ethnic communications tends to intensify the awarenss of one's own ethnic heritage. It is doubtful whether

> . . . . the traditional view among ethnographers that it is the village that tends to preserve distinctive ethnic features, while the cities with their standardized material culture and a mixture of ethnic components are viewed as something anti-ethnographic, can now be substantiated (Pokshishevskyi, 1971).

However, the ethnic consciousness which is thus intensified by the experience of an urban environment cannot be said to be the 'authentic' ethnic culture. The consciousness of being Welsh and of the Welsh language as one's native tongue, though far more intense among the Welsh of Cardiff or Swansea than in the villages of Carmarthenshire or Meirionethshire, is not a consciousness of the historical ethnic culture which the folk memory is thought to preserve. The urban ethnic consciousness is modified as well as intensified by the urban experience. What is intensified is an awareness of the ethnic culture in contact with another, and those who are conscious of the one are simultaneously conscious of the other. Those who are identified with this modified culture are sometimes regarded as 'marginal men' who are said to behave according to an 'alternation model', adopting industrial and urban norms in some contexts and traditional norms in others. A great deal has been made of this concept since it was first administrated by Park (Hughes, et.al., 1950), but valid though it is it needs to be refined if it is to meet the demands made upon it in different contact-situations. The classical paradigm as set out by Park carried with it pejorative connotations, but there is nothing particlarly reprehensible about having a dual set of norms, nor should we identify the possession and co-existence of different valuations or orientations in the same individual with a schizoid, unstable personality. According to the classical praradigm a person is said to be marginal when he/she is not a full member of a well organised and supportive group, or more precisely when he/she is on the margins of the social spaces occupied by the groups in contact. Marginality, so defined is usually associated, in these terms, with social isolation and cultural as well as self estrangement, with a loss of personal identity in some circumstances (Goldberg, 1958 : 25). This may be a fair account of the condition of some persons when contact is first established and when the two cultures and the two languages have not adjusted to each other. It was the case in the mining valleys of Wales, and particularly in towns like Merthyr Tydfil during the initial phases of industrialization and culture contact. Such conditions during the last century were at the root of the many religious revivalist movements which expressed the deep social rather than religious insecurity of the urbanised populations.

The classical paradigm is not applicable in Wales any longer, nor to persons who live and have lived for several generations in a long standing mature contact-situation. We in Wales are in the position of the Spanish during the eighth century. As the Arab invasion spread and the Moors gained control over large parts of the Iberian peninsula Spaniards were attracted to the Moorish way of life, technology, science, economic organisation and literature. They became bilingual and produced a literature which was an organized development from the two literatures in contact. The great Spanish heritage now enjoyed in Latin America as well as in Spain itself is a refinement not of the 'pure and authentic' pre-Moorish culture but of the fusion, albeit in unequal parts, of the two cultures, Spanish and Arabic. Similarly, the authentic English culture of our day was itself once a marginal or contact culture reflecting the influence of the Norman French and the native English. In time a contact culture acquired its own authenticity. At present the Welshman who may not be totally committed emotionally to either language exclusively, Welsh or English, has been conditioned from birth to such an uncommitted existence on the borders of both cultures, or at least not at the centre of either, like his parents before him. We share this 'marginal' condition with a very large number of individuals in our primary groups: we belong in fact to well organised and supportive groups in much the same way as the "authentic" Welsh and the "authentic" English do. The history of this group stretches far back beyond the seventeenth century. The periods of our individual growth, maturation, and even adulthood find us participating in 'marginal' institutional activities which are conducted by very many others like ourselves.

Finally, there is no way in which the so called "marginal" position, or failure to affiliate exclusively to one or other culture and its associated language results in any major, or for that matter, minor, blockage or frustration of our learned expectations and desires. In fact those expectations have been shaped over the last two or three centuries by 'marginal men' like ourselves. So far as Wales is concerned then, it is possible to adopt a dual model of two entirely separate cultures and their languages, or a model of three such cultures that is, Welsh, English and a contact urban culture served by two languages, or a single model, a matrix of several gradations of the contact of the two primary cultures, with a cultural reservoir or repetoire which draws on either indifferently. So far as the two languages are concerned this is the model which Gumperz (1962) proposes for language contact situations in several countries.

Demographic Change

The industrial change giving rise to urbanization and culture change were made possible by, and have led to, large increases in the population of a few areas and this selective increase is characterised in turn by considerable migration - in the first instance from the neighbouring rural areas of Wales and later in large numbers from England. Table 10:1.

The rural counties which had traditionally been regarded as the main bulwarks of the Welsh language, namely, Anglesey, Caernarfon and Meirioneth in north Wales, Brecon and Montgomery in mid Wales, Cardigan, Pembrokeshire and Carmarthen in south west Wales are heavy and consistent losers by out-migration almost from the beginning of the era of intense industrialization. They contributed considerably to the satisfaction of the early manpower requirements of the industrial growth areas in Glamorgan, Monmouth and Flintshire. Because of such local migration the populations of the south west Wales coalfield increased nearly six fold. The period of general industrial depression between 1920 and 1936 helped to reverse the process of out-migration from the rural Welsh-speaking areas only slightly and accelerated out-migration from industrial areas.

Four periods or phases of migration may be distinguished. Up to 1850, the needs of Welsh industry were met largely by migration from the neighbouring Welsh-speaking counties with some slight support from south west England. This compares with the early phase of industrialization in the Soviet Union and contrasts with the

United States of America where early industry was far more dependent on immigrant foreign labour than on the indigenous rural populations. Wales follows the general

Table 10:1 Net population change per thousand due to migration in each Welsh County 1851-1971

County	1851 -61	1861 -71	1871 -81	1881 -91	1891 -1901	1901 -11	1911 -31 (20 years)	1931 -51 (20 years)	1951 -71 (20 years)
Anglesey	+25	+96	+58	-32	-31	-35	+13	+49	+4
Brecon	+35	-46	-98	-47	-48	-21	-34	-11	+4
Caernarfon	-19	+33	+15	-32	-9	-43	-15	-2	-2
Cardigan	-62	-45	-99	-133	-63	-21	-34	-11	+4
Carmarthen	-58	-48	-33	-45	-43	+67	+10	-65	+3
Denbigh	-6	-44	-27	-22	-16	+2	-9	-4	+7
Flint	+158	+24	+51	+83	+24	+22	+132	+120	+40
Glamorgan	+133	+45	+144	+166	+54	+92	-191	-109	+20
Merioneth	-61	+106	-12	-62	-54	-104	+14	-14	+13
Monmouth	-38	+35	-65	+59	-4	+119	-123	-111	+3
Montgomery	-72	-75	-96	-118	-90	-80	-50	-64	-11
Pembroke	-54	-74	-81	-99	-64	-73	-35	-24	-5
Radnor	-115	-83	-145	-116	-90	-80	-50	-64	-11

Source : Extracted from Official Census Returns 1851-1971

pattern in much the same way as does the Soviet Union. When industrial growth is very rapid, the influx of the non-indegenous workers tends to exceed the influx of the indigenous into towns and cities. However, when the economy develops at a more moderate rate the share of indigenous populations in these towns tends to be higher (Pokshishevskyi, 1971 : 61-2).

The major turning point from moderate to rapid industrial growth in Wales did not occur until about 1850 and up to that point the industrial and urban revolution may be said to have worked in favour of the Welsh language to the extent that consciousness of Welsh ethnicity was intensified so that several Welsh religious causes were established in parts of Wales which had long been thoroughly anglicised, as was the case in Monmouthshire and especially in Newport. The second phase which lasted from about 1850 to 1910 was the period of very rapid influx of English populations, and it is this second phase which was responsible for the cataclysmic change in the fortunes of the Welsh language. What happened in the third phase and the fourth could do very little to modify the strength or to change the direction of industrial influences on the language, espcially in south Wales. So far as the rural areas are concerned, whatever fluctuations occurred in the years following 1850 were slight compared with the processes of continuous out-migration at a fairly consistent rate.

Geographical Distribution of the population

Without exception the predominantly rural counties, those in central Wales and the isolated north and south west manifest a regular and continuous outward migration. Among all the counties of England and Wales which belong to the losing group throughout the period from 1851 the Welsh rural counties rank among the highest. The rural population reached its peak in 1871 and in fact, the rate of population increase had been slight since 1801. At that date, all the counties except those who were to become the centres of industry aggregated 359,000. In 1971 the figure was 834,000, an increase of 130 per cent while the total population increase was 364 per cent. The three industrial counties had experienced an eleven fold population increase.

However, the depopulation of the rural counties was not a total loss to the Welsh language, any more than it has been to the ethnic languages of the Soviet Union as we have already noted. The period 1851 to 1871 in Wales is characterised by short distance migration, much of it from adjacent counties. The condition of the language in south Wales at present would be much poorer than it is if the migrations from England had not previously as well as simultaneously, been offset by the deployment of the internal resources of Wales. During the period 1850 to 1871, about 70 per cent of the migrants to Glamorgan came from neighbouring Welsh-speaking counties. A large proportion of these were monolingual Welsh or nearly so. It was between 1871 and 1881 that long distance migration really set in, so that only 38 per cent migrated from the five neighbouring counties, while migration from England caught up at 37 per cent. One feature of short distance migration from Welsh speaking counties which the census figures cannot reveal but which was of considerable importance was its seasonal character. Farm workers and owners of small holdings were accumstomed to move into the iron works and mines during the slack agricultural period and returned home when the farms required their presence. This constant mobility had two contrary effects. It helped to reinforce regularly the existing Welsh character of the industrial areas. As the same time, it helped to break down the settled traditional pattern of Welsh rural life, to promote the acceptance of new ideas and to prepare the way for the forces tending towards the anglicisation of even remote rural areas. This commuting aspect of migration is a factor in the language situation of the Soviet Union, the anglicisation of the American Indian tribes moving in and out of reservations, as well as areas such as Luxembourg (Tabouret Keller, 1972).

The history of in-migration into Wales is largely, though not entirely, the history of changes in the economic life of the south Wales coalfield. Using their migration index Friedlander and Roshier (1966) estimate that in 1851 to 1861 Glamorgan of all counties in England and Wales witnessed a flow of migrants second in strength only to that of another Welsh county in the process of industrialization, namely Flintshire. In the second decade, 1861 to 1871, it was second only to London and the home counties. During this phase over 70 per cent of the immigrants were recruited locally from Monmouthshire, Cardiganshire, Pembrokeshire, Carmarthenshire and Brecon, in that order. In the next decade 1871 to 1881 Glamorgan was at the top of the list of Counties in England and Wales so far as migration was concerned and during this period over 57 per cent of the in-migrants came from England, a flow which continued to 1911. Between 1861 and 1911, the number of non-native born inhabitants of Glamorgan reached 390,000, representing a residuum of nearly 430,000, over 55 per cent of them English monolinguals. The ratio of non-native to native born remained constant between 1861 and 1911 at around 35 per cent and this constant ratio is due to the equally constant reinforcement by in-migration. After 1911, the ratio falls to 21 per cent because of the cessation of in-migration. But the decline in the ratio is no consolation from the standpoint of the language because the second and third generation in-migrants though native born were predominantly English in speech.

The fate of the Welsh language in Glamorgan is due partly to the fact that industrialisation began in the strongest Welsh speaking areas and was fed by migrants from other Welsh-speaking areas. This is the first phase. It is a consideration of this phase which has led some researchers (Thomas, 1950) to maintain that industrialisation and in-migration did not affect the Welsh language adversely. This contention is valid for this phase and for it alone. During the second phase the balance of 'cultural advantage' finally swung decisively to the side of anglicisation and with it went the last hope of preserving the 'authentic' historical Welsh culture in the coalfield (Jones,

Table 10:2 Glamorgan immigrants 1861-1911.
Numbers (in thousands) and percentages according to areas of origin

Date of Census Return	Grand total of migration to Glamorgan	Welsh Counties												Total of Welsh Migrants	Welsh Migrants % of Grand Total	Migration from England.
		a. Anglesey	b. Brecon	c. Caernarfon	d. Cardigan	e. Carmarthen	f. Denbigh	g. Flint	h. Meirioneth	i. Monmouth	j. Montgomery	k. Pembroke	l. Radnor			Total
1851/71	21.0	-	2.1	-	1.5	5.7	0.1	-	0.1	2.3	0.4	3.7	0.4	16.3	78	4.7
1871/81	76.7	-	3.6	0.3	4.1	4.9	0.2	0.1	0.2	10.1	1.4	5.8	0.7	31.4	43	43.3
1881/91	108.8	0.6	4.3	1.9	7.6	9.3	0.7	0.4	1.6	10.5	4.1	5.5	1.4	48.2	44	60.6
1891/1901	105.0	0.4	4.2	1.0	3.8	11.6	0.3	0.3	1.1	13.5	1.4	7.1	0.7	55.4	53	49.6
1901/1911	128.5	1.0	3.8	3.9	2.9	6.8	1.1	013	2.5	11.6	2.2	5.5	1.3	42.9	33	85.6

Source : Extracted from Official Census Returns

1970 : 92). The second phase was characterised by a predominantly English speaking labour supply, which though it reached its peak in a relatively short time was massive in scale. The first phase gave the Welsh language an opportunity to adapt to change while in the second phase in-migration was too intense to allow of the English being assimilated. This fact was stressed by the Commission of Enquiry on Industrial Unrest (1917). Until 1895,

> .... the inhabitants in many respects showed a marked capacity to stamp their own impress on all new comers and communicating to them a large measure of all their own characteristics. Of more recent years the process of assimilation had been unable to keep continuing pace with the influx of immigrants.

The fate of the Welsh language is associated inextricably with the inflow of English in-migrants and the outflow of Welsh-speaking rural populations into the industrial areas of the increasingly English speaking south Wales.

The changes did not occur uniformly throughout Glamorgan, the rate of migration and population growth varied from district to district. The most rapid changes were experienced in Merthyr and the Rhondda Valleys. In 1851 the former had a population of 50,000, over 40 per cent of whom came from other Welsh counties and 12 per cent from neighbouring Welsh speaking districts within Glamorgan. Only a small proportion of the remaining 20 per cent came from England. It is here that the significance of the historical isolation of the uplands of Glamorgan from the anglicised and conquered lowlands appears. Unlike the lowlying agricultural areas of Glamorgan, Merthyr and the Rhondda Valleys had remained strongly Welsh speaking. Consequently, of the in-migrants into Glamorgan the Welsh-speaking element was attracted to the coalfields in the hills and did not replace, as is generally the case, the local migrant agricultural labourers who were nearer the point of industrial development. The English-speaking migrants to Glamorgan, on the other hand, were drawn in the first instance to the more congenial English-speaking lowland areas to provide the labour replacement we have referred to. For example, in 1891, the 252,000 life time in-migrants to Glamorgan as a whole were divided almost equally between the Welsh and the English. However so far as the limited areas of the coalfields are concerned Welsh migrants outnumbered the English by four to three. Outside the coalfield the ratio of English to Welsh migrants was reversed, it was nearly five to two in favour of the English.

If it was the traditional linguistic and cultural character of the Valleys which drew Welsh in-migrants to those areas, their presence in turn reinforced that tradition for a short time, and in the period of very rapid transition they ensured that the process of anglicisation was delayed, and the English assimilated to some extent. In 1840 before long distance migration began to affect Merthyr, but at a time nevertheless when, because of short distance movement, the population of the town and surrounding villages had increased from 13,000 to 85,000 in less than fourty years, the religious situation, reflecting the linguistic division between the Church and the non-conformist sects, was highly favourable to the latter, by a factor of nine. In one small but typical part of the town consisting of two very long rows of tenement houses

> . . . . standing behind each other and close to the works - a fair average of the whole, seventeen of the twenty families were Welsh; ten of the husbands could read Welsh and four of the wives could read the Welsh Bible (Tremenheere, 1840).

In 1846, only 12.3 per cent of the population was English and even this small proportion declined within five years to 9 per cent due to local migration. Twenty years later the position had not changed greatly though the children were by now becoming bilingual.

> In such towns as Merthyr, Aberdare and others where the different races converge large numbers speak English for the purposes of necessary communication with their neighbours, who beyond the very scanty nomenclature used for this end are entirely ignorant of the language. Welsh is their vernacular for the fireside, for general conversation and for all the ordinary purposes of life . . . . They would be recent emigrants from the agricultural western districts of Wales. However, among the children, knowledge of English is in advance of the population. In these instances, the parents have been longer located in the district and the children are native to it or brought there very young. And from intercourse with companions of their own age and other sources they not only are habituated to English in their earliest years but aquire and make more use of English abroad than they do of Welsh at home (Jenkins, J., : 453)

Nevertheless, in assessing and acknowledging the value to Welsh language maintenance of the concentration of Welsh-speaking migration on Merthyr and the Rhondda the fact should not be ignored that the same concentration deprived other areas in Glamorgan on the border of the lowland English and the upland Welsh-speaking areas

Table 10:3 English and Welsh speaking populations of Wales 1891 - 1971

(Note: The totals of the language categories d) & e) do not, as they should, equal the totals in a) because of ommisions in languge data returns. No Census was taken in 1941.

	a.	b.			c.			d.			e.		
		Welsh Only			English and Welsh			Total Welsh Speaking b + c			English Only		
		1	2	3	1	2	3	1	2	3	1	2	3
Year of Census	Total population in thousands	Total in thousands	1 as % of a.	percentage difference from previous return	Total in thousands	1 as % of a.	percentage difference from previous return	Total in thousands	1 as % of a.	percentage difference from previous return	Total in thousands	1 as % of a.	percentage difference from previous return
1891	1813	508	29	-	402	24	-	910	51	-	759	41	-
1901	2013	281	14	-45	649	32	+61	930	46	+2	928	54	+22
1911	2421	190	8	-36	786	32	+21	976	39	+5	1108	46	+30
1921	2656	153	6	-19	746	29	-5	900	36	-8	1467	63	+33
1931	2593	98	4	-36	820	32	+10	909	36	+1	1552	64	+5
1951	2472	41.1	2	-57	673	27	-18	714	28	-22	1758	72	+13
1961	2518	26.1	1.0	-38	629	25	-7	656	26	-8	1862	74	+6
1971	2602	32.7	1.3	+30	510	19.6	-20	542	21	-20	2060	89	+20

Sources: Census of England & Wales - Reports on Welsh speaking population

of similar much needed Welsh language support. Consequently, outside the coalfields the language collapsed more rapidly than it might otherwise have done. But from whatever angle it is examined the consequences of the early reinforcement of the Welsh-speaking population of Merthyr and the Rhondda Valleys at the beginning of the industrial expansion were apparent throughout the period of intensified industrialisation and are far from having disappeared completely.

The Decline of the Welsh Language

The proportion of the population which is bilingual rose consistently up until 1951 with the exception of the period 1911 to 1921 and has been falling since. In 1961, the percentage was only slightly higher than in 1891 at 24 per cent. The continuous decline in the proportion of monolingual speakers of Welsh has been very much steeper, from 29 per cent in 1891 to 1.0 per cent in 1961, rising slightly to 1.3 per cent in 1971. The rise in the proportion of the monolingual English is continuous from 41 per cent in 1891 to 74 per cent in 1961. It is clear that the bilinguals are shifting to monolingualism in English very rapidly and the monolingual Welsh are becoming only temporarily and transitionally bilingual. The only decade when this transference of language affiliation was retarded is 1921 to 1931, the depression years when Wales experienced the highest rate of out-migration. With the almost complete disappearance of Welsh monolingualism, except among children aged 3 to 5, there remained after 1931 no pool from which bilinguals could be recruited. From that time the curve of bilingualism has declined from 32 per cent in 1931 to 25 per cent in 1961 and 19.6 per cent in 1971. While the population of Wales increased from 1.8 millions in 1891 to 2.6 millions in 1961 and 1971, the number of monolingual Welsh dropped 540,000 to 26,000 in 1961, rising contrary to all historical precedents to 32,700 in 1971. The population increase represented a rise of almost 44 per cent but the number of speakers of Welsh, monolinguals and bilinguals dropped by 16 per cent. Looked at nationally the picture of Welsh language maintenance has no variation, no complexities, no light and shade but rather a uniform and deepening gloom.

Regional differences in the density and distribution of Welsh

However, the description of the national trends in the demographic incidence of Welsh can not do justice to the variation from one type of locality to another. The analysis needs to be pursued according to geographic distribution, type of locality, whether urban or rural, the age and sex composition of the population, as

Table 1O:4 Welsh speaking population by categories and according to Counties 1971 (In thousands)

Area	All persons aged 3 and over			Speaking Welsh														
				Total			Not speaking Welsh			Speaking English			Reading Welsh			Writing Welsh		
	persons	males	females	persons	males	females	persons	males	females	persons	males	females	persons	males	females	persons	males	females
Wales	2,6O2.O	1.261	1,341	542	255	286	32	15	16	5O9	239	269	448	2O8	245	297	189	1O8
Anglesey	55.4	27.6	26.O	37.O	17.8	19.1	2.5	1.2	1.2	34.5	16.5	17.9	32.4	15.5	16.9	31.1	14.9	16.2
Brecon	51.1	25.4	25.7	11.7	5.6	6.1	O.5	O.2	O.3	11.1	5.3	5.8	9.1	4.2	4.8	7.6	3.9	3.7
Caernarfon	117.9	54.6	63.1	73.1	34.2	38.8	5.1	2.5	2.5	62.9	31.5	36.2	55.O	3O.2	34.7	62.2	28.9	33.3
Cardigan	52.9	25.4	27.3	35.7	17.O	18.7	1.9	O.9	O.9	35.8	16.O	17.7	32.6	15.3	17.2	31.O	14.6	16.4
Carmarthen	156.6	75.2	85.8	1O3.8	49.7	54.O	4.5	2.2	2.2	99.3	47.5	51.8	87.6	41.1	45.9	76.8	36.5	4O.3
Denbigh	176.4	83.9	92.4	49.5	23.7	28.8	3.1	1.5	1.6	46.3	22.1	24.2	4O.8	19.2	21.5	36.5	17.3	19.2
Flint	166.6	85.O	86.O	24.4	11.5	12.8	1.4	O.6	O.7	23.6	1O.9	12.O	18.7	8.7	1O.O	16.1	7.4	8.7
Glamorgan	1,99.2	581.4	617.5	141.O	63.9	77.O	8.6	3.9	4.6	132.3	6O.O	72.3	1O7.3	47.1	6O.1	84.9	37.4	47.5
Meirioneth	33.5	16.O	17.8	24.8	11.8	13.O	2.6	1.3	1.3	22.2	1O.5	11.7	22.8	1O8	11.9	22.1	1O.9	11.2
Monmouth	439.1	216.1	222.9	9.2	4.5	4.7	O.6	O.2	O.3	8.6	4.2	4.3	6.2	3.O	3.2	4.9	2.4	2.5
Montgomery	41.2	25.5	2O.6	11.5	5.8	5.7	O.5	O.2	O.2	11.O	5.6	5.4	9.9	9.O	4.9	9.O	4.5	4.5
Pembroke	24.3	46.2	48.O	19.4	9.4	1O.O	O.9	O.4	O.4	18.5	8.9	9.5	15.9	7.6	8.3	13.9	6.6	7.3
Radnor	17.5	8.6	8.8	O.6	O.3	O.3	O.O3	O.O1	O.O1	O.6	O.2	O.3	O.4	O.2	O.2	O.4	O.1	O.3

Source: Census 1971 Report on the Welsh Language

Table 10:5 Welsh speaking population of each county in thousands, expressed in percentage of total population of the county, and as percentage of the national Welsh speaking total 1891 to 1971

	Wales	Anglesey	Brecon	Caernarfon	Cardigan	Carmarthen	Denbigh	Flint	Glamorgan	Meirioneth	Monmouth	Montgomery	Pembroke	Radnor
1891														
Total Welsh speaking total	910	40	29	107	73	100	52	27	320	58	39	32	24	1.0
Intensity index	52	94	40	90	95	90	66	68	51	95	20	52	37	10
Distribution index	100	4.4	3.2	12.0	8.0	11.0	5.7	3.0	3.5	6.3	4.4	3.5	2.6	1.0
1971														
Total Welsh speaking total	542.0	37.0	11.7	73.0	35.7	103.8	49.5	24.4	141.0	24.9	9.2	11.6	19.5	0.65
Intensity index	19.6	61.2	21.8	57.6	63.9	63.6	26.3	13.8	11.0	65.7	2.0	26.8	19.7	3.6
Distribution index	100	6.3	2.4	13.5	6.8	11.6	9.4	5.6	26.4	4.8	1.9	2.2	3.8	0.1

Notes: a) Intensity Index is the Welsh speaking total expressed as percentage of total population in each country

b) Distribution Index is the Welsh speaking total of the county expressed as percentage of national Welsh speaking total.

well as according to the two dimensions of the local incidence of Welsh. The first dimension is the proportion of Welsh speakers to the total population in any area. This is the measure of the local or regional density of Welsh and is referred to as the 'intensity index'. The second dimension refers to the proportion of the national total of speakers of Welsh which are found in any one area and this is referred to as the 'distributional index'. The two indices represent different aspects of the demographic status of Welsh consequent on modernisation, and, as we shall see, they are negatively correlated in almost every instance.

In 1891, the thirteen counties, in terms of the intensity of Welsh, can be organised into three clearly distinguished groups. There are five with percentages of Welsh speakers of 90 per cent and over: Cardigan, Merioneth, Anglesey, Carmarthen and Caernarfon. Next there are four counties which range between 51 per cent and 68 per cent the highest being 20 per cent below the lowest of the five counties. Those in the second group are Flint, Denbigh, Montgomery and Glamorgan. Then there are four counties ranging between 10 per cent and 51 per cent: Brecon, Pembroke, Monmouth and Radnor. It is not insignificant that the first group, the high intensity areas, are heavily if not exclusively agricultural in 1891 with very low population densities, and the second group were either dominantly industrial in their general trend. The third group, those with lowest intensity of Welsh, are either in the English border or, as in the case of Pembrokeshire possess English language plantations. Monmouth, in the third category, is both an industrial county and on the English border so that its intensity index was nearly the lowest of all. It is noticeable too, that the counties in the high intensity Welsh group all appear to behave identically during the period 1891 to 1961, the rates of attenuation of Welsh in these counties is synchronised. The four counties in the middle range of Welsh speaking intensity also behave consistently as a group. Glamorgan and Flint suffered a 66 per cent and 60 per cent loss respectively, while in the same period, Denbigh and Montgomery, who retain a strong agricultural element suffer losses of approximately 40 per cent.

There is thus a close knit group of counties which have become identified with a relatively high intensity of Welsh. They have maintained their statusin spite of population change. As is the case with all the other counties their Welshness has diminished but to nothing like the same extent as the average, the Welshness of the whole of Wales has declined at a much sharper rate than in the first group from 32 per cent in 1891 to 26.1 per cent in 1916. To that extent the high intensity counties are not characteristic of the whole of Wales. Furthermore this anomaly has increased with each decade so as to produce a polarization, in terms of intensity of the incidence of

Welsh, between the agricultural and heavily industrialised and semi-industrialised counties.

This polarization has been aggravated by another characteristic of the demographic status of Welsh. The five counties in the high intensity group have a mean of 92 per cent in 1891 and 75 per cent in 1961, but they are very low judged on the distributional index, contributing only 40 per cent to the national total in 1891 and 1961. The industrial counties in 1891 had a relatively low intensity index of 50 per cent and a very low mean of 18 per cent in 1961, but they contributed far more than half to the national total of Welsh speakers in 1891 and 1961. Generally speaking increased industrialisation correlates with a declining intensity of Welsh in an area, but at the same time, if we exclude Monmouth, which as we have pointed out is a special case, increasing industrialization correlates with high status on the distributional index. The great majority of speakers of Welsh live in highly industrialized and urban areas and though they maintain the Welsh language their attachment to the language becomes very much less assured though they may become more intensely conscious of their being of Welsh origin. The polarization which we have noted between the industrial and agricultural counties is unlikely to be purely demographic. The authenticity of Welsh for the latter is a matter of historical continuity, it is to be sought in the past. The Welsh of the industrial areas are in the process of developing a contemporary authenticity for Welsh involving a non traditional urbanized consciousness which is nevertheless intense and self-conscious. They tend to see the language as an expression of a different Welsh ethos from that favoured by the minority.

Other Responses to Modernization

So far we have referred to two major responses to modernization in Wales. One is a qualitiative response, namely the emergence and stabilization of an urban marginal or contact culture. The other is a quantitative response, namely a very great decline in the numbers of those who speak Welsh. There are other responses which can at this point be referred to only very briefly. Earlier in the discussion we referred to differentiation and specialisation of institutionalised and personal roles and functions, the diffused responsibilities of primarily institutions like the family are articulated and become the responsibilities of separate and specialised institutions, including education. Such a differentiation of roles and functions is a major consequence of modernization. This role differentiation is also an aspect of the social division of labour and this is reflected in the relation of the roles of languages in contact. In a traditional bilingual society the roles of the two languages are undifferentiated. The use of one language rather than another is not formalised and is not governed by rules or conventions, it is a matter of the interlocutors rather than of topic or situation. Where the bilingualism is institutionalized within the system of education oral bilingualism becomes literate involving the ability to read and write at least one and possibly both languages. The use of both languages tends to be formalised, they divide between them the communication requirements of soceity not on an ad hoc basis but according to fairly fixed rules and conventions of social usage (Lewis, 1978). One of the consequences of role differentiation as it affects Welsh, because of its withdrawal from a dynamic industrial and technonlogically orientated society, was that the language suffered status rigidity. It had acquired a set of historical roles and was trapped within that set. It was associated with exclusive groups so far as its literary use goes, and was identified with a particular way of life inflexibly. It reflexted particular occupations and for this reason it also reflected a degree of social distance between those who spoke the two languages. The status of English on the other hand, associated with a dynamic society was flexible rather than rigid. The one language was backward-oriented seeking legitimization in an authentic historical tradition; the other was geared to change and to the search for change. They fitted into different and opposed social slots and for that reason, attitudes to the two languages were polarized (Lewis, 1978).

Another aspect of modernization to which reference has been made is convergence on all social levels, demographic, cultural, linguistic and psychological. Demographic convergence produces social heterogeneity; cultural convergence results in new contact cultures, and linguistic convergence produces bilingualism which results in structural changes in the languages involved and ultimately in language shift. However, as is the case with almost every aspect of modernization, the consequences in this case are ambivalent. Modernization redefines group boundaries, it restructures society and to that extent it produces a new social synthesis. All this is true, but so far as ethnically heterogenous societies are concerned, it is only partly true. The Deutsch (1966) model of modernization predicts that as the modernization processes advance, regional and ethnic sub-cultures will become increasingly assimilated into the main stream of society. However, such assimilation does not occur across the board, nor where it does occur, does it advance at the same rate or to the same extent on all levels of social life. In socio-economic terms the assimilation of the Welsh has been almost complete. On the cultural level it has occurred far less rapidly, and so far as the demographic status of Welsh is concerned although the language has declined it has not been completely lost under the influence of English. The unilinear assumptions of political integration and assimilation of sub-groups into the dominant 'national' framework as a result of modernization may not appear in plurilingual societies, and it has not been manifested in Wales. In the same way as urbanization intensified ethnic consciousness the general processes of modernization forces a society to reconceptualize itself. Such a rconceptualization is inevitable, though it may be long delayed as in the case of Wales. The reconceptualization may be attempted in several ways, and the one adopted in Wales has been guided by a romantic search for some historically authentic identity which ignores the transformations of modernized society. The role of the Welsh language in contemporary society is determined by the manner in which the reconceputalization is managed. At present therefore, because of its aversion to the processes of modernization, the issues of language maintenance are almost completely identified with the negative aspects of modernization economic and social disruption. The issues of bilingualism and bilingual education, in turn are surrogates for far more fundamenal economic and political concerns. The theory of language maintenance is identical with a theory of political action or it is no theory at all. At the same time the political action which alone makes language maintenance a relevant social issue may, once it is successful, change attitudes to the maintenance of the language, as it appears to have done in Ireland. Once the goals of political action have been achieved, of which the language issue was a symbolic feature rather than a substantive component the need to stress the language will have lost much, if not most of its significance.

The last stage of the process of modernizaton is the mobilization of the total population as participants in the political system. So far as language maintenance is concerned the movement towards participation is identified with on the stages of the development of the theory or the rationales of bilingual education. There have been four such stages and four rationales corresponding to them, each succeeding the other in the same order in mature bilingual countries such as Belgium, Ireland, South Africa, Canada, the Soviet Union and Wales. The first step towards political participation is the provision of literacy by means of a system of education which embraces the total population. The rationale for this first stage is literacy in which every language is the more convenient. The second phase, once universal literacy has been promoted if not completed is cultural assimilation, the creation of what Disraeli called 'the one nation'. Without literacy there is no cultural assimilation and without the latter there is no possibility of participation. Consequently, the system of bilingual education is governed by a 'code' which includes a selection of the most representative English literature together with a study of the historical roots of that culture. But there is a third stage between assimilation and participation which reflects that aspect of modernization we have referred to as differentation, with which goes an emphasis on individual achievement rather than ascribed status. The main stream system of education reflects differentiation and individuation in the shift which occurred from a stress on the three R's to the three A's - age, ability and aptitude. These are certain criteria, and developmental in their orientation, rather than being static as are the criteria of literacy and assimilation. The child in the first phase was judged by his/her command of two languages and only by that criterion. In the second phase he/she was judged additionally by his/her acquaintance with a core curriculum in literature and history which gave the grounds for assimilation. The third phase of bilingual education was judged according to whether such an education was able to produce an integrated and rounded individual able to undertake the tasks of a highly specialised technological society, requiring individual flexibility as well as the characteristics of the first two phases.

The fourth phase, which becomes possible only on the foundations of the first three, takes account of the fact that modernization rather than resulting in a totally convergent society has tended to produce, at least on certain levels of society and social action, a deepening awareness of ethnic, cultural and linguistic independence. This fourth phase is that of 'political pluralism' disguised by many commentators by the use of the term 'cultural pluralism'. The justification of bilingual education and the maintenance of the Welsh language is no longer simply to produce a literate child, nor to enable that child to be aware of the cultures with which the two languages are associated, nor simply to enable him/her to develop as an independent and flexible individual, it is to safeguard the political integrity of a particular group. At the same time 'political pluralism' is not a uniform concept, it includes the possibility of consociational democracy as is the case in Switzerland, or segmental pluralism as is the case in Belgium and tends to be accepted more and more as the aim of Celtic countries. On the other hand, it may be subordinated pluralism as is the case in the U.S.S.R., and in a different sense in the United States of America, where ethnic languages tend to be allocated certain limited roles in society while the lingua fanca, Russian or English is superordinate.

CHAPTER 11

NATIONALISM IN NINETEENTH CENTURY WALES : THE DISCOURSE OF MICHAEL D. JONES

Glyn Williams

It is generally conceded that the recent political expression of nationalism in Wales is not a new phenomenon but one that can be traced at least to the last century. While it is emphasised that this development achieved its widest expression towards the end of the nineteenth century (Morgan, 1963, 1981) there is an awareness among political historians that nationalism was of interest to some Welsh leaders much earlier in the century. At the end of the eighteenth century there were various forces which tended to draw Wales into a closer integration with England. For example Burke (1959 : Vol.2, 29-37) argued in favour of integrating the legal processes of the two countries by eliminating the quarter sessions in Wales. He deplored a situation in which Wales did not come under the direct authority of the King but rather had its own legal and financial structure. This integrating tendency coincided with the expansion of industrial capitalism into Wales, an expansion which created a new form of economic articulation between the two countries. This new economic order also led to various demands for integration at the superstructural level.

Yet there were other forces which were generating a contrary reaction to the expanding capitalist system while also stimulating a heightened sense of ethnic and national awareness. Both the French and the American revolutions had an impact upon the development of political ideas in Wales at the end of the eighteenth century (Williams, 1950: 168-175). These movements served to give meaning to a developing radicalism which objected to royalty, the established church, the power of the ruling class and the limitations of the democratic order. However the discussion which was generated by the developments in France and the U.S.A. tended to focus upon the issues of individual freedom rather than national liberation. Yet it did bring into focus the very issues around which the nationalism of the following century were to mobilise. The radicalism of the last quarter of the eighteenth century was subdued by the opposition to France that was associated with the Napoleonic war. In contrast to other European countries the two revolutions failed to generate any direct movement for national liberation in Wales.

The extension of industrial capitalism created a tension in the social order, a tension which the proletariat expressed in rural insurrection in the form of Beca, and industrial risings at Llanidloes, Newport and Merthyr (Williams, 1978). It was evident to the centralised ruling class that such reactions had to be eliminated and that the ideological influence of education was a powerful force by which this could be undertaken. It was also evident that in terms of education, Wales had been ignored. The need for a control of the industrial proletariat in order to further the interests of the capitalist order was directly responsible for the awareness of the limitations of the educational structure in Wales. It was not lost on some that the existence of the Welsh language presented a potentially powerful revolutionary force in that it served to keep the majority of the population of Wales aloof from the influence of the ideological forces of the dominant class which were almost exclusively expressed in English. For example, it had been noted that English played but a minor role in the education offered in the schools where the various aspects of unrest had occurred and that many of those who had participated did not understand English. Some went so far as to blame the Welsh language for the unrest. Undoubtedly, the Welsh language was also seen as a hindrance to the smooth operation of the industrial capitalism that was primarily owned and operated by non-Welsh interests. The language either had to be expropriated or eliminated (Williams, 1981 n.d.).

These interests led to the inquiry into the state of education in Wales the published report of which became known as the 'Treason of the Blue Books'. Its importance to nationalism in nineteenth century Wales lies in the reaction which the report created among the leadership in Wales and the manner in which this reaction served to generate a heightened sense of national identity. Of course it was not this report alone which was responsible for the growth in nationalist sentiment. The changing economic order was strongly controlled by a bourgeoisie which was drawn from outside of Wales and this constituted a threat to those aspiring to such a status within Wales. Indeed the change in the social structure prompted by the economic developments created tensions both between and within social classes. The new political orientation was a manifestation of this threat. It is also evident that the influence of what was happening elsewhere in Europe (Connor, 1977) also played a significant role in the formation of a nationalist political philosophy.

If we consider nationalism as involving a desire for political independence that derives in part from a sense of injustice associated with the existing political order it is necessary to consider the nature of the economic integration which serves as the basis for the perceived injustice, the institutional order which serves to legitimise the economic order, and the organisational structure around which the emergent nationalism can be mobilised. In nineteenth century Wales this involved the expanding capitalist mode of production, the forces which existed to further the interests of capitalism and the various nonconformist sects. The interaction between them as manifested in a nationalist philosophy was expressed most clearly in the writings of Michael D. Jones.

The name of Michael D. Jones is usually cited as the most influential of nationalist leaders in 19th century Wales and it is therefore surprising that, apart from a biography published in 1903 (Pan Jones, 1903) no-one has attempted to analyse the nature and content of his ideas. This is particularly so in view of his influence upon national consciousness in Wales, and on the ideas of politicians who perhaps carried a greater influence than Jones himself. Among these politicians and leaders were Emrys ap Iwan, O.M. Edwards, Tom Ellis, E. Pan Jones and Lloyd George. While his ideas were complex Michael D. Jones had the ability to present them in the popular press in such a way that they were widely influential.[1] His ideas had a wide appeal and were influential in crystalising the opposition to the hegemony of the landed gentry and the Tory party in Wales at a time which Morgan (1963: 13) has described as one when

> . . . . the expansion of nonconformity and the rise of popular radicalism as a political creed went hand in hand.

Analyses of political ideas generally begin by considering the relevant influences which these ideas are held to derive from. It is not my intention to pursue such an issue with reference to Michael D. Jones but rather to focus attention upon the central points of his ideas. However, it might be useful to mention that among those who are claimed to have influenced his ideas are various philosophers including Paley, Locke, Butler, Cudworth and Stuart whom he studied at Highbury College, London (Pan Jones, 1903 : 21); European nationalists such as Kosuth,[2] Davis Garibaldi and Mazini; and various social reformers including Spinoza and Robert Owen whom he cites in some of his works. (Y Celt, March 16th, 1883).

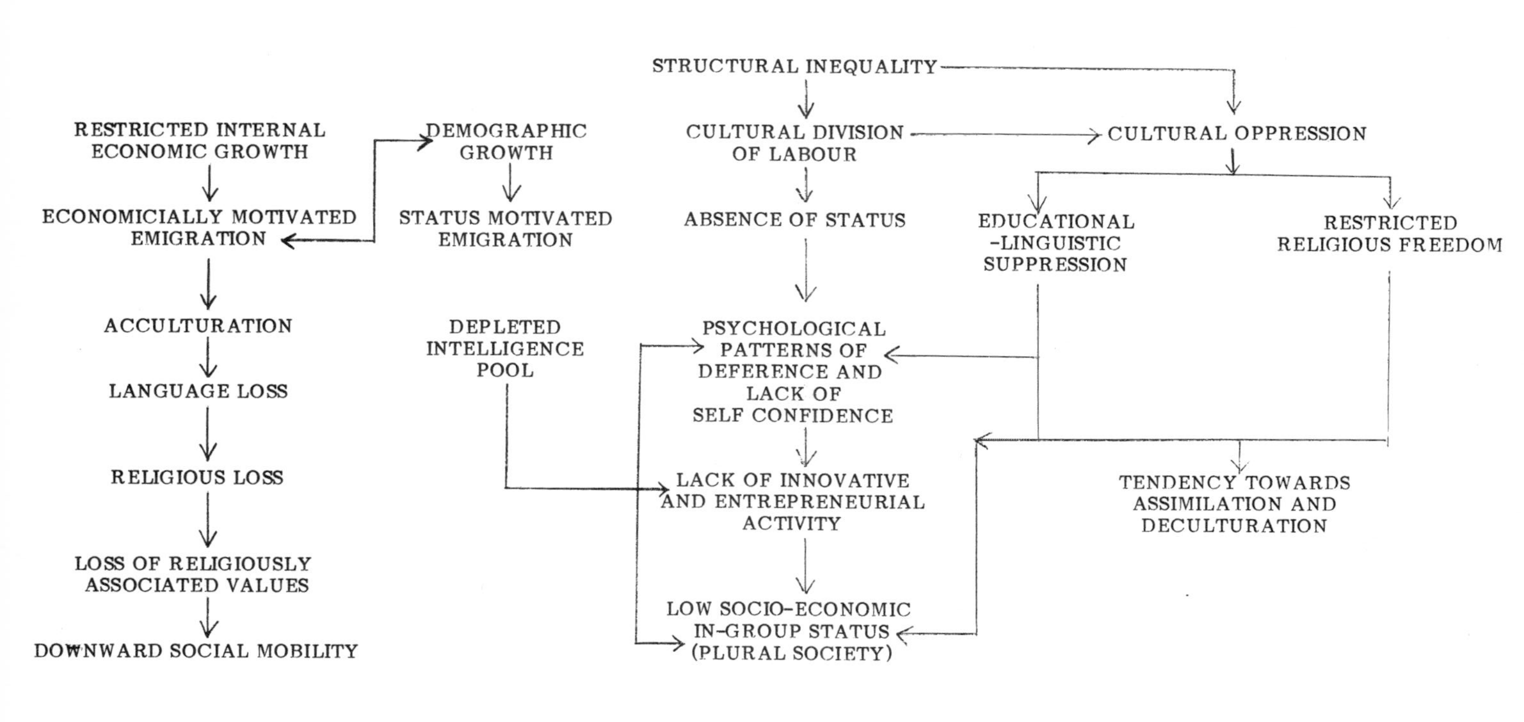

Figure II:1. Schematic Model of Jones' central argument

In figure 11:1, I have attempted to synthesize Jones' understanding of social and economic forces in nineteenth century Wales. This scheme should prove useful in following the argument presented below and especially in explaining linkages between disparate ideas. The concepts derive from contemporary sociology but their meaning is synonomous with that of Jones, as we shall see in the subsequent discussion.

The independent variable in Jones' thesis involves the nature of the economic structure in Wales. He envisaged a conspiratorial link between the Tory gentry and the state through the hegemony which the former held in the world of politics at a variety of levels. The gentry and the state conspired to,

> .... deprive the worker of the rightful reward of his labour.
> (Y Cenhadwr, November, 1848)

the net result of which was an inevitable poverty in the rural areas of Wales. Implicit in this idea of the expropriation of surplus labour value was the idea of exploitation. However, this apparent class division was complicated by a tendency to associate the gentry in Wales with fundamentally English interests both in terms of speech and religion. This manifested itself in several ways. The Tories opposed the disassociation of the church and the state and used both to further their interests. Jones claimed that the gentry used their economic power to guarantee their political position against the interests and will of the majority and also manipulated the Church of England, an essentially alien institution in Wales, in order to retain their hegemony. This influence was nowhere more evident than in the issue of the church taxes which were mandatory even for non-members. The equation of the gentry with the Tory party guaranteed their control over the proletariat and agricultural tenants. This control, based upon class relations, Jones saw as the major factor in the interference of the wealthy with the issues of freedom and equality. As Morgan (1963: 27) has pointed out, once this implicit class conflict became highlighted into contrasts of a linguistic, religious and political nature, it came to involve an ethnic dimension; they,

> . . . . were to transform the injustice of a class into the indictment of a nation.

Various authors (Pan Jones, 1903; Dictionary, 1953) claim that the leading role in the development of an awareness of such dimensions of inequality was played by Michael

D. Jones many years before such views became popular in Wales towards the end of the century.

His conception of social class appears to have been developed during the 1840s but was elaborated in subsequent years. At the top of the stratification was Royalty and those of the ruling class who sought to gain access to the royal lineage (Pan Jones, 1903). The British constitution, he claimed, supported this alliance between royalty and the ruling class consisting of the gentry, the military leaders and the church officials. This alliance in turn, supported as it was by the constitution, allowed royalty, as a result of nothing more than a blood qualification to be supported by the 'productive labour' of the working class (Y Celt, March, 1892)[3]. Jones made little reference to the petit bourgeoisie other than in terms of encouraging the peasantry to seek social mobility to petit bourgeoisie positions via the educational system while also indicating that the minor squirarchy tended to align with the ruling class in order to exploit the labour of the workers by mediating the deferential process. His main conception of class focussed upon the conflicting interests of the ruling class and the peasantry and proletariat. This resulted partly from his preoccupation with rural Wales although he does make reference in his later work to the industrial proletariat.:

> . . . . justice should be done to the worker since it is the workers who carry society on their backs. They produce our food, make our clothes, build our houses, construct our roads, build our ships, work our minerals and our trade in every direction: but they have been given little political authority in our country until recently, for which reason their rights have, until recently, been ignored by the middle and upper classes. (Y Genhinen, 1897)

He drew widely on the scriptures to support his position of equality and liberation for the workers. This contradicts the recent work of some social historians of Wales who claim that the nonconformist doctrines as preached in nineteenth century Wales exclusively emphasised the ethic of individual salvation at the expense of the predicament of the worker. Indeed Jones went as far as to state:

> It is time that we put aside the idea that religion is something for the next world, so that we suffer injustice in this world as patiently as Job. (Y Genhinen, November 1893)

He recognised that the problem of the proletariat was implicit in capitalism

> The same greed for wealth burns the breasts of capitalists in working light industry, opening coalmines, slate quarrying, iron, copper, gold, and silver mining. While the workers are scarcely able to survive on their earnings, and many of them are in desperate need, the greedy rich are making hundreds of thousands in order to live in pomp and revelry for the rest of their days, leaving behind them huge endowments. It is little wonder that the workers unite to sell their labour on the highest market, and are in revolt against the existing social organisation. The oppression of landowners and the lust of capitalists for wealth has enraged the masses against them, to the extent that democracies based upon socialist principles are gaining such ground that the rich of all countries tremble in surveying their future. The capitalist press and the classes supported by unjust laws roar protest against movements which seek greater social equality . . . . The objective is to overthrow the order which gives the wealth to the masters so that they can fill their pockets while the workers suffer. It is the wealthy who have been making the laws which give them so much power. Their sympathies lie wholeheartedly with the system which impoverishes the masses in order to enrich the wealthy. (Y Genhinen, 1897)

While recognising that not all members of the proletariat in Wales were subject to the extreme of poverty which left them undernourished and worried about their ability to support their families he claimed that most working class families in Meirionydd and Montgomeryshire, the areas he was most familiar with, were subject to such conditions. The tenant farmers were included in this category, especially at times of agricultural depression when the gentry tended to demand extra labour without remuneration in order to sustain their profits. He claimed that as many as twenty per cent of Welsh families were undernourished (Y Cenhadwr, November, 1848). This was particularly true of large families with the workers' income being insufficient to sustain a number of dependants and the ability of the worker to use his labour declined with age. During the 1840s he saw emigration to north America as a partial solution for such families, arguing that the economic conditions for the immigrants were such that the labour value was high enough for the industrious to accumulate capital and thereby to rise above poverty. In Wales the converse was true with wages being fixed by the owners at a level that did not allow accumulation but rather at a level which barely allowed survival.

The ethnic conflict which was so obvious to Jones in the agricultural sector was also apparent in other economic sectors. He focused attention upon what he felt was an unfair exploitation of the natural resources in Wales. For him the economic problems of Wales at the middle of the last century derived largely from the tendency for Welsh resources to be extracted by English interests who removed them to England for processing:

> It is true that it is mainly, if not entirely, English companies which develop the resources of Wales . . . . As a result the English take all the profits of the Welsh labour. (Jones, 1863 : 17)

He cited the example of the woollen industry where the exploitation of the Welsh worker involved the use of his/her labour to extract the resources of Wales at a low cost before removing the commodity to England to be processed at a high cost in terms of return to the labour force. This left Wales at a disadvantage in two senses. Firstly the value of the resources was realised outside of Wales and secondly the work that was generated in the processing was denied the Welsh people who were restricted to the labour use in primary production.

He seems to have developed some of these ideas as a result of his experience in the U.S.A., during the 1840s. He claimed that the government in the U.S.A. held the right to land and the mineral resources only by right of conquest and force. The authorities encouraged immigration but as a result of their hegemony insisted that the immigrants learn English while also allocating to them the hardest and lowest paid work. From this he employed the idea of the rights of conquest and the idea of exploitation deriving from the resulting hegemony to the historical background of Wales (Y Cenhedwr, December, 1848).

The idea of hegemony seems evident in his discussion of the colonial situation although it is also clear that he did not entirely disassociate Wales from his discussion. He claimed that in every colonial situation there were two elements consisted of the colonial force which dominated the situation to the extent that any non-member of the colonial group had to conform to their interests and thereby became part of the assimilative force (Jones, 1863). In part at least, the assimilation which he referred to was akin to the acculturation thesis in which contact between two different cultures involved the exchange of the traits of the minority group for those of the majority group. Certainly the idea of power relationships between the colonial and the conquered is evident in these ideas. He recognised the power of language in terms of closure, with the formal elements using their language to preserve their hegemony in commerce, law, religion and leisure. The ability of the English to impose the assimilative process '. . . gives them the advantage of being foremost in influence and allows them to control every position of status, profit and comfort' (Jones, 1863). The net result was a cultural division of labour in which the assimilative element assumed the lower occupational categories. He also emphasised that the superstructure was firmly controlled by the formal element.

This congruence of ethnic and occupational stratification was a major facet of his perception of the situation in Wales. The English control of both the infrastructure and the superstructure was a dominant theme. He argued that the monoglot Welsh were at a severe disadvantage in the law courts, the schools and public administration in their own country since these institutions were administered through the medium of the English language. He campaigned widely for Welsh speaking judges in the law courts. Because the Welsh had been conquered in their own country they had lost their nationhood and national rights with the result that it was impossible for the individual Welshman to be socially mobile as a Welshman (Jones, 1863). It was this which was responsible for the tendency for the Welsh to depricate themselves as a nation.

He regarded deference as a 'national weakness of the Welsh' (Jones, 1863) which derived largely from the insecure position of the Welsh people, who were predominantly of a proletarian class background, in the economic structure. For many of them survival demanded a deferential relationship with powerful overlords. He saw the association referred to above between the squirearchy on the one hand and royalty, the lords and others of the ruling class on the other, as an allieance which facilitated the development of a deferential attitude on the part of the workers. This deference in turn served the interests of the ruling class who tended to despise those of the proletariat who retained an element of self respect (Y Celt, March 1892). He was not specific about how the ruling class achieved the imposition of deferential attitudes among the workers but implied that it related in some way to their control of the infrastructure and superstructure. He clearly saw deference as a correlate of power. He referred to a chain of hierarchical control where, for example, the squire's agent could influence the tenants not to draw upon the services of an independent local craftsman if he so wished. Thus the squire and his representatives, by controlling the labour market could control even those economic sectors of local activity not under their direct control. Control by the gentry on a local level was nowhere more evident than in Jones' home area of Meirionydd where, during the election of 1859, a number of tenants, including the widowed mother of Michael D. Jones were evicted as a result of voting against the local landowner. (Pan Jones : 236). There were numerous accusations of coercion and bribery on the part of the Tory candidate and his agents and in his evidence at a select committee of the House of Commons, Jones offered evidence to substantiate these accusations while defending the integration of politics into non-conformism.

He claimed that the controllers of the infrastructure were also patrons of the Church of England and this also resulted in a persecution on religious grounds. The families of non-conformist ministers were summarily evicted from their holdings without any evident reason as were the families of numerous chapel deacons. This he saw as an interference with the principal of religious freedom stating: 'Despite the extent of their (the gentry's) power they will not suppress non-conformism and freedom' (Pan Jones : 235).

It was this loss of control of the infrastructure which was responsible for the irrational tendency for the workers and tenant farmers who voted for a political party which so clearly opposed their interests:

> Because the Welsh are a conquered people in their own country and because they constitute the assimilative element in the colonies they have lost their strength and self-confidence. The Welsh don't believe in their ability to achieve on their own and subsequently their achievements are few. Like slaves, they believe that ability is the prerogative of the master, for which reason their national talents collapse. Because they have been oppressed they tend to become deferent .... Presently our main weakness as a nation is our servility (Jones, 1863 : 9).

The power of the gentry was institutionalised to the extent that many tenants believed that political support for the landowner was part of their tenancy agreement. This did not mean that Wales did not produce talented and able people. However the absence of opportunities in their own country led many Welsh people to emigrate to serve other nations: 'Our circumstances cause us to lose the services of the nation's best talents' (Jones, 1863 : 9). He emphasized that Wales had both the talents and the resources to push the nation forward but that the structural inequality prevented their adequate deployment.

Jones also wrote extensively about the manner in which the control of the superstructure by a majority group influenced the self-concept of members of the minority group:

> After the English defeat a nation they place her at such a disadvantage that she is obliged to assimilate to the English nation, and mobility is not possible by any other means. Law can only be adminstered in English, which is the only medium of education, apart from some small concessions such as the use of Welsh to explain the English. This spirit has produced such servility in our nation that the Welsh will not conduct commerce

> in any language other than that of the conqueror . . . . The Welshman can not succeed socially as a merchant without becoming English . . . . Most of the doctors, many of our lawyers and different government officials take the same stance - from our members of parliament to the 'bwmbeiliaid' . . . in order to achieve individual mobility according to the order which the English have cunningly formed to serve their own interests, and in order to oppress the Welsh (Y Genhinen, October 1894)[4]

The focus of his attention in this respect was the educational system with English medium education being seen as discriminating against the monolingual Welsh speaker:

> Doubtless English medium schools, and an entirely English language education in Welsh rural communities are no more than useless. When a Welsh child receives his education to the age of thirteen, in a language which he does not understand, he is often turned out to the world, completely unsuited educationally for the circles in which he will turn . . . . What reason is there that law continues to be administered in Wales through the medium of English . . . . All of these are branches growing out of the English tree of oppression in the same way that the English medium education in our schools is another piece of the same plan. The government's English medium schools are seeking to complete that which the English sword has started (Pan Jones, 1903 : 264)

In another source he stated:

> The government's present English medium education is one of the most effective means of killing the Welsh language, and for thousands of Wales' children it is not an education but a means of making them more stupid than before they went to school, more fearful and more incomprehensible. (Pan Jones, 1903 : 267)

These were among the forces which contributed to the cultural assimilation of the Welsh people. E. Pan Jones claimed that Michael D. Jones was not critical of the English as people but rather he '. . . . disliked their superior and arrogant spirit and could not come to terms with the idea that every language should submit to the English language' (Pan Jones, 1903 : 330). Michael D. Jones also alluded to the fact that '. . . . ignorant English people described the Welsh language as 'a crude peasant language' and there was a tendency for many Welsh people to accept this stigmatization and to reject the Welsh language (Pan Jones, 1903 : 348). However, it is clear that for him this was not simply a matter of how the superstructure could be manipulated to guaranteee minority acceptance of majority stereotypes since, as we have seen above, he recognized the importance of market forces and the function of language in the relations of production and in commerce as important contributing factors in language rejection. The associated phenomenon of 'passing' was discussed within this context. He was aware of the tendency for those seeking upward social mobility to do so by associating with the markers of those who controlled the means of production while simultaneously disassociating themselves from markers of the minority ethnic identity which they felt to be stigmatic. He makes it clear that English was the language of individual mobility ('personal success'). 'It is not possible for a Welshman as a Welshman to hope for any form of upward mobility in the public sector, and he must be satisfied on personal and religious achievement' (Jones, 1863). In his view the only occupation which afforded social mobility within the context of the Welsh language was that of the non-conformist minister of religion. Yet even here he expressed the concern about a tendency for some non-conformist ministers, after receiving an expensive training, to defect to the better paid and more prestigious English language religious institutions. However he realized that being voluntary associations there was less room for concern in the area of religion than in areas such as education and law which were firmly under state control. He advocated Welsh medium education in primary and higher education and the college of which he was principal was the only institute of higher education in Wales which taught through the medium of Welsh. He also argued in favour of the appointment of Welsh speakers to posts in Wales. (Y Genhinen, October 1894)

So much for his conception of the power relationships in Wales, what were his solutions? At a local level he saw the non-conformist chapels as serving a function to alleviate the poverty and powerlessness of the working class. The chapels were to have a welfare function and the scriptures were drawn upon to underline the altruistic nature of the religious values. The chapels were ethnic institutions which integrated all Welsh people in a common struggle against the influence of the ruling class. While there was a recognition of the possibility of individual ability and action leading to success it was emphasized that strength lay '. . . . in the unity of many' (Y Cenhadwr, November, 1848). It was argued that the ethics of accumulation should involve a willingness to use it for the good of others. He went as far as to suggest that those Welsh migrants who had succeeded in the United States should contribute, through their respective denominations, to alleviating the poverty of their fellow Welshmen in the homeland. (Y Cenhadwr,

November, 1848) This welfare function of the religious institutions was the basis of integration on an ethnic and a political level.

Jones advocated that all workers should be given a house and a little land so that a minimum subsistence level could be achieved (Y Cenhinen, October, 1895). This was in keeping with his views on land reform through land nationalization (The Times, 25th September, 1890) and he maintained that it was poverty that was responsible for crime and that such reform would empty the prisons. He advocated expanding the rights of the workers stating:

> The numerous strikes which occur from time to time have awakened the public's awareness of the rights of the workers. The government thus far has done little to improve the conditions of the worker, but the workers have political power now and soon they will have more, they can not continue to be ignored. (Y Genhinen, May, 1897)

Yet while recognizing the increasing power of the workers, advocating support of their cause and the associated social reform, his pacifism led him to condemn any suggestion of achieving the objectives of the workers via violent revolution.

Being frustrated with the hegemony of the ruling class whose association with the political machinery meant, for example, that they could pass laws which would extend their land holdings in rural areas, led him to encourage the formation of Trade Unions and to advocate land nationalization but he also wished to encourage the population to support those politicians who represented their interests. On the other hand, he was also frustrated by the inability of the democratic process to serve the interests of the people of Wales as Welsh people in that any majority of Welsh members of parliament would have to bow to the desires of the more numerous English members thereby '. . . . thwarting the desires of the minority'. This tyranny of the majority he also related to the other Celtic nations:

> The Welsh, the Scots and the Irish are all represented in this country but our representation can do nothing but accept that which the English majority chooses. (Pan Jones, 1903 : 241)

One context in which this tendency gave him much concern was that of British imperialism which he felt was an English concern which Wales was drawn into. He saw the ruling classes of the European countries as supporting one another in oppressing the workers and, in some cases, in suppressing the national aspirations of small nations. In this sense he also identified the struggle for national identity and self-determination in Wales with parallel cases such as Scotland, Ireland, Hungary and Italy. Clearly his objection to British imperialism stemmed from the equation of such imperialism with English dominance in Britain. He simultaneously condemned the British presence in India and the role of Lord Derby as a member of the ruling class in supporting the suppression of Italian aspirations:

> It is not fair that they (the English) lord over numerous nations, to turn their taxes to work out English schemes, and to fill English coffers. (Jones, 1863:19)

However, this nationalism derived from a belief in republicanism rather than in separation. In this respect he appears to have been influenced by Kosuth's writings concerning the rights of nations to rule themselves, albeit within a republican context. His model in this respect appears to have been the state governments in the U.S.A. Every nation had the right to pass judgement on matters pertaining to that nation, leaving matters of the Empire to the general government. However in such matters he expected that Wales, Scotland and Ireland be given equal status within the United Kingdom. He advocated 'home rule all round' years before Gladstone thought even in terms of home rule for Ireland. (Pan Jones, 1903 : 238)

He claimed that despite internal variations the people of Wales constituted a single nation whose aspirations were thwarted by the dictates of a centralist political system. He regarded the Welsh language, customs, the peculiar forms of non-conformism, and the associated morals and values as the basis of the distinct national identity. Materialism was the converse of these morals and values which to him were selectivist in that it developed an individualistic orientation which emphasized self aggrandisement and display in the form of conspicuous consumption. Furthermore his assimilation thesis led him to see the growth of materialism as involving the exchange of one set of morally based behaviours for another; the exchange of sobriety, honesty, altruism etc. for arrogance, vanity, materialism etc. The emphasis on materialism and self aggrandisement would, in his view, lead not only to a form of moral corruption but also to the decline of craft skills and work achievement. In a sense materialism was seen as the converse of the protestant ethic. Yet he was not a conservative in the sense of wishing to preserve the existing economic order by rejecting the new forces of production. On the contrary he insisted that Wales had to expand industrially but that it should do so within the context of the existing cultural order albeit within a quite different hegemonic order.

The most important ingredient of nationhood for Jones was the existence of the Welsh language and he claimed that the loss of the language would inevitably result in the loss of the other 'Welsh' features. It was clear to him that the existing political and economic relationships with England would inevitably result in the type of development which he feared. However his argument concerning the relationship between language and the economic order is most clearly expressed with reference to expatriate Welsh populations. Referring to north America it was stated that the inability of the Welsh to control land and other economic resources in sufficient quantity meant that it was unlikely that the Welsh immigrants would be able to regroup upon arrival in north America in sufficient numbers to be able to resist assimilation. As has been discussed above, his understanding of the colonial situation involved a need on the part of the immigrant to adopt the linguistic norm of the colonial power of their political followers. Consequently the linguistic assimilation of the Welsh was inevitable and with it, given the lack of institutional support for the Welsh language, the erosion of that language. He does not specify why, but claims that the erosion of the Welsh language would be accompanied by a secularization process as a result of which the second generation Welsh would lack the values which derived from the protestrant religion and which he saw as essential in order to generate upward social mobility. Consequently, given the structural situation of the Welsh within north America, it was inevitable that their assimilation would be at a low socio economic level. Hence the need for a location where the Welsh would corporately own the means of production and where the assimilative forces could be resisted. (Jones, 1863).

While there were Welshmen in north America who saw immigration as an opportunity to import and exploit cheap Welsh labour there remained the question of liberation from the capitalist system. There were advantages in the New World. There was a scarcity of land and capital and an excess of labour in Wales. Social mobility would be curtailed, wages depressed and rents increased. In the New World on the other hand the availability of free land and the smaller demand for capital in countries where labour was scarce afforded a much greater possibility for upward social mobility. It meant that the price of labour was increased to the point where it often allowed the individual to finance the capital investment for his family farm from his labour earnings. Thus although the worker had only his labour to offer it did have more meaning in the New World than in Wales. On the other hand there were those who exploited their ethnic cohorts and the Patagonian settlement was seen as the basis for settling the problem of capital and labour by removing the issue of ownership and maximizing the value of labour (Y Ddraig Goch, August, 1877). Outside of agriculture the economy was to be organised on a cooperative basis, the worker not being subject to supervision by any owner but at the same time earning a share of the profits (Y Celt, 6th June, 1890).

There was little doubt that the work of Michael D. Jones is best remembered for his contribution to the theoretical nature of the emigration debate in nineteenth century Wales (Williams R. B., 1962, Willliams, G. 1975). Furthermore his work on the existing social and political situation has been ignored in favour of that over employed concept of 'cultural nationalism' (Jenkins, 1935). This concept appears to imply that political autonomy is conceived of solely in terms of cultural conservation without any reference to economic forces, or that the cultural discussion bears no relation to economic factors. Certainly in the case of Jones there was a strong preoccupation with the cultural effect of the existing political and economic condition. However it is equally clear that he understood that the impact upon cultural resources related to the economic order and the related political dominance. He saw the Welsh both in terms of class and ethnicity, the overlap between social and ethnic stratification being a dominant facet of his argument. He sought to awaken the public's awareness of themselves as Welsh people by highlighting the injustices accorded them as workers. Without emphasizing the Welsh language he felt that the Welsh nation and the sense of nationalism could not exist.

It would appear that the ideas of Michael D. Jones which had a far reaching influence on Welsh political awareness in the nineteenth century are a contradiction of the impression currently circulating that nineteenth century nationalism is held to derive from the elements of non-conformist ideology which emphasized individual salvation and an associated anti-socialism. He saw religion not only in spiritual terms but also as a basis for political mobilization:

> Few Welshmen achieve fame, and these without exception are ministers of religion, this is the only institution which holds the nation together, if it were not for Welsh preaching ninety nine percent of the nation would be Uncle Toms. As a nation the Welsh have died in everything but their religion . . . . we need Welshmen to look after people's bodies rather than turning their whole energy to protect their souls (Y Drych, 22nd August, 1857).

He freely used the scriptures to support socialist principles and we should be aware that it is possible to employ the religious ideology of non-conformism to support almost any social principle. What is required is not a dogmatic generalizaton but rather a careful study of the contextual relationship between religious and political discourses. While in the Calvinistic ethic each individual may be answerable to God for his/her errors, without mediators, and receives from the Lord the mark of grace as evidenced by material wealth, it does not appear to be correct that this can be equated with an anti-socialism that would apply across the board to non-conformism in nineteenth century Wales.

The ideas of Michael D. Jones had a profound influence upon several of the political leaders who emerged to positions of prominence towards the end of the nineteenth century and yet his nationalism did not attain a meaningful institutional base. Jones' influence was most forcibly expressed in the form of Mudiad Cymru Fydd a movement which David Williams (1950:280) described as a 'Young Wales' movement but which had an impact upon several of the nation's representatives at Westminster. These Welsh members threatened to form their own party and forced a conflict between Welsh and English Liberalism. The diaries of Michael D. Jones suggest that in 1886, the very year when 'Mudiad Cymru Fydd' was formed, he was collecting subscriptions to form an official nationalist party (BMS 11292). While this did not develop, the rebel Welsh members did put pressure upon the Liberal Party to give more attention to Welsh matters, especially after four members, including Lloyd George, formed an independent party. The nationalism of this group is expressed by Lloyd George in an essay which he wrote for the journal 'Young Wales' (October 1895) in which he contrasted the Celts with the Teutons and claimed that it was a folly to offer the Irish a separate government to discuss Irish affairs while expecting them to send members to London to discuss 'Imperial affairs'. He claimed that it was impossible for the Celts and the Teutons to co-exist and that political independence should be given to the Celtic nations. Not that this was an expression of extremism at the time since parliament voted by 128 votes to 102 in favour of establishing separate parliaments for the four nations 'in principle'.

The failure of this movement lay in its involvement in the Liberal Party. Within this party there developed a rift between the nationalism of those such as Tom Ellis and Lloyd George on the one hand and the liberalism associated with capitalist interests as represented by Lord Rhondda and Sir Alfred Mond (Jones 1950:124). The later interests felt threatened by the idea of a politically independent Wales. One prominent leader claimed that nationalism could not succeed while

Welsh Liberalism was tied to English liberalism.

> If English Liberalism conflicts with the nationalism of Wales, then we will be non-conformists in our politics as well as in our religion (Young Wales, 1905).

The potential rift was resolved in part by buying off the more prominent Welsh leaders, most notably Tom Ellis and Lloyd George. Mudiad Cymru Fydd came to an end at the turn of the century and thereafter the ideas which Michael D. Jones had nourished in a generation of political leaders rapidly receded.

There are several surprisingly contemporary perspectives in the ideas of Michael D. Jones but there are also some interesting contradictions. By identifying the cause of the social and cultural changes which were identified in the economic order he drew upon an argument which in many respects is reminiscent of the recent discussion of economic dependency. It is also here that we recognize that it was the economic structure for Jones which was the root cause of poverty and inequality. This orientation is not surprising in that there is an explicit nationalism in the dependency argument. It is claimed that the external control of the means of production generates an internal impotence which means that any economic developments are geared towards the external interests. However, it is also recognized that for this articulation to occur it demands a degree of either military control or the active co-operation of the members of the dependent nation who are, as a result of the relationship, placed in a situation of power within that nation. This of course is perfectly clear in the argument presented by Jones. Some claim that this dependency argument misconceives the situation and that it is best accounted for in terms of the uneven development associated with capitalism. It is pointed out that there is the problem of the articulation between different modes of production. Yet Jones did recognize that the petty commodity enterprises were forced to compete with the capitalist interests and that in this competition there was a tendency for an intensification of the existing mode of exploitation to occur. The problem as he recognized it was that the means of production of the capitalist mode were owned outside of Wales while those of the petty commodity mode, which in general required but little capital, tended to be owned by Welsh owners. Thus as one mode of production exploited, expropriated, or even eliminated the subservient mode it involved an explicit power relationship between capitalists drawn from different ethnic groups. He understood very clearly that the petty commodity productive system came under the domination of the capitalist system.

While recognizing and emphasizing the ethnic dimension of inequality Jones did not entirely ignore the class dimension. He linked class and ethnicity in terms of the cultural division of labour, a concept which has recently been developed by Hechter (1978). This was inevitable given the recognition that both the capitalist system and the associated means of production were exclusively in the hands of the dominant ethnic group. Of course, with the development of the coal industry, which had a significant amount of Welsh involvement, at least in its initial stages, the empirical basis of this argument was questionable.

Jones' statements concerning migration also carry a contemporary ring. While much of the more recent work has emphasized the role of the individual in terms of the personal attributes which are held to account for the propensity to migrate, the patterns of adaption at destination or the role of background cultural features in facilitating or blocking migration, the more recent approaches have tended to include what Middleton (1979) refers to as a historico-structural analysis. Here the focus is upon the relationship between development policy and migration with the emphasis being upon the external nature of the economic decisions which affect the migration, both internal and external. This is very much in line with what Jones saw as the fundamental cause for migration. Undoubtedly he was influenced by a desire to see the Welsh people remain in Wales and therefore was preconditioned to conceive of population movement as something that was imposed upon people rather than something which derived from the free will of the individual.

Yet at the same time as he was emphasizing these structural features as explanatory forces in terms of change and deprivation, Jones tended also to introduce arguments which were much more in line with the individualism of a more liberal philosophy. Thus for example economic development was related to two tendencies which appear to contradict the above approach, the individualism of entrepreneurial behaviour and a form of protestant ethic thesis. The emphasis upon the individual derives from an attempt to relate the individual to his position in the social structure as it relates to economic causality. This does tend to become tautological in that there is a claim that the individual is influenced by the economic structure while also claiming that it is the action or condition of the individual which is responsible for the economic. This need not necessarily be the case had he been more clear in his specification of what aspects of the economic structure, as they relate to social formations and social relationships, were responsible for the psychological conditions while also clarifying the manner in which this condition placed constraints upon individual action.

The protestant ethic thesis derived from his claim that economic success derived from a posession of the values which were held to derive from non-conformism. This tendency to give primacy to ideas rather than structures would appear to contradict his other statements about the individual and the role of rationality in economic action. Of course, we should not lose sight of the fact that Jones was dedicated to his particular form of religious expression and undoubtedly found it useful to stress the role of that religion in generating social mobility. In this sense a discussion of ideology itself becomes part of ideology. In fairness it should be said that these individualistic orientations were related to the economic order rather than being an argument couched in terms of individual psychologism.

In terms of his ideological stance a powerful ingredient was the tendency to draw upon the liberal concept of freedom and to relate it to power and control as they derived from control over the economic order. This would appear to contradict the above protestant ethic thesis in that, rather than claiming that material success depends upon the individual and his/her relationship to a particular source of values, he is maintaining that the individual is constrained in his/her actions by his/her lack of control over the economic order. Thus success is conditioned by a willingness to align with the interests of the controlling forces. This, together with more direct forms of intimidation tended to restrict freedom of action on the part of the individual who is expected to forsake his/her cultural and institutional affiliations in order to achieve.

It should be evident that the work of Jones does show a degree of contradiction and it is quite possible that this derives from his attempt to give his ideas a political expression, to use them explicitly as ideology. This could lead to the fragmentation of his overall thesis with the result that any overall theoretical model is absent. Nonetheless his ideas had a wide influence in Wales, some might even claim that they have persisted to the present as the underlying framework for contemporary nationalism in Wales.

It is in this sense that the relevance of his influence becomes most evident. It has been argued that non-conformism in nineteenth century Wales constituted an ideological order which countered the ideological hegemony of the dominant order. From the sixteenth century the implementation of state control was facilitated by the ideological role of the Church of England. Despite the linguistic and cultural separation of the aristocracy from the community they exerted a powerful influence over the economic and institutional structure of the community and in this capacity served as intermediaries linking the control of the ruling class to the community. The increasing importance of non-conformism represented a struggle over the community and in the community. The struggle in the community was between the new Welsh bourgeoise and petit-bourgeoise on the one hand and the aristocracy on the other over the control of the proletariat. The struggle over the community on the other hand focussed upon the inability of the state to control the devolved non-conformist institutional structure. Thus there developed an ideological order which stood in contradiction to the ideological hegemony of the dominant order. It is in the writings of Michael D. Jones, and in particular in the manner in which the non conformist principles were fused with a political economic analysis, that we begin to come to terms with the specific nature of this counter ideology.

CHAPTER 12

WELSH NATIONALISM AND THE BRITISH STATE[1]

Charlotte Aull Davies

The most important external factor shaping the Welsh nation and Welsh nationalism has been its dominance by the English, later British, state. As early as the 1536 Act of Union, the rulers of the state clearly stated their desire to impose cultural unity into their domain. Practically, however, the imposition of cultural uniformity was well byond the capacity of the medieval state. For nearly three centuries, the effect on the Welsh language and culture of political subjugation by England was limited primarily to the upper landowning class. This class allied itself to the monarchy and became anglicized within a few generations. Thus, the Welsh language lost its traditional literary patrons; but the bulk of the population remained thoroughly Welsh in language and culture. Furthermore, certain actions of the state, namely, the translation of the Bible and the Book of Common Prayer into Welsh, actually helped compensate for this loss of patronage. These actions also suggest the preeminence of religion over language as a form of social control during this period.

The growth of the system of industrial capitalism in the eighteenth and nineteenth centuries produced fundamental changes in the nature of the state. The powers of the state were gradually assumed by the new bourgeoisie, who espoused an ideology of democratic control. At first this class was primarily concerned with eliminating feudally based restrictions and obligations which interfered with the free development of the new industrial order. Gradually, starting in the second half of the nineteenth century, they began to use existing state institutions and to develop new ones for more positive forms of social control in order to promote their economic goals. This fusion of political and economic ends was apparent in the role played by the second wave of imperialism in bringing the capitalist system out of the serious depression of the final decades of the century. During this period the new state elite also began to attempt to exercise more direct forms of social control within the boundaries of the state, a development made feasible by rapid improvements in communication and transportation.

The fact that the state was beginning to play a more direct role in the lives of ordinary citizens, linked with its legitimizing ideology advocating democratic control and investing ultimate sovereignty in an elected parliament, was, to an extent, a two-edged sword. As the state assumed a more active role in everyday life, it came to be seen as a potential mechanism of reform through political action; and democratic ideology could clearly be employed in support of the extension of political rights to disenfranchised classes. Thus the past century has witnessed a gradual widening of political rights and, with the coming of the welfare state, a significant increase in social equality as well. While the state has not been fundamentally transformed, in terms of those groups that ultimately hold power, there have been significant changes in its nature, changes which have profoundly affected groups struggling to further alter the body politic.

The history of Welsh nationalism over the past century has been greatly influenced by the changing nature of the British state, in that this state provided the arena for its activities as well as being a major protagonist in its struggle to alter Wales' political status. The focus of Welsh nationalism can be seen to have varied in response to the opportunities and challenges presented to it by variations in the British state. Thus the institutional focus of the nationalist movement may be seen to have shifted from religion to national history and the Welsh language to economic issues and the bureaucracy. However, there has not been a simple linear progression; in particular, the roles of language and economy have fluctuated, even becoming intertwined over the past decade. Only the importance of the bureaucracy can be said to have consistently increased.

Nonconformity and Nationalism : The Nineteenth Century

During the nineteenth century the central state exercised very little direct control over ordinary people. One of the main areas of contact between state and people was the institution which had been of major importance for social control in the medieval state, namely, the state church. For a period which is meant to be one of very little direct state interference in everyday life, the activities of the state church - collecting tithes, registering births and deaths, controlling place of burial, and assuming considerable responsibility for poor relief - represented a very high level of involvement in community affairs. Furthermore, in Wales, the state church, the Church of England, had become a completely foreign institution. It was patronized by the anglicized gentry while the bulk of the population had been converted to the nonconformist faiths and attended chapels where Welsh was the language of worship. The democratic structure of these chapels had facilitated the creation of a local elite who were leaders of a social structure relatively divorced from that of the English-orientated aristocracy (Verdery, 1976). This nonconformist elite was active in the agitation for electoral reform and was soon able to assume the position of political leadership opened up by the electoral reform acts of the second half of the nineteenth century.

The local power bases of this Welsh nonconformist elite were the highly sectarian nonconformist chapels, and their nationalism was affected by this dependency. Although they did support Welsh culture and their campaigns were conducted naturally enough in the Welsh language as the only language the bulk of the population understood, they made no attempt to formulate a broad national political appeal based on the Welsh language or on Welsh national history and aspirations. Predictably their concern was almost exclusively with nonconformist related issues, such as disestablishment, Sunday opening and education. Their relative lack of concern for Welsh political unity is indicated by the fact that the only overarching institutions giving some organizational unity to their movement were both British based. The earliest one was the Society for the Liberation of Religion from State Patronage and Control, which was willing to concentrate its efforts on Wales as an area ripe for disestablishment. Later this unifying role was assumed by the North Party. Cymru Fydd was the only political organisation whose formally stated goals called for separate Welsh political institutions. However, its membership was drawn almost entirely from Welsh Liberal leadership and it never developed any popular base of support. Hence its pursuit of Welsh separatism was somewhat ephemeral, and the organisation foundered within a few years, having enjoyed no significant political success.[2]

Thus the relatively high interference of the state church in local affairs provided the major stimulus of the Welsh nationalist movement of the late nineteenth century. The issues that concerned its leaders were nonconformist related concerns, and their primary goal was the reducation of Church influence in their communities. They pursued this goal through legislative activity, a path opened up to them by electoral reform. Judged in terms of its primary aims the nineteenth century nationalist movement was quite successful, but judged in terms of accepted nationalist political goals, it had very little impact, and some of its activities may actually have been harmful to the nationalist cause of the future generations. The movement was successful in reducing the power of the state church and in removing disabilities suffered by nonconformists, although it did not win formal disestablishment until 1914. Welsh Liberals also obtained special legislation for Wales in areas such as Sunday opening and education. They also established Welsh national institutions, notably the Welsh Museum, the National Library and the University of Wales.

These were several reasons, besides the nature of its own power base, for the failure of the Welsh elite to seriously pursue nationalist political goals. In the first place, except for the area of religion, the central state was not perceived as being of great importance to everyday concerns. In fact, once the nonconformist elite had gained control of local government, as it succeeded in doing in the elections of 1889, it was in charge of that area of government that most affected its life and the lives of its constituents. The legitimizing of local political institutions by this election may have actually acted as a barrier to the propogation of a broader Welsh identity, reinforcing instead of the localised folk cultures and chapel loyalties characteristic of Welsh society in that period (Jenkins, 1935).

In the second place, there were no obvious positive incentives, at least in the short term, for increased Welsh unity or autonomy, and there were few external resources on which Welsh organizations might be built. Virtually the only means of pursuing such Welsh institutions was through formal legislation. Here the Welsh elite did enjoy some success, particularly in the area of education, which was an area of increasing interest to the central state.

The Welsh Liberals managed to obtain legislation that established a system of education in Wales considered to be in advance of that available in England. However, from a contemporary nationalist perspective, the system thus created was actually harmful in that it was a major factor in bringing about the decline in the numbers and percentages of Welsh speakers that came close to destroying one of the most powerful markers of a separate Welsh identity. The Welsh elite had based its case for these educational measures on the only argument that had credence under existing assumptions about the purpose of educating the masses: that is, that to become intelligent participants in the British political process, Welsh children had a special disability to overcome, namely the Welsh language. It thus succeeded in equating education with English language achievement and left a legacy of Welsh language decline.

The campaign for improving education in Wales was led by the London-based Welsh elite. Although the political power of this influential group rested on their Welsh roots, many of its members were increasingly drawn toward English culture and society, where they were on the whole very successful. Their concern for Welsh culture was thus primarily one of reflected self-image. They wanted to demonstrate that Welsh culture and the Welsh language were not deserving of the contempt heaped upon them by the English establishment in such noted examples as the 1847 Blue Books Report on education in Wales (Report on Education, 1847). Their desire to be accepted as part of English society and culture was enhanced by the position of England as an imperial power successfully exporting her language and culture throughout the world. The Welsh elite thus seized upon the concept of British identity to allow it to share in England's imperial greatness, and it was concerned to show that Wales had contributed in its own small way to the growth of the British state.[3] To this end it encouraged the growth of a romanticized version of Welsh history, a chronicle of princes culminating in the assumption of the English crown by the Welshman Henry Tudor in 1485. The Welsh language was promoted as an esoteric and romantic academic pursuit; but there was little concern with the maintenance of Welsh as a living language. The purpose of education for Welsh children was to acquire the fluency in English that was essential for them to be full participants in the opportunities of the empire.

Therefore, the crucial role of the British state in nineteenth century Welsh nationalism is apparent: the state's interference via the state church determined the main motivation of the movement; it facilitated the movement through electoral reform and channeled its activities into the realm of legislation; it inadvertently imposed certain limitations on the appeal of broader Welsh political institutions by allowing Welsh elite control of local political institutions; and its overseas imperial successes profoundly affected the attitudes and actions of the Welsh elite.

Building a National Identity : 1900–1945

Of course, once a tradition of Welsh historical and cultural studies had been established and institutionalised by the creation of a national University, Library and Museum, the field developed its own momentum, especially given the relative intellectual independence of academics. In the early years of this century, a few scholars with nationalist sympathies embarked upon a new direction in Welsh historical studies; they began to write Welsh history with Wales, rather than the English monarchy, as its focus and to analyse events and historical personages in the light. In other words, they began to create a genuine Welsh national history. This tradition was already established by the time of the foundation of Plaid Genedlaethol Cymru (the Welsh Nationalist Party) in 1925. It was to serve as an inspiration to the movement and several of the party's early leaders were to make important contributions to Welsh literary and historical studies. In fact, the impetus to establish such an independent political party was the concern of its leaders to safeguard Welsh culture and the Welsh language, an end, they believed, that could only be achieved by securing self-government for Wales.

The party was established just as Wales was entering a period of severe economic crisis that was to worsen throughout the 1930s. However, support for the new nationalist movement did not increase as a result of these economic conditions; rather the 1920s and 1930s saw the consolidation of the power of the Labour Party in the Welsh industrial areas. Indeed the overriding concern of the Welsh Nationalist Party with the language and cultural preservation must have seemed largely an irrelevance to those suffering the worst effects of the depression. Nationalists were not insensitive to the tragic consequences of the existing economic system. Some of their leaders perceived clearly the links between economic deprivation and cultural denigration (Davies, 1979; 77-78; 93-4). However, the solutions they offered, even in their relatively few economic pronouncements, depended upon the existence of a Welsh government. Such solutions had little political impact under external circumstances that required action to force the British state to intervene in order to relieve the immediate suffering. The Labour movement, which had a significant Welsh dimension in its early stages, bowed to this external necessity and constituted itself, organizationally and ideologically, along British lines. This was the same path that nineteenth-century nationalism had taken. Plaid Cymru, however, held to its nationalist principles and hence remained independent of the British-based political parties, rejecting equally English cultural dominance and English political rule.

The price the party paid for its independence was to remain a very small and somewhat elitist movement throughout the pre-World War II period. It did succeed in building a dedicated core of nationalists, but they had few opportunities to acquire political expertise. The central state did not offer much scope for pressure-group activities in that period.[4] About the only avenue open to nationalists under the circumstances was sporadic protest action against the intrusions of the British state, particularly in Welsh speaking Wales. The most important act of this sort was the 1936 burning of some workmen's huts at the R.A.F. bombing range under construction in the Lleyn Peninsula, a facility that nationalists had argued would do irreparable harm to the language and culture. The incident received a great deal of publicity and three Plaid Cymru officials who claimed responsiblity won wide public support in Wales. However, it did not lead to a significant growth in party membership, not did it signal a new direction in party campaigning.

With the coming of the war the party became entangled in opposition to conscription, with little real succes. Faced with massive public support for the war, party morale fell to a very low level; and many nationalists joined the armed services, although maintaining some links with the movement (Davies, 1979 : 225-239). However, toward the end of the war, there was an improved prospect of combining protest against state intrusion and increasing centralisation with positive steps to gain some measure of Welsh control over the administrative processes generated by this state activity. Plaid Cymru quickly recognized both the potential and the danger in government planning for the postwar period, and it was active in agitating for Wales to be treated as a unit in various government schemes for the nationalisation of industry as well as for economic planning for the post war world.

Nationalism and the Welfare State

The late 1940s saw massive central government involvement in local affairs through the setting up of the new welfare services. This activity tended to weaken such local institutions as the chapels, local government and, in the valleys, the union lodges that had, to some extent, been a barrier to Welsh unity since the nineteenth century. Furthermore, the central state became directly involved in economic affairs, both through the nationalisation of basic industry and through its new interest in economic planning. Plaid Cymru responded quickly to these altered circumstances. Party publications argued strongly that Wales should be treated as a unit both for economic planning and in the new nationalised industries. Their arguments used Welsh culture and historic identity as a basis for claiming a separate status for Wales within the various government programmes, rather than stressing cultural preservation as the primary goal. The popular appeal of this altered tactical approach was reflected at the polls while economic organisation along Welsh lines was a real possibility. Plaid Cymru made a much improved showing in the 1945 general election and in four by-elections in 1945 and 1946, three of them in primarily non-Welsh speaking constituencies in the south east, which were fought mainly on economic issues.[5] However, toward the end of the decade, economic organisation had become set, for the most part, along British lines, and the political nationalist surge dwindled accordingly.

Only in rural areas did economic life remain directly dependent on central state bureaucratic activity. This dependency was due mainly to the price-setting policy established by the 1947 Agriculture Act. Furthermore, rural economic measures were administered through a separate Welsh department within the Ministry of Agriculture. For this reason, it is quite significant that one of the first Welsh organisations to be established outside the bureaucracy was the Farmers' Union of Wales (in 1955) and, further, that the Welsh speaking rural areas were virtually the only areas where Plaid Cymru did show some electoral growth through the 1950s.

Once economic organization had been determined along British lines it was necessary for the focus of nationalist activity to shift to other areas. Given the massive build up of the bureaucracy needed to administer the various programmes of the welfare state, it is not surprising that this became a major focus of nationalist activity in the 1950s and 1960s. During the late 1940s most of the newly created or reorganized ministries had established Welsh departments. The next decade and a half witnessed a gradual accumulation of Welsh based organizations, primarily within the bureaucracy, culminating in the establishment of the Welsh Office in 1964. In the campaign to secure recognition for Wales within the bureaucracy, the Welsh language has been a vital resource for the nationalist movement. It was used to argue for special organizational arrangements on the basis of he particular needs which its existence created. The earliest such Welsh organization had been in education and agriculture, areas where the case for special treatment was particularly good. Once the special Welsh departments were established in these areas, their very existence provided a stronger argument for expanding Welsh-based organization than did the reality of Wales's separate cultural identity.

> The degree of decentralization in the field of education and agriculture, where in certain respects the difference between Wales and England is very evident, has fallen manifestly short of that in health, housing and local government where, it could be argued, the difference is not so obvious (Randall, 1972 : 357).

The important distinction in these latter areas seems to be that they were created, or fundamentally reorganized, after the administrative precedent for treating Wales as a separate unit had been firmly established.

The overall constitution of the Welsh infrastructure in the area of education reveals much about the importance of the Welsh language in the process of winning bureaucratic recognition for Wales. The major resource available from the bureaucracy for creating a Welsh infrastructure in education has been the 1944 Education Act, which established a system of comprehensive education and created a Minister of Education who was to have the power to ensure that local authorities implemented the provisions of the act (Bruce, 1968 : 320). One of these provisions, that within certain limits children were to be educated in accordance with the wishes of their parents has been used by Welsh-speaking parents to force local authorities to establish ysgolion Cymraeg (Welsh medium schools) in anglicized areas. Another very important organisation in the Welsh educational infrastructure is the Welsh Joint Education committee, which was established in 1948 under the 1944 Education Act. A separate Welsh teachers' union (U.C.A.C.) was set up in 1940; since the late 1960s it has been quite successful in attracting members from the Welsh-speaking areas of north and west Wales as well as among the staff of the ysgolion Cymraeg. Finally, the Welsh Nursery Schools Movement (Mudiad Ysgolion Meithrin) established in 1971, has been a major factor in making Welsh-medium education available to children from families where Welsh is not the language of the home.

It is significant that the most effective basis for creating a Welsh educational infrastructure was the Welsh language, which is spoken by a minority of the population, rather than Welsh national history. The major reason for the greater efectiveness of language in this regard seems to be that provision for the study of other cultural markers, such as national history, can more readily be made within the existing educational structure through relatively simple additions to the curriculum. Language, on the other hand, if it is to be used as a medium of instruction, requires a different set of educational materials, different training for teachers, and different examinations in all subjects. Its use thus encourages the growth of separate organisations to address these special educational needs.

The language has also proved to be a valuable resource for forcing other forms of recognition of Welsh cultural distinctiveness from the bureaucracy. In fact, the most active and vital part of the nationalist movement in the mid 1960s was, without doubt, the campaign for official status for Welsh - in the courts of law, on official forms, and on roadsigns - conducted with considerable success by Cymdeithas yr Iaith Gymraeg (Welsh Language Society).

During this period, there was relatively little growth in the political nationalist sphere and little internal change in Plaid Cymru. The party's popular support, judged by its vote in general elections, was very low; in fact, its proportion of the vote actually decreased in the 1964 and 1966 general elections.[6] In contrast to some of the pamphlets produced in the late 1940s party pronouncements were concerned mainly with the cultural nationalist argument, stressing Wales' historical identity and the preservation of the language. However, in the mid 1960s, Plaid Cymru began to attract many more activistis from anglicized areas, its tactics and ideology were transformed, and within a few years, this internal growth was reflected in greatly imporved electoral performances. As in the postwar period, this second period of political nationalist growth has been associated with increased central state involvemet in economic life, in particular with the post war years which directed new industry to the periphery had fallen into disuse by about 1950, once it became apparent that the high levels of unemployment that had followed the First World War had been avoided (Manners, 1964 : 45-47). However, beginning in the early 1960s, state involvement in the Welsh economy again accelerated in response to an economic recession and rising unemployment. At first, the economic programme had a highly localised, rather than a regional, orientation, hence they did not provide a viable resource for Welsh economic organisation until 1966, when broader development areas replaced local districts as the units for the new economic measures (Davies and Thomas, 1976 : 28). Significantly, in this same year, Plaid Cymru achieved its first major electoral breakthrough with the victory of its president, Gwynfor Evans, in a parliamentary by-election in Carmarthen. This victory was followed by two very closely contested by-elections in the Rhondda and Caerphilly in 1967 and 1968, when Plaid Cymru came near to defeating the Labour candidates in these industrial constitutencies. Although Gwynfor Evans lost his seat in the 1970 general eletion the party's proportion of the total vote reached its highest level ever (11.5 per cent) and the nationalist political advance continued in the 1974 general elections, when the party won first two, then three parliamentary seats.

Thus, while the political nationalist advances associated with the advent of greater central state involvement in economic decisions in the postwar years soon dissipated, Plaid Cymru's breakthrough of the late 1960s heralded a period of sustained growth of over a decade for the party and the nationalist movement. A major factor responsible for the difference in the two periods was that the existence of the Welsh Office in the latter period meant that there was an element within the bureaucracy advocating economic planning on an all-Wales basis. Whereas in the late 1940s the nationalists stood almost alone in arguing that Wales be treated as a unit for purposes of economic planning and were largely unsuccessful in their efforts along these lines, in the 1960s, they had an important, if unwilling, ally in the Welsh

Office. With the assumption of economic planning authority by the Welsh Office, and despite the inadequacy of the planning document it produced, (Welsh Office, 1967) Plaid Cymru was able to concentrate on specific economic issues and develop its own economic plan for Wales without continually having to answer the argument that such an exercise was futile or foolish. Instead, the concept of economic planing for Wales was generally accepted through its having received official endorsement by the government.

Another important consequence of the development of the Welsh Office, and especially of its assumption of some economic powers, is the fact that the two major economic factors outside the government, namely the labour movement and business interests, found it advantageous to establish Welsh branches of their principal organisations in order to deal directly with the Welsh Office. The importance of such organisations to the nationalist movement is that they help bring decision-making powers to Wales, even if they themselves are opposed to nationalist principles. The Welsh branch of the highly centralized Confederation of Busines and Industry enjoys considerably more autonomy than some of the larger offices in the English regions. Also the Wales Trades Union Council, which was formed in the period 1972-74, was, by the late 1970s, advocating the devolution of significant political power to Wales, although it remained quite hostile to nationalism in general and to Plaid Cymru.

The year 1979 marked the end of the quite impressive nationalist advanced that had begun with the by-elections of the late 1960s. On March 1, 1979, the Labour Government's proposal for an elected assembly for Wales was defeated in a referendum; and in the general election in May, Plaid Cymru's support fell sharply to 8.1 per cent of the total vote, although the party's M.P.s in Caernarfon and Meirioneth easily retained their seats. That election brought to power a Tory Government determined to undertake a general withdrawal from the commitments of the welfare state. In particular the Government wanted to reduce state involvement in economic life. Given the close association between regional economic programmes and popular support for Plaid Cymru, its decline in electoral fortunes in the wake of the Tory victory was probably unavoidable.

Nevertheless, the party seems unlikely to return to the position of the 1950s. In the first place, the extensive Welsh infrastructure now in existence will not disappear. This infrastructure provides vital support for the movement, both by giving administrative reality to a separate Welsh identity and by helping to bring a degree of administrative, if not political, independence to Wales. It also provides a much more accessible target for nationalist protest and pressure-group activities.

Secondly, the nationalist movement has shown considerable resilience in its ability to move the focus of its activity away from the strictly electoral process. This was apparent in the campaign to ensure that the new fourth television channel would be used in Wales to provide a Welsh-language service. Cymdeithas yr Iaith Gymraeg had been campaigning on this issue since the 1960s and all major political parties had agreed to such a service by the 1979 election. However, when the new Tory Government reversed its position on this issue, shortly after the election, Plaid Cymru entered the fray in earnest, organizing direct action in which nearly two thousand people refused to pay their television licence fees. Gwynfor Evans' announcment of his intent to fast to death if necessary unless the Government backed down inspired the support of thousands, and this support became apparent in a series of rallies held throughout Wales in the spring and summer of 1980. The Government's acceptance of defeat on the issue in September of that year represented a very significant victory for the nationalist movement and greatly helped to raise morale after the 1979 setbacks.

The successful involvement of Plaid Cymru in this campaign also signalled a determination that was explicitly set out in the 1981 Report of the Plaid Cymru Commission of Inquiry to place less emphasis on the electoral process and on strictly reformist policies. The party has declared itself ready to undertake campaigns involving unconstitutional methods in order to achieve a genuine transformation of Welsh society. The most recent manifestation of this new direction has been the party's water rates protest in which members were urged not to pay their water bills as a protest against the differentials between water rates in Wales and in water authorities in England that receive water from Wales. Tied to the party's change of emphasis has been its recent explicit committment to socialism. This commitment was made official by motions at the 1981 and 1982 Annual Conferences incorporating it in the party's three basic aims.[7]

Thus changes in the central state have been a major determininat of the focus of nationalist activity in the contemporary movement as well as in the nineteenth century. The British state between the wars offered little scope for positive actions to enhance Welsh unity or autonomy; and the Welsh Nationalist Party was unable or unwilling to mount a sustained campaign of direct action against the state, restricting itself instead to a handful of symbolic protest actions. However, the opportunities presented to the movement by the coming of the welfare state were very different and this change of circumstances was rapidly reflected in nationalist activity. The major factor enabling Plaid Cymru to recruit significant electoral support has been a perceived possibility of winning control over Welsh economic affairs. Such a possibility appeared in the late 194Os and again in the late 196Os with the emergence of various government economic programmes and regional planning. However, the first of these prospects was short-lived. With the effective withdrawal of state support from such regional economic measures by about 195O, the nationalist focus shifted to the area of greatest state activity, namely, the extension of social services and their attendant bureaucracy. During the 195Os and 196Os, the accumulation of Welsh organisations within and peripheral to the state bureaucracy was massive. In this process Welsh cultural distinctiveness and particuarly the Welsh language, proved to be valuable resources for the movement. When the opportunity for Welsh economic planning and control reapppeared in the late 196Os, Plaid Cymru was able to reap the benefits of the build up of a Welsh infrastructure and the winning of administrative recognition for Welsh identity, especially for the Welsh language, in the intervening years. The recent withdrawal of state support for regional economic measure has predictably meant a change of focus once again for the nationalist movement, with Plaid Cymru trying to shift its emphasis, to some extent, from the electoral process to pressure-group activities. A degree of radicalisation may also be observed, both in the great willingness of Plaid Cymru, to support direct action campaigns and in the increasing recognition of the links between socialist economic solutions and measures to ensure the survival of the Welsh language.

CHAPTER 13

UNEVEN DEVELOPMENT AND THE POLITICS OF CULTURE

Phillip M. Rawkins

In a recent paper, Glyn Williams (1981) has sought to take stock of the strengths and deficiencies of recent work relating to Wales, culture and nationalism. His main concern has been to deplore what he views as the tendency to de-emphasize social structure and class relations as the basis for analysis and explanation. Perhaps rightly, it is to this tendency that he attributes the rash of primarily cultural explanations for what Emyr Humphreys termed "The Welsh condition". Thus he argues that cultural consciousness is in no way prior to or more "natural" than other forms of consciousness. Rather, it is suggested, under certain circumstances, changes in economic structures and group relationships prove conducive to the emergence of a group consciousness emphasizing ethnic symbols or markers, and territorial rather than functional group divisions.

For the most part, Williams' argument represents a useful corrective to approaches which fail to place culture in their structural context. However, in demolishing the primordial notion of culture, it appears to this author at least that there arises the danger of removing culture from the picture altogether by viewing it as entirely reducible to its structural base. It will be argued in this paper, following Weber (Gerth and Mills, 1949; Giddens, 1971; Cohen, 1976) that culture should be perceived as enjoying a <u>relative</u> autonomy from structural determination. In other words, cultural phenomena exist within limits set by social structure. Within these limits, there fall a considerable array of possibilities, further, under certain conditions, the limits may be considerably wider than is usually the case. In recognition of this, an attempt will be made to locate culture in the context of an approach to the analysis of political change based principally on political economy and specifically on the model of core-periphery relations.

Nationalism and Uneven Development

To accept the argument that nationalism in any or all its forms is best understood as a "natural" phenomenon, or an historical coming of age meeting a universally-felt need, is to fall prey to the romantic nationalist interpretation of history. As Elie Kedourie (1960:9) has pointed out, "nationalism is a doctrine invented in Europe at the beginning of the nineteenth century". However, there may well be powerful factors - economic, social, and political - which, in certain circumstances, have the effect of making the nationalist idea, in the context of these particular conditions, appear as a natural and irresistable response to historical developments. (Gellner, 1964:150)

Nineteenth century European nationalism is best seen as a response to the development and diffusion of the modern, capitalist, industrial economy. Despite the assumptions of the linear conception of progress, in nineteenth century Europe, as in colonial Asia and Africa, a century later, the impact of modernization has been highly uneven in terms of its geographical effects. As a result, nationalist history has been characterized by the straggling emergence of an erratic procession of local nationalisms, as the institutions and agencies of the modern economy touched particular regions at particular times, in particular ways.

Nationalism has always and everywhere had an ambivalent character: part reaction against economic modernization and the concept of progress, and part carrier of modernity. Overwhelmed by the force of capitalist expansion, the emergent elites of peripheral regions, one after another, have sought to resist such expansion, while at the same time harnessing its forces for their own advantage (Nairn, 1975; Smith, 1971).

Hence nationalism has the character of both a unifying and a divisive force. It is important to grasp that its ambivalence is a direct consequence of the uneven impact of modern economic forces. In its non-imperialist variant, nationalism may thus be understood as the compensatory ideology of peoples relatively distant, culturally and geographically, from the centres of capital concentration. Such peoples experience the disorder brought about by economic change, but find themselves unable to enjoy its promised benefits to the full.

It will be argued that the emergence of regional discontent and minority-nationalist opposition to the maintenance of the present structure of nation-states may be similarly related to the process of uneven development. However, in the context of the modern world-system, and particularly with regard to the advanced industrial-technological society, the relationship is one of considerable intricacy, requiring the specification of a number of intervening variables.

Technological advance in transportation, communications, and in the production process have facilitated enormous developments in what Max Weber termed the "rationalization" of economic life. Increasingly, scientific and technical development is integrated with the forces of production in the institutional context of the global corporation, diversifying investment in a number of industries in many countries. Technological change has made possible the growing concentration of capital investment in a few metropolitan regions, and in the hands of an ever-decreasing number of vertically, and horizontally, integrated companies.[2] A multinational system of trade and payments has emerged, such than an expanding volume of trade is conducted between the same firms in different countries.

In north-west Europe, the expansion of heavy industry in the late nineteenth century resulted in a massive increase in demand for labour, as well as for raw materials. By contrast, corporate growth in the advanced industrial state has taken the form of an increasing rate of capital investment per worker. Associated with this trend is the growing significance of technological innovation, as compared with the surplus value of labour productivity over labour cost, as a basis for profitability. A sharp division of labour has been created between a concentrated, high-wage, advanced technology, high productivity industrial core in western Europe, north America and Japan, and a more extensive, low wage, low technology and low productivity sector in the less developed countries. (Hymer, 1972; Holland, 1975).

In such circumstances, the economic advantages of those regions of western Europe whose economies were dependent primarily on a small range of extractive and heavy manufacturing industries have disappeared. Hence the economic difficulties of such regions as the Walloon south of Belgium, south Wales, the Scottish Clydeside and the Belfast area of the north of Ireland. Despite substantial financial inducements offered by national governments, the prospect of investing outside areas immediately adjacent to metropolitan centres has become unattractive for major national and international corporations.[3] The result is high unemployment, the emigration of the young, and the breakdown of communities and established social structures.

Similarly, the relative poverty of rural areas of the periphery such as the interior and west coast of Brittany, the French Basque Country, Galicia, Corsica, southern Italy, the Scottish Highland interior and north and mid-Wales has been exacerbated. Such areas are offered little prospect of a viable economic future, and it becomes clear that the chief function of their populations is to act as a territorial pool of reserve labour, or as service employees maintaining a summer playground for the wealthier inhabitants of the metropolis.[4] Though the agencies of the welfare state may assist the casualties of economic progress by attempting to equalize incomes on a geographical basis, such efforts are limited, and are necessarily confined to compensating for an imbalance, the source of which is built into the system, and whose impact will continue to be felt. Young people are obliged to leave in search of work. Those fortunate enough to find employment locally are priced out of the housing market by city-based purchasers of second homes.

For the United Kingdom, the post-war period has brought a belated recognition of the fact that the country is no longer part of the core of the world-system; rather, it occupies a position in what has been termed the semi-periphery. In order to clarify the meaning of such a status, it may be useful to consider briefly what is involved in the conceptual apparatus of the world-system perspective.

As Wallerstein (1978) has put it, the relation between core and periphery is based on unequal exchange between the products of two related sets of production processes. Drawing on the work of Emmanuel (1972) he goes on to emphasize that there is an extra dimension to be added to the transfer of surplus value from the producers to those who obtain the surplus:

> If there are two sets of producers and receivers of surplus-value, (N.B. one in the core, one in the periphery) . . . the receiver of one pair acquires part of the surplus-value of the other pair. This is not given at the expense of the producer of the second pair, because he has already given up his surplus-value, but rather . . . at the expense of the receiver.
> (Wallerstein, 1978:220-221)

Within the world-system, "core-type activities" and "peripheral-type activities" are unequally distributed within and among world-regions. A semi-peripheral state, then, would be one which has a roughly even balance of the two forms of activity. Similarly, Johann Galtung (1971) has referred to "go-between" states, mediating between the core and periphery in much the same way that the metropolis within a peripheral state mediates between the territory which it dominates and those at the core of the world-system.

In some senses, the relation of the United Kingdom as an economic entity to the European metropolitan core is becoming roughly similar to that of Wales to the United Kingdom economy. However, the links of the United Kingdom with the European core, and, more generally, its place in the international financial system, has been such as to enable it to retain a fiscal framework sufficiently strong to prevent major social contrasts emerging between different regions [5] (Seers, Schaeffer and Kiljunen, 1979).

Despite the now diminishing flow of oil revenues, present trends would suggest that in the late 1980s it may prove to be beyond the capability of the British state to maintain this state of affairs. As Stuart Holland (1977) has pointed out, regional development policies have not been designed to confront the inter-regional imbalance of industrial structure. Certainly in Britain, at least since the defeat of the Labour Government of 1964-70, regional policy has amounted to little more than an ad hoc programme for subsidising multinational companies. Since the late 1970s, as Doreen Massey and Richard Meegan (1982) have argued, as the general rate of U.K. wide unemployment has inreased, and as the number of regions experiencing a high rate of net job loss has grown, so the government has tended to simply abandon its committment to regional policy as a whole. Hence it seems likely that, in the coming years, the state will prove both unable and unwilling to mask either the realities of structural unemployment and de-industrialization or the spacial inequality of the distribution of their social costs. At the same time, precisely because of the integration of Wales into the British economy and political system, the state is unable to offer foreign investors the docile and controlled labour market which Ireland, unambiguously a part of the European periphery, has been able to provide.

As the United Kingdom as an entity has become more peripheralized, so the inter-regional relations within the territory of the state have been transformed. The relegation of the United Kingdom from the metropolitan European core has led to a greater tendency to concentrate investment in the south east of England, the region whose links with the core remain strongest and whose economic structures are the most diversified. Similarly, at a regional level, within Wales, the tendency has been for a flow of jobs and investment away from the rural areas and the valleys of south east Wales to the more prosperous south coastal area, accessible to the M4 motorway. The increasing economic integration into the metropolitan economy of this more prosperous "bridgehead" zone goes along with a growing tendency towards marginalization elsewhere in the region.

The significance to the Welsh economy of the steel closures of the late 1970s puts into perspective the growing marginalization of the region as a whole. It is surely a sign of the growing peripheral status of the British economy more generally that the government has been obliged to intervene in an ever-widening range of economic sectors (Selwyn, 1979). However, the exceptional degree of dependence of Wales on public sector investment seems to provide some measure of its distance from the core of the British economy, where the relative importance of government as both employer and decision-maker is substantially less.

Nationalism in Wales has taken on an unusual importance in two epochs: the late nineteenth century and the 1960s and 1970s. It is no coincidence that each period represented a time of economic transition and of a change in patterns of core-peripheral relations at international, British and Welsh levels. Naturally, the effects have been felt quite differently by social groups throughout Wales, formed not only around class-based economic interest, but also mobilizing as status-groups, defining themselves by an ideology linked to territorial location and language. It is the varying impact of changing and intensifying patterns of social inquality, and particularly the growing pressure on occupational opportunities, and on locality-based patterns of class relationships, which underlies the relative strengths and weaknesses of nationalist politics in Wales.[6]

The accentuated economic dependency of Wales has provided the crucible for both nationalism and the integration-orientated politics of the Labour Party. Devolution and the referendum debacle indicated the strength of the politics of integration in a country which is internally divided by social class, by differential regional patterns of relationship to the metropolitan core, and by language. As appropriate to a periphery within a semi-periphery, Welsh politics reflect the pattern of dependency that its economic structure would lead us to expect. However, it should be born in mind that the core-periphery framework does not yield pleasingly tidy patterns of dependency relationships. Rather, it yields interlocking networks of interaction at different spatial levels of economic organization. In turn, these networks produce a modification to patterns of class relations. Hence class antagonisms are broken down and expressed at a local level by groups with conflicting interests and incompatible territorially-based reference-groups. The most obvious example is the growing polarization in Gwynedd between the locality-oriented Plaid Cymru supporters and the cosmopolitan metropolis-oriented Conservatives. Conflicts over such policy areas as language-in-education, tourism and recreation and industrial development rflect the clash between two different status-groups, with radically different territorial and class reference groups (Rawkins, 1979; Madgwick and Rawkins, 1982; Williams, 1980; Betts; 1976).

Since the mid 1960s, the Labour Party's ability to integrate a population whose interests are increasingly divided by a series of cross-cutting cleavages has declined. Yet it is the conservatives, not the nationalists who have benefitted. As a periphery, Wales is characterized by the absence of regionally-integrated communications network and the general weakness of patterns of interaction carried on entirely within Wales. The lack of effective local control provides an issue but denies the means to nationalist politicians in their efforts to create an "anti-metropolitan" politics. Unlike Quebec, and to a lesser extent than Scotland or the Basque provinces of Spain, Wales lacks the institutional basis for the articulation of a national response to its economic crisis. In any case, internal divisions resulting from economic changes set in motion in the nineteenth century have eroded the language which at one time represented a potent mobilization symbol for ideological opposition to "the politics of the centre".

International Capital and the Advanced Industrial State

To understand the failure of the state to combat the impact of uneven development, it is necessary to turn to a consideration of those factors which have led to a transformation of the role of the state in the world economic system. The internationalization of capital concentration and economic enterprise has brought about not only a structural transformation of the world economy but also a severe limitation on the powers of the nation-state to influence events. As Barnet and Muller (1974:302) have commented:

> Loss of control over money, increasing concentration of income and wealth, failure to maintain emloyment and mounting debts are symptoms of the permanent managerial crisis that now afflicts advanced industrial societies as well as poor countries . . . Territorially-based government lacks the imagination and the power to develop political response to the dynamic global economic forces which, more and more, are shaping our lives.

Yet, paradoxically, the power of the state vis a vis the citizen, and the encroachment of the state bureaucracies on day-to-day life have grown considerably in recent decades. The internationalization of capital has not suppressed the state. Rather, it has increased its difficulties in performing its role as manager and guarantor of full employment, social peace and political consensus. The power of international capital is such that it is able to induce the state to assist it in achieving its general goals. Though conflicts of interest have inevitably emerged between nation-states and global corporations, the general trend has been towards cooperation (Poulantzas, 1974; Hymer, 1972). The result has been a decline in the ability of the state to plan and pursue its own destiny. Where the state seeks to take actions consistent with the broad interest of capital it does so at the risk of creating complex problems of finance and administration (Scott, 1979). In turn, it may lack adequate resources to respond adequately to such strains in the economic or political order.

As Stephen Hymer (1972) has pointed out, the array of governmental policy instruments involving, for example, monetary, fiscal and wage policy, becomes progressively less effective the more open the economy, and the greater the proportion of foreign investment. The concentration of capital, technology and scientific expertise in the hands of the global corporations makes it essential for governments to meet the terms presented by international capital as a means to promoting economic growth and maintaining relatively high levels of employment. The pressure on government to provide a satisfactory R & D structure to assist private industry in the high technology field is a particularly noteable feature of the political economy of the 198Os.

The European Economic Community has been seen by many comentators as a means to improve the competitive power of European corporations vis as vis their international rivals. Ironically, it has been the non-European corporations which have gained most from the creation of the tariff-free market. Such corporations have been able to apply the benefits of scale of operations, already enjoyed in domestic and world markets to this new arena of production and marketing. Hence they have come to enjoy substantial advantages over the majority of European corporations, thus further increasing their global dominance, and their ability to play off one national-state against another (Holland, 1977, Swann, 1975). Despite the relative decline of the U.S. economy since the end of the Vietnam War, the dominance of U.S. corporations in the more advanced industrial fields, particularly in computor hardware and software and telecommunications, continues.

It is the adaptation of the state to the international corporate system, and an acceptance of the system's values, rather than a literal transfer of powers to trans-national economic and political institutions, which has reduced the state's ability to cope with ruptures in national unity (Poulantzas, 1974; Murray, 1971). Rather than providing an alternative to the international system, the European Economic Community has become a powerful bulwark of the system.

The peripheral regions cannot expect relief within the existing political framework. Hence, solutions to their problems presuppose a rejection of prevailing political structures and values. The question of values is particularly significant, as is emphasized by Kari Levitt (1972:2-3) in her essay on Canada, Quebec and the multi-national corporation:

> Underdevelopment, ... is perpetuated above all by our collective mentality of dependence and impotence with respect to the supposed superiority of the economic, political and even the cultural institutions of the dominant metropolis. It follows that the first step towards an escape from under-development and hinterland status is the self-definition and self-assertion of a society in its own terms. . .

The Significance of Culture

Nationalism is more than simply a romantic variant of regionalism, and it would be erroneous to seek to comprehend the emergence of minority nationalist movements on the European periphery merely in terms of a demand for regional planning and a redistribution of the benefits of growth. The dimension of values, of culture and thus of ethnic identity is all-important. In seeking to understand this, the nature of the broader impact of the international corporate order must be clarified.

As has been argued above, the impact of economic change and hence of social disruption has been particularly marked in the periphery. A consequence of this has been a modification in the role of culture, defined by Ernest Gellner (1964:155) as "the manner in which one communicates in the broadest sense". Though culture is always important, generally its importance lies in the fact that it reinforces social structure, and that cultural forms symbolize and emphasize the character of the substance of existing structures.

As established social structures undergo transformation and disruption so the link between structure and culture is broken. Formerly individuals found their identity in their place in the social structure, with their identity symbolized and reinforced in culture. In transitional society, Gellner (1964) argues, culture replaces structure as the realm for definition of identities. The range of roles that individuals now occupy fails to accord with their self-perceptions. Hence their culture, their style of conduct and expression, becomes their identity, and there exist the circumstances under which individuals may come to classify themselves self-consciously according to nationality.

The relevance of such considerations to the phenomenon under consideration arises from the concentration of the ill-effects of the most recent phase of internationalization of concentration of capital and technology, and hence of the disruptive effects of uneven development, in the European periphery. Thus the effects of social disruption become concentrated on the historical and cultural fault lines of what have always been undermined by the impact of external forces, so cultural and historical symbols emphasizing ethnic distinctiveness have become increasingly significant as a focus for personal identity.

Uneven development thus tends to stimulate ethnic awareness while at the same time undermining social indicators of ethnic diversity. Hence the common phenomenon among the educated, urbanized young of western European national minorities of renewed interest in indigenous cultural forms, languages, national history and rural traditions. (Mayo, 1974; Jacob, 1975) As Ernest Gellner (1964:162) has put it, "the self-image of nationalism involves the stress of folk, folk-lore, popular culture, etc. - in fact, nationalism becomes important precisely when these things become artificial".

In seeking to carry out political mobilization on the basis of culture and ethnic identity, the nationalist movements are standing against the process termed by Weber the "rationalization" of the modern world. Through this concept, Weber was attempting to express and explain the effects of scientific technical progress on the institutional arrangements of societies undergoing "modernization". Essentially, Weber peceived an ever-expanding application to production and bureaucratic administration of scientific-technical rules based on analytic knowledge (Habermas, 1971).

Like Marx, Weber observes that the application of what may be termed "the rationality of technique" is characteristic of the development process in Western industrial society. But the application of rationalization does not stop with the economy, but also extends to the conduct of government and the administration of public and private institutions of all types. Consequently, bureaucratization becomes the chief organizational dynamic of society.

In such a society, no problem need be consigned to the realm of magic or the unexplained. All mysteries, in principle, may be solved through the application of methods and information available within the inventory of scientific knowledge. Hence rationalization of action becomes the leifmotif of Western culture, penetrating even the arts and popular entertainment (Giddens, 1971: 180-4). Accordingly, Weber argues, there is no longer any place in "the disenchanted world" of public life for the expression of "ultimate and sublime values" which "have retreated from public life into the transcendental realm of mystic life or into the brotherliness of direct and personal relations" (Weber, 1948: 155).

Weber's view of the world was a bleak, unpromising one, in which the process of secular rationalization would continue to percolate through all aspects of social organization and daily life. However, as Ernest Gellner has argued, while Weber's analysis of developments in the economic system and in the character of complex organizations, public and private, has been vindicated in its essentials, the process of diffusion of rationalization has not continued into other sphers of life. What now exists, Gellner (1974: 193) suggests, is "a complex symbiosis of diverse conceptual styles", such that the world of serious discourse is insulated from other spheres of society. As a result, there exists a noteable lack of continuity within the culture of advanced industrial society. In striking contrast to Weber, Gellner (1974: 194) sums up the situation of Western society with a quotation from Gaston Bachelard: "the world in which we think is not the same as the one in which we live".

Culture continues to be disseminated as before, and indeed, through the increasing reach and density of advanced communications networks, probably reaches societal members more effectively than before. However, lacking internal integrity, the cultural material which is disseminated fails to reinforce the authority of the social order. While this is unlikely to produce either social collapse or revolution, it allows for the appearance of additional social space in which meanings and identities may be negotiated. In other words, the "receivers" of the disseminated culture possess greater room for manoeuvre in responding selectively, and distancing themselves from the values and sets of ideas transmitted by the state and the networks emanating from society's dominant institutions. From a materialist perspective, culture is taken to refer to the whole

> . . . . complex sphere of legal, political, economic and philosophical discourses which comprise the dense, ideological complex of a modern capitalist society (Hall, 1977 : 324)

following Marx's discussion in The German Ideology and Capital, Volume 1, but also drawing on Gramsci and Althusser, Stuart Hall suggests that despite the growing social complexity of advanced industrial society, and the demolition of the over-arching "canopies of legitimation", ideological coherence and consistency is maintained as a result of the work of such agencies as the mass media (Hall, 1977 : 340-2). The ideological work performed by the media serves to provide an interpretation and encoding of the various expressions of diverse lifestyles and alternative collective representations, with the result that out of an apparent disorder and pluralism of outlooks an "acknowledged order" is negotiated. As a result of continuing ideological work, a consensus is negotiated, the effect of which is to maintain the legitimacy of the dominant order.

In the process of "negotiation", there is room for the expression of minority views. The discourses arising from these "subordinate ideologies" are encoded in such a way as to enhance the legitimacy of the moral order and of the media which help sustain it. In the argument presented here, it is suggested that the system is rather less coherent than this. In the negotiated space available, oppositional forces have room to develop alternative outlooks more profoundly at variance with the dominant order than is suggested by Hall. Ideological or cultural space is never safely occupied but remains a sphere of conflict and contention.

Bearing this in mind, in examining the historical process of the incorporation of territorially peripheral groups into a centralized state, it will be far from surprising to discover that in many cases some aspects of the minority cultures, their symbols and values, will have been maintained in the interest of achieving accommodation, while minimizing the likelihood of conflict between peripheral groups and the State. Such "cultural fragments" may be seen by those directing the State apparatus as harmless symbols: as elements making for a healthy social diversity. However, the meaning attached to these symbols as well as their political salience, may come to change with history.

The concept of cultural innovation, and the emphasis on culture as interaction and process which goes along with it, represents a necessary corrective to prevailing interpretations of culture. For all this, the imagery employed in evoking the active character of culture overdramatizes a situation, which, in many ways, is remarkably mundane. Minority nationalism, rather like the phenomenon of fundamentalist religous cults, is attractive to its adherents and interesting to its analysts precisely because of the underlying shallowness of the mainstream culture, by comparison with which it stands out so strikingly.

The discontents of recent decades, whether expressed by collective action or by withdrawal from political participation, have raised serious questions concerning the capacity of state bureaucracies and private corporations to provide for social needs. Centralization of the location and control of both economic and political resources, along with what might be termed the 'cultural means of production', in the form of the mass media of communication, has led to an erosion of local social institutional networks, which at one time mediated the relationship between the individual and centres of economic and political power.

Ethnicity has not only become more salient as a focus for group identity for the Scots and Welsh, it has also become more relevant as a basis for political action. The indecisiveness of the state, referred to above, has coincided with the growth of areas of state responsibility and a corresponding increase in what Jeffrey Ross (1981) has termed 'politically relevant access points'. Further, with the increasing scope of the role of government, the state becomes the legitimate target for an expanding range of public demands (Bell, 1973). This state of affairs produces substantial changes in political organization:

> The spread of political decision-making forces the organization of persons into communal and interest groups, defensively to protect their places and privileges, or advantageously to gain place and privilege. The multiplication of groups increases community conflict (Bell, 1975 : 144-6).

However, as Bell (1975 : 174) points out, the new-found saliency of ethnicity does not amount to its political predominance. On many political issues, functional interest groups and social class affiliations may be more important than ethnic and communal groups. Thus it appears that the popularity of the nationalist parties in Wales and Scotland faded in the late 1970s as economic issues - apparently deemed more important in the context of state-wide elections than the national question - came to dominate public debate.

In both Wales and Scotland, the evidence derived from the 1979 General Election survey of public opinion suggests that there exists a widely-held attachment to national identity. In both cases, however, this attachment has little political saliency. While nationalism is acceptable as a vehicle for political opposition, it may be discarded where other means of raising political demands appear more viable. In other words, while the nationalist parties lack the advantages of the major state-wide parties (financing, mass media exposure, leadership visibility), they share their current problems. The decline of class-based partisan alignment, and the emergence of the calculative, selective voter as the norm, affects Plaid Cymru or the S.N.P. as much as the Labour Party (c.f. Crewe, 1979; Himmelweit, 1981). Given this substantial change in the character of voting behaviour throughout Britain, both the timing of nationalist success and the volatility of nationalist support becomes more readily explicable. With the rise of the Social Democrats, both nationalist parties have seen their support decline at local elections in 1981, as a new oppositional force with little to offer in the way of cultural or ideological innovation, but with far greater resources has appeared on the scene. The relative success of the S.D.P./Liberal alliance, and the uniformity of its advance throughout Britain is yet another reminder that the cultural gap separating England, Scotland and Wales from one another is less significant than the commonality which binds them together.

Wales in Comparative Perspective

The nationalist parties in Scotland and Wales have succeeded in accomplishing what might be termed cultural innovation: in moulding an ideology of opposition around national identity, ethnic difference and territorially-defined interest. Yet the very conditions which have favoured cultural innovation and which have made possible a nationalist challenge within the political arena, have also made it unlikely that the nationalists will succeed in mobilizing and maintaining significant levels of mass support (Rawkins, 1983).

Something rather different has occurred in Quebec, the Basque country and Catalonia.[7] In all of these cases, a bridge has been built between the intellectuals, activists, and native speakers, who may be seen as constituting the core of the nationalist sub-culture, and the surrounding society. The nationalist elite has succeeded in creating a social and political organization which has tapped into the deep vein of cultural themes, myths and symbols, and has done so in such a way as to mobilize popular sentiment and give it a new political expression.

Where Spain and Canada are concerned, the relatively late formation of the state system, and the relative weakness of its capacity to integrate regional collectivities, distinguished from one another by significant cultural barriers, stand in striking contrast to the situation which prevailed in the making of the British state. Neither the direct and indirect demolition work on pre-existing regional cultures, nor the process whereby the new state asserted its authority, was so extensive in scope and intensive in character as was the case in Britain or France.

For these reasons, in all three cases listed above (as in pre-independence Ireland), the character of the relationship between the minority nation and those exercising the authority of the state has been such as to constitute a significant division around which political mobilization may occur. This has not been the case with the Scots and the Welsh and their relationship to the governing authorities in London. Where the Catalans, Basques and Quebecois are concerned, there is clear evidence of a substantial history of differential political treatment accorded to the minority, along with the presence of many of the factors associated with Hechter's cultural division of labour.

It has been political conflict, and the intervention of the state in determining the territorial distribution of valued rewards, and not culture as such, which has created the conditions for nationalist mobilization. To be simplistic, as an aspect of individual identity and community integration, culture is as much in evidence in Aberystwyth or Aberdeen as in San Sebastian or Quebec City. In the latter two locations, however, it is the long-standing conflict with state power which has served to politicize culture, endowing national identity with a political significance quite different both in kind and intensity from that encountered in Scotland or Wales. Without this cutting edge of a deeply-rooted conflict with the state, in political terms, nationalism in Wales and Scotland, at least for the presnet, represents little more than a minor variation in the struggle of interest groups for political spoils. The maintenance of a distinct national identity may not add up to much more than a form of local pride quite consistent with strong adherence to the British state and society.

At an activist level, however, the situation is rather different. In both Wales and Scotland, there have come into being what have been termed nationalist sub-cultures. For members of these significant minorities (perhaps five to seven per cent of the voting age population in Wales, between ten and twelve per cent in Scotland), nationalism has become a major element in their view of the world.

As a process, except in times of political breakdown or in such commercialized forms as fashion, advertizing, or rock music, cultural innovation amd refinement is normally carried on through a social movement. Such a movement works at two levels. On the one hand, it becomes an organizational home and a fundamental frame of reference for a circle of insiders: those for whom participation in the movement becomes a focal aspect of life. On the other hand, the movement operates at the level of ideas, serving to transmit and circulate new values and concepts in an informal and diffuse manner throughout the wider society. In a directly political sense, the ability of Welsh nationalism to attract mass electoral support has been limited. However, at this less specific, less focussed level, nationalism has had considerable impact.

For most ordinary citizens, Scottish and Welsh identity are rather peripheral aspects of their daily lives. For the members of the nationalist sub-culture, national identity has become a definitive element in their relations with the world at large. Similarly, nationalist ideology has become an organizing principle for their perceptions of the surrounding world. Further, at the level of the elite and intelligentsia in the two countries, those who are most likely to be engaged in processes of cultural production and decision-making, the national idea has percolated to a considerable depth. In education, current affairs journalism and television, drama and literature, as well as in certain aspects of local government administration, the Scottish and Welsh dimensions have taken on a new importance since the 1960s. In Wales, this is particularly noticeable, with the continuing growth of Welsh language education, and the success of the campaign for a Welsh-language television channel.

Among minority nationalist movements, like the Scots, the Welsh occupy a middle position. There has been sufficient space to allow for the creation of new movements, which have taken full advantage of the opportunities available. However, the breadth and depth of their popular appeal has been limited by the very openness of the political space in which they must operate. Thus it has not proved difficult for non-nationalist parties to co-opt or obscure the position of their nationalist opponents.

Conclusions

In the earlier discussion of the process of the "rationalisation" of social life, the implications of the disjunctions within the cultures of advanced industrial society were sketched out. To develop the earlier sketch in a little more detail will facilitate the placing of minority nationalism, especially in Wales and Scotland, in broader perspective.

As Ernest Gellner (1974) and Daniel Bell (1970) have argued, what we might term the "organisational culture" of advanced industrial society is characterised by the application of what Weber termed "formal rationality". The realms of science, the law, public administration and complex social and economic organisations are detached from the realm of everyday life. Consequently, the culture of the advanced industrial state lacks internal inconsistency. More than this, within it, there coexist modes of thought and codes of language which are diametrically opposed to one another.

The culture of rationality, formidable though it may be, provides no moral guidelines for the practices of everyday life. Yet, at the same time, the cognitive power of science and rational thought is such as to undermine the security of a society which lacks an alternative cultural code of sufficient coherence and depth to stand against it. As a result, ordinary life and leisure has a certain provisional or interim character to it (Gellner, 1974 : 198; Giddens, 1981 : 154).

With the development of the modern industrial economy and the modes of work associated with it, as Durkheim noted, the normative integration of work and social life has broken down. A large part of life has become routinized, but has also come to lack either a moral or a rational content. As secularization and routinazation have advanced, so they have eroded tradition. In the process, it appears that the "materials" from which new authoritative customs and mores might be constructed have been destroyed.

In such a society, both personal and collective identities are hard to form. Citizenship is a given rather than an active status. Much of life is guided by habit and routine, not by authoritative values and a sense of purpose. In these circumstances, and under favourable conditions, people may become readily available for mobilization by political movements, whose status is in keeping with the times. However, given the lack of depth of the culture, the deauthorization of cultural symbols, and the growing cynicism towards the political process, such movements are unlikely to succeed in converting large numbers of voters or adherents into committed partisans.

In terms of theories of cultural change, the phenomenon of minority nationalism in Western Europe draws attention to the dangers of assuming that culture is a direct response to, or a reflection of, social and economic structure. The new prominence of the politics of ethnic identity within Western states is one result of economic and political change. It is not, however, a necessary result, and its development, along with its somewhat ephemeral quality, underscores the importance of understanding culture and the development of interpretations of reality as part of a dynamic process of change, where individuals and groups possess considerable latitude for action in assigning new meanings to old forms. The significance of their doing so, however, is restricted by the very disintegration of the culture which makes innovation so characteristic a feature of our time.

CHAPTER 14

THE SOCIOLOGY OF EDUCATION AND WALES

Catrin Roberts

Despite the fact that education in Wales would appear to cry out for attention from sociologists since it represents the interplay of the structural, the ideological and the cultural, its accorded analysis is limited. However perhaps this is not too surprising if we take the view that the concerns of an English sociology must, by definition, be very different from those of a Welsh sociology. By this, I mean that the former has rarely had occasion to focus on issues such as domination, exploitation, ideological and cultural control and has been concerned to concentrate on class-based inequality as the central sociological variable. On the other hand, the impetus given to the development of a distinct Welsh sociology by recent work deriving from non-English sociology (c.f. inter alia, Hechter 1975; Williams, 1978; Rees and Rees, 1980) has allowed it to dispense with the traditional orientations of English sociology, and begin to look at inequality in Wales in far more subtle ways than merely regarding it as another facet of class, geographical or spatial inequality.[1]

As far as a distinctive sociology of Welsh education is concerned, the possibility was effectively negated for many years by the normative concerns of pre-1971 British sociology of education. Since the preoccupation of the latter was with the ideal of equality of educational opportunity, and the achievement of this ideal through the equalisation of access to all forms of educational provision, then the case of Wales was relatively unproblematic. A comparatively large number of grammar school places had traditionally been made available in Wales, so that the proportion of working class pupils taking up grammar school places was always higher than in England. Also, in recent years, the problem of lack of opportunity for working class pupils was somewhat appeased in Wales since 'natural' comprehensive schools already existed in many areas. The small numbers of pupils within the catchment areas of these schools was insufficient to support separate grammar and secondary modern schools. However, although the concerns of traditional British sociology of education were not mirrored in Wales, and although a distinctive Welsh sociology of education has been slow to develop, there is a wealth of commentary on education in Wales which has taken as its theme that which clearly differentiates education in Wales from education in England : the Welsh language.

Three main sources contribute to the contemporary analysis of education in Wales, reflecting official government reports, social historical accounts of the development of education in Wales, and the more recent spate of feasibility research into bilingual education. Although these sources are separated into three strands, it is as well to bear in mind that this is an analytical convenience which is not necessarily reflected in reality. Indeed, there is a strong case to be made for the unity of the three sources in terms of their approach since they overwhelmingly tend to consider the relationship between education and social mobility in terms of the individual rather than seeking explanation of educational arrangements in terms of socio-structural variables.

The main difficulty surrounding official government reports on education in Wales is one which has been identified as 'for Wales, see England', namely that educational policy is formulated for England and Wales as a unity. In the past, this has tended to restrict the amount of discussion given to the specific state of education in Wales. This is particularly true of the nineteenth century (with the notorious exception of the 1847 Report of the Royal Commission) where, for instance, a Report entitled 'The State of Popular Education in England' (Education Commission, 1861) actually also included a discussion of education in Wales. The position has eased somewhat in the twentieth century, especially in the wake of the establishment of a separate Welsh Education Office, so that, for instance, the Plowden Report on primary education (CACE, England, 1967) had its Welsh counterpart in the Gittins Report (CACE, Wales, 1967). However, the beginning of this century was characterised by few reports relating specifically to education in Wales. Where these did exist, they tended, even then, to refer to the Welsh language as an anomaly (see Ministry of Education, 1927; CACE, Wales, 1953). In general terms, the theoretical underpinnings of the government publications discussing education in Wales reveal the same bias as their English counterparts, namely the proposal of policy based on a traditional individual liberal analysis of the role of education in society.[2] Perhaps this in itself is not too surprising, but the hegemony of this particular tradition is further enhanced by the research into bilingualism pursued by linguists, psychologists and educationalists in Wales since the 1920s. The difficulty with this research tradition is that although it concentrates on the very important question of the relationship of individual bilingualism to intelligence and achievement (see, inter alia, Saer, 1922, 1928, 1932; Saer et.al., 1924; Smith, 1923; Jones, 1949, 1950, 1955, 1960, 1966; Barke, 1933; Barke, et.al., 1938), it has not been sufficiently supplemented by considerations of the societal effects of bilingualism, and particularly the associated question of the differential status and prestige of Welsh and English. Current research work in the area has unfortunately tended to consolidate rather than compensate this deficiency, reflecting a concern with the acquisition of bilingualism in children (Harrison, et.al., 1981) and the elaboration and implementation of programmes for the teaching of Welsh as a second language (Dodson, 1962, 1966; Dodson, et.al., 1968; School Council, 1972, 1978). However, the seminal work of Lewis (1974, 1978, 1981) has contributed to analysing the neglected area of the societal effects of bilingualism primarily in terms of a comparative perspective, and another notable contribution is provided by the work of Sharp et.al. (1973) which attempts to relate school children's attitudes to the two languages to variables such as geographical location, sex, age, social class, ability and mother tongue.

Turning to social history as a source of information about the nature of education in Wales, we are immediately confronted with the issue of whether a specific Welsh history exists, or is possible. The paradoxical nature of this issue is evident today in the schools of Wales. Current emphases on local studies and area studies within the curriculum reflect a growing concern throughout the latter half of the twentieth century that schools become more involved in the communities that house them. The idea that educational institutions are not atomised entities which are geographically dispersed in an arbitrary manner is not new, but its embodiment in specific curricular practices is a recent development, and one which raises significant epistemological issues. If the curriculum is to give official recognition to local history as a valid area of study, it reflects a concomitant recognition by the established hegemony that local areas have some degree of autonomy of their own. In other words, this development involves recognition that 'national'[3] history may not be the same as 'local' history, and consequently that 'national' interests and concerns may not always reflect 'local' interests and concerns. Indeed, if this line of recognition is followed through, then it involves an awareness that 'national' and 'local' interests may in fact be opposed to each other.

This has particular significance with reference to the development of a specific history of Wales. Traditionally, the history taught in Welsh schools was British history, which consisted of the history of England and Wales as a unit, and in practice tended to reduce to the history of England, with very limited reference to

Wales. The implication of this practice appears to be that, firstly, there is no specific Welsh history and, secondly, that Wales is, anyway, a part of England. Thus the possibility of generating a particular 'Welsh' standpoint deriving from an adequate understanding of the historical processes which culminated in the emergence of modern Wales is effectively precluded. The potency of history as an ideological tool is a much publicised phenomenon (c.f. Whitty and Young, 1976), and recently its significance both in the making and remaking of an effective dominant culture (Williams, 1973) and in generating counter-hegemony through the specific agency of the organic intellectuals (Gramsci, 1971) has received considerable attention. If the latter argument is accepted, then it provides one explanation for the fact that the development of a Welsh history which is substantively different from an English history and which expresses a distinctive approach to its substantive concerns has taken so long to materialise. Another contributory cause may be that the existence of a specific Welsh history (or English history, for that matter) was a white elephant, given the tendency of historians to argue the existence of a value-free, objective and, therefore, universally applicable historiography.

Thus, it should not be too surprising that until recently the limited reference to the history of Wales derived from descriptive historical analyses which were traditional in reflecting dominant class and cultural concerns. It is not that 'nationalist' (Morgan, 1981) or 'socialist' (Smith, 1980) histories of Wales have not been written, but that they have been rare, and their sanction for the purposes of education rarer, in comparison with more traditional and conventional historical interpretations.

It is in this sense that the paradox engendered by contemporary British developments in the curriculum is exposed. On the one hand is the inclination to regard a historical knowledge of the area in which one lives as desirable, and its inclusion within the curriculum as legitimate. On the other hand, it may be that such a knowledge has far-reaching ideological implications. It is with reference to the latter that we can argue that 'legitimate' Welsh history in schools has been tempered by drawing upon a liberal ideology with its associated emphasis upon the individual, the role of diffusion in overcoming isolation and parochialism, and the integration of a society devoid of structural differentiation.

Since sociologists must use historical analysis, for the sociology of education, or any sociology for that matter, must take into account the historically and situationally specific character of its phenomena, the documentation of education in historical accounts in both Welsh and English provides an invaluable source. However, whilst emphasising the present 'system's' nineteenth century antecedents, there has been a tendency to associate education in Wales predominantly with religion and language to the exclusion of a consideration of its relationship to economic and structural features (see, for example, Jones, 1981). An exacerbating feature of this tendency is the way in which education is often described as a 'given', the desire for it being almost implicitly assumed to be primordial and therefore not really to be explained in terms of existing social structure, and thus not really within the province of social scientific enquiry. It is a tendency borne out in popular references to the Welsh as a nation of education lovers (see, for example, Thomas, 1973), suggesting an endemic quality of educability in the national 'make-up'. The following quotation provides an apt example of this type of reference:

> The Welsh have, for example, traditionally regarded themselves as having an unusually high respect for education, which has often been taken to mean that they set special store not only by the academic but by the cultured individual (CACE, Wales, 1967 : 2).

Whilst accepting that sociologists certainly have many lessons to learn from history and historians, the quest for causality or real explanation makes much of the historical material frustrating, and surely points to a re-interpretation of the existing data within an explanatory theoretical framework.[4]

Having argued the need for a coherent theoretical framework to explain educational practice within Wales, the next question to be addressed is clearly that of determining which theoretical categories are to be used, and why. It is at this juncture that we might usefully turn to some of the theory generated by recent developments in 'main-stream' sociology of education with a view to evaluating the pertinence of research directions indicated by such theory for analysing the Welsh situation.

It is now self-evident to most sociologists of education that despite presenting itself as an empirical, and therefore atheoretical, enterprise, traditional sociology of education was heavily predicated on the theoretical underpinnings of positivistic structural-functionalism. As such, its validity was open to challenge by the logical criticism which challenged structural-functionalism within the parent discipline of sociology, namely the teleology of explaining social phenomena in terms of societal needs. In practice, however, this challenge was not forthcoming in the sociology of education until the publication of a collection of papers edited by Michael Young in 1971 (Young, 1971). In revealing the weakness in traditional perspectives on the sociology of education, this publication effectively provided a radical restatement of the aims of the sociology of education achieved by raising the question, so long considered non-problematic, of : what is to be educated? The nature of the problem thus shifts to what counts as valid knowledge, and how is this knowledge organised and made available in society. Young's thesis is that what is regarded as knowledge is a social construction. The implication of this for the sociology of education becomes one of directing its enquiry into the social organisation of knowledge in educational institutions. In practice, this brought the school, the classroom and the curriculum firmly to the fore as areas of educational research.

Durkheim, Marx and Weber were concerned with the social organisation of knowledge rather than the sociology of the educational system, and consequently it is paradoxical that the sociology of education and the sociology of knowledge evolved as two distinct areas of enquiry. Young's model serves to collapse the two, with important theoretical consequences. If the sociology of education is to treat knowledge as:

> . . . . neither absolute nor arbitrary, but as available sets of meanings which in any context do not merely emerge but are collectively given (Young, 1971 : 36)

then it also becomes the task of sociological enquiry to define the legitimising categories, to investigate the doctrine of control.

Although Marx wrote little specifically about education, his proposition of the infrastructural and superstructural nature of capitalist society by implication has the question of who defines and legitimises knowledge at its core. Thus Marx's topographical metaphor is central to a theory of culture in which the infrastructure reflects a society's productive activities which, in particular structural relations, constitute the foundation of all other activities, termed superstructural. Some degree of a causal relationship exists in the base-superstructure relationship; the one is determining, the other determined; the former representing the real relations of production, the latter the reflection or reproduction of this reality in social relations.

Applying an orthodox Marxist critique to traditional sociology of education challenges the assumptions of that approach on the grounds of their inability to express the nature of education or knowledge, as in any way prefigurated or determined by the economic infrastructure of a given society. For Marx, knowledge incorporates not only the 'formal' knowledge transmitted by educational institutions, but also the more pragmatic knowledge of everyday life, and those aspects of it which can loosely be referred to as 'culture'. The traditional assumption of education as an enclosed, encapsulated system within 'developed' countries, and the separation of knowledge from day to day existence through the establishment of institutions and organisations specifically concerned with the 'education process' becomes questionable.

This assumption has also been challenged by the concept of the hidden curriculum, which encompasses the non-academic but educationally significant consequences of schooling that occur continuously and at all levels, but which are not normally made explicit, factors including the inculcation of values and dispositions, discipline, obedience, manners and political socialisation. What Marxism suggests is that these factors which were previously considered by-products of the schooling process, have developed into the primary exigency of the education system. In other words, in an increasingly complex technological society, the social control function of education has become 'hidden', since its overt expression would be incompatible with the liberal, social-democratic ideology pervading British education. Nevertheless, it is argued (Apple, 1979, inter alia) that social control, as a legitmising agency for the activities of the base, through schooling, is the single most important function of education being the agency for perpetuating existing class relations and ultimately the status quo.

The liberal ideology of education, characterised by calls for educational expansion and education for all, and assuming the desirability and the possibility of redressing social inequality by equalising educational opportunity, is consequently also called into question. If the primary function of education is to socialise into an already existing and pre-determined system, then social inequality cannot be overcome by access to an educational system that has already internalised the inequalities inherent in the basic relations of production. Education is seen as reproducing and reinforcing already existing relations of production, and thus as an agency for legitimising the status quo and its attendant inequality, rather than as an agency for the liberation of human potential. This contradicts the third traditional assumption, namely of education as a source of social change through its role in determining the level of technological knowledge and rate of economic growth of a given society. Marxists argue (c.f. Bowles and Gintis, 1976, inter alia) that the direction of the relationship is the other way around: education is a conservative force serving to reproduce the social hierarchies of the class structure.

Although Young's (1971) 'new directions' was related to the Marxist indictment of conventional perspectives on education, in the sense that he also argued for a fundamental questioning of the taken-for-granted assumptions and towards an awareness of the social construction of knowledge, the work generated by his rethinking was far from complementary to the Marxist school. Young, drawing on contemporaneous developments in sociology, derived his theoretical stance not so much from Marx as from the phenomenology of Schutz and the symbolic interactionism of Mead. Thus, central importance in his work was attached to the individual's construction of his or her own reality, and his/her subsequent interpretation of this reality. Practical research work capitalising on this particular theoretical stance involved taking actors' accounts as the only 'true' accounts of educational reality (c.f. Esland, 1971; Keddie, 1971, inter alia). In many ways this has a basic similarity to the modus operandi of the older cultural anthropology which was concerned to see the world through the eyes of those being studied. However, a distinction is occasioned by the fact that the analytic unit within cultural anthropology was the collectivity, the group of people sharing the same 'culture'. Within phenomenology, in contrast, the analytic unit becomes the individual. This is problematic for a sociological explanation which has traditionally been viewed as an exercise in generalisation to facilitate predictive outcomes, which involves the articulation of causal relationships between phenomena.

If phenomenology adopts the individual as its analytic unit, then it follows that the individual's construction of reality becomes 'true' in a philosophical sense. Marxists, on the other hand, would argue that the construction of individuals' reality may constitute a false consciousness. Blum (1971) clearly makes this point when discussing philosophical revisions of the corpus of knowledge in order to achieve 'true' knowledge. The main criticism of phenomenology from this position is that its concentration on the individual's reporting of his/her own reality prevents it taking into account the fact that individuals may have their reality constrained and defined by their position in society. The possibility of action which is based upon group mobilisation or collective consciousness is precluded. Thus, as far as sociology is concerned, what phenomenology tends to accomplish is an explanation of reality which ignores reference to collective constraints and conflicts. From a Marxist viewpoint, this can be summarised by the following:

> .... it is also true that any society has a specific organisation, a specific structure, and that the principles of this organisation and structure can be seen as directly related to certain social intentions, intentions by which we define the society, intentions which in all our experience have been the rule of a particular class (Williams, 1973 : 5).

The lack of consideration of issues of conflict and collective mobilisation and, implicitly, of power relations, has also been characteristic of much of the work concerned to analyse the nature of ethnicity. Ethnicity has invariably been viewed as a primordial attachment of the individual rather than as a means by which individuals may be mobilised in order to further certain group interests. Thus it is hardly surprising that any consideration of the adaptive significance of the ethnic group, and the structural features of ethnic group survival, should have been ignored despite the evident fact that most societies are bi-ethnic or multi-ethnic rather than mono-ethnic. Within the work on ethnicity, four major approaches are discernible (Williams, 1978).

The first approach is concerned to follow the fate of non-indigenous ethnic minorities in a host society in terms of integration with the host society. The process of integration is regarded as one of ethnic acculturation along a continuum, with the two poles of the continuum representing primitive non-alignement with the host society due to insufficient exposure at one end, through to the ultimate point of assimilation into the host society at the other end. There is a certain evolutionary inevitability about this view of ethnicity; any associated change is seen as an automatic 'shedding' of indigenous cultural traits in the face of increased interaction with the host society, and the pressure to adopt the cultural markers of the host society. Failure to do so, as reflected in the persistence of minority ethnicity, is explained as either individual backwardness or as the inability of the ethnic group to see the undoubted desirability of 'progress' through alignment with the majority ethnic group and the adoption of opportunities for individual mobility.

The second approach concentrates upon the adaptive significance of ethnicity, thus seemingly solving some of the problems associated with the above-mentioned acculturation studies. Again, however, there is a failure to explain why ethnic group closure is or is not exerted, together with a failure to take into account the development of ethnic group institutions and the degree of salience of these institutions.

The third approach, transactional analysis, focusses upon the individual, upon how the individual operates or fails to operate ethnicity in line with the cognitive model of the ethnic boundary held. Although this approach has the advantage of pointing to ethnicity as a dynamic rather than a static phenomenon, in the sense that individuals exercise a rational choice in operationalising it, it falls prey to criticisms previously made about the inability of approaches focussing upon individual action to reveal collective sources of conflict and action.

Finally, the fourth approach is associated with structural analysis. Inexorably linked to the tenets of structural-functionalism, this approach holds that the ethic of increasing technological industrialisation is incompatible with the persistence of ethnicity and ethnic heterogeneity. Ethnic adherence is seen as at odds with the rational orientation of technological society, the claim is that increased communication within industrialised settings must give rise to ethnic homogeneity. Paradoxically, it is ironic that even in advanced capitalistic societies, ethnicity persists, and shows very little signs of disappearing. It is also ironic that ethnicity features as a major source of fission and division within these societies. Indigenous ethnic groups continue to be involved in widespread liberation struggles, whilst immigrant ethnic groups pose a paramount 'problem' for social order. Thus it appears that to consider ethnicity from the point of view of consensus is to fail to explain either its origin or its persistence.

The alternative perspective of ethnicity as a source of conflict poses its own problems. Central among these problems is the question of the relationship of ethnicity and class as dimensions of inequality. If the ethnic group is viewed in Weberian terms as a status group, then seemingly it can be said to mobilise individuals across class lines, as another element in social stratification. However, this entails the separation of class and ethnicity as analytic categories, but this is a separation which is not borne out in reality, since in practice there is clearly a dynamic relationship between the two dimensions. The poverty of Marx's analysis of ethnicity has resulted in neo-Marxists claiming that ethnicity should be anlysed solely in terms of social class, so that ethnic consciousness reduces to a form of false consciousness. The unhelpfulness and rigidity of the Marxist approach in this respect lies in its inability to cope with certain obvious problems such as the absence of a necessary congruence between class and ethnicity. Not all members of ethnic groups enter the class structure at the same point.

What the above argument seeks to indicate is that whilst the relevance of class should not be ignored, its primacy over ethnicity should equally not be presented in an unproblematic way. Class and ethnicity require to be discussed in tandem. In the meantime, it should be borne in mind that ethnicity may serve as a conscious agency for the mobilisation of group members in the expression of economic interests which may be very different from those of the majority ethnic group. In this sense, the two dimensions of class and ethnicity are not mutually exclusive, since the existence of ethnic groups does not preclude the existence of social class. What is important is to remove ethnicity from the traditional terrain of structural-functionalism, to cease analysing it as a 'given' and view it as a variable, and to introduce it to mainstream sociological analysis as a much-ignored but highly significant aspect of stratification. In order to achieve this, we must look at ethnicity in relation to other analytic concepts such as class, culture, infrastructure and superstructure. Only thus will ethnicity be brought into a central position in the explanation of the social formation in much the same way as education is discussed.

This sharpening of focus with regard to education was achieved by increasing interest in Marxism in Britain during the 1970s. The growth of the New Left and the increasing availability of European Marxist texts in English has generated a number of critiques from within sociology of the traditional view of schooling, attaching central importance to the problem of relating the institutions and ideologies of the superstructure to the economic base in the formulation of a theory of social control. There is, however, a continuing controversy about how this is best achieved, a controversy reflecting varying interpretations of the degree of causality exerted by the base on the superstructure. In part, this largely derives from differing interpretations of Marx deriving from the failure of Marx to extend his idea of social being determining social consciousness to a systematic analysis of the education process of his time comparable to his analysis of the economy.

In a discussion of some of the revisions of Marxist cultural theory which attempt to accommodate the fact that in practice the reality of the base is seldom directly reflected, imitated or reproduced in the superstructure, Williams (1973) outlines some of the notions put forward to try and explain this. The notion of time-lags, of various technical complications and of indirectness, was first introduced in explanation. A more fundamental reconsideration gives rise to the concept of mediation, in which something more than simple reflection or reproduction, indeed something which may be essentially very different from either, actively occurs. The current sophistication involves homologous structures, where the similarity between base and superstructural process may not be directly apparent but where there is an essential correspondence of structures discernible by analysis.

Williams, (1973) suggests that these refinements to the concept of superstructure are, however, relevant only in combination with a revised notion of the base, the latter being in his view the more fundamental of the two concepts, while also being the neglected concept. He argues that the base has come to be considered in essentially uniform and static ways, and that this is a false consideration for:

> . . . . while a particular stage of development can be discovered and made precise by analysis, it is never in practice either uniform or static (Williams, 1973 : 17).

He suggests a revaluation of the base away from the notion of a fixed economic state and towards the specific dynamic activities of men in real social and economic relationships, and a revaluation of the superstructure in the direction of a related range of cultural practices and away from a directly reflected content.

It is stressed that this sophistication must not be at the expense of sacrificing the notion of intention in society. Williams is dismissive of theories such as Lukacs's, which view the social formation as a totality, and thus are unable to attribute a superstructural element to areas of social and political thought, law, institutions and ideological activity. The danger is that these may be hailed as having universal validity without the qualification that they also legitimise the domination of a particular class.

Of course, if we are to agree with the Marxist formulation of a dialectical base-superstructure relationship, it becomes incumbent upon us to consider the mechanisms by which reproduction, in all its various forms and guises, is ensured. It is to this end that the concept of ideology is introduced as the legitimising agency. The debate surrounding the nature and function of ideology is particularly relevant, since it contains the key to the 'split' between the 'deterministic' Marxists and the 'humanistic' Marxists.

'Deterministic' Marxists stress the superstructural origins of ideology, its merely secondary derivation, and thus, since education is closely linked with the transmission of ideology, view education as having little or no potential for change which is unsolicited by the economic base (c.f. inter alia, Bowles and Gintis, 1976; Sharp and Green, 1975; Althusser, 1971). In contrast, the school of 'humanistic' Marxism, drawing upon the work of Gramsci (1971), views education as a potential site for conflict and change. This may be achieved through challenge to hegemony, which is the extension of ideology, to represent something far more fundamental and all-pervasive and which, by being more fundamental, acquires the character of being the potential arena of class struggle (c.f. inter alia, Apple, 1979; CCCS, 1981; Freire, 1977). The implication of the concept of ideological hegemony for education is significant. For whilst education may still be viewed as superstructural in the sense of being secondary to an economic analysis, its role as prop to the transmission of ideological hegemony suggests that it is no mechanistic process which ensures the legitimisation of the reproduction of the relations of production but a subtle and complex process which justifies a great deal more investigation.

It is to this end that current discussion within the sociology of education has centred on relating economic production to the key processes of social and cultural reproduction. Amongst the pioneers were Bowles and Gintis (1976), who sought to show how the economic system in the U.S.A. shaped the nature and content of eduction and thus ensured the reproduction of the social class structure and dominant cultural practices of that country. Indeed their analysis suggests that this process occurs through a reproduction of consciousness, of specific types of dispositions, through schooling. Their attempts to isolate the mechanisms of reproduction have met with a good deal of criticism and this is hardly surprising given the crudity of the model with which they worked. Their major shortcoming was to suggest too close a 'fit' between the activities of production and schooling, a 'fit' reminiscent of earlier work in the structural - functionalist tradition (c.f. inter alia, Hopper, 1971) which allowed no room for endogenous change and accorded education no autonomy from the base. A further criticism concerned the deterministic and passive ontology adopted by Bowles and Gintis which regarded man as a mechanism dictated to and moulded by the requirements of production, and thus negated the possibility of human conflict.

The work of Bourdieu (1973, 1976; Bourdieu and Passeron, 1977) has also deployed the concepts of social and cultural reproduction in trying to explain the social significance of education. Bourdieu attributes central importance to the school as the primary agency in the conversion of economic capital to cultural capital in contemporary society. His thesis rests upon the case that it is no longer sufficient to be born into the class which owns economic capital: this cannot now be sufficient to guarantee the perpetuation of that class's monopoly on capital as it once was. The economic capital with which the individual is born, in the sense of wealth, prestige and status, is converted into a scholastic heritage of cultural capital, the habitus, by means of the highly selective nature of schooling. It is for this reason that Bordieu regards the school as a highly inegalitarian institution whose sole purpose is to perpetuate inequality through selecting for certain qualities that are structurally denied to the greater proportion of the school population, a process referred to as 'symbolic violence'.

One of the difficulties with Bourdieu's work is his use of the term 'culture'. In his theoretical work, culture is identified with a symbolic scheme, representing the values and mores associated with the dominant class. In his empirical work, however, Bourdieu operationalises the concept to refer to the institutions of 'high' culture, or the institutions concerned with the articulation of this 'high' culture, such as theatres, concerts, cinemas and museums (see Bourdieu, 1973). What remains problematic is that whilst access to this 'high' culture, or the institutions concerned with the articulation of this 'high' culture, may be selective in the way Bourdieu suggests, how do other aspects of culture, such as working class culture, for instance, relate to the central process of dominant cultural reproduction? Confusion seems here to centre on the concept of culture, as indeed seems to have been the case since the time when culture initially assumed importance as an explanatory social variable within cultural anthropology. There appear to be three major usages of the concept of culture, all three of which are often to be found in use within the same piece of work (Williams and Roberts, 1982). Firstly, there is culture as it relates to behaviour or life-style, embodied in social customs, practices and traditions. Secondly, culture is used to denote the rules that govern behaviour, in the sense of systems of values, beliefs and moralities. Thirdly, it is sometimes taken to refer to world view, and it is in this context that ideology becomes most pertinent as the agency which serves to structure and define world view. It appears that Bourdieu's conceptualisation of culture involves drawing primarily upon the second usage in his theoretical work, and the first usage in his empirical work. What this achieves, by implication, is a view of sub-cultures simply as passive adaptive responses to a poverty of access to dominant culture. Thus, Bourdieu's analysis is unable to explain the existence of 'minority' forms of culture, since his usage of the term culture denies any dimension of conflict. Effectively, this means that working class sub-culture, or any other alternative culture, is automatically reduced to a form of false consciousness.[5]

There are also problems with Bourdieu's use of the terms social and cultural reproduction. It is not clear whether these processes should be taken to refer to the reproduction of culture and social structure from generation to generation, indicating a historical process, or whether reproduction is to be viewed in the more Marxist sense as the process involved in the translation of the economic relations of the base into cultural and social relations. Whatever the nature of the process, it appears that culture is discussed as the independent variable, so that cultural reproduction ultimately acts as a facilitator of social reproduction in the sense of legitimising the perpetuation of the social structure. Thus social and cultural reproduction are assumed to be essentialy congruent processes, they are assumed to work in tandem at all times. Consequently, the possibility of social and cultural reproduction operating in opposition to each other, does not arise. This is clearly an inadequate framework for the description of situations characterised by the existence of minority cultures. This reflects a general tendency within sociology to discuss social structure in terms of class without reference to culture and ethnicity. Where the latter concepts are considered, they are viewed simply as legitimising agencies having no autonomy of their own and thus are denied as potential sites of conflict and change.

In the above respect, Bourdieu's view of education may be interpreted as characterised by a pessimism and determinism equal with that of Althusser (1971). Both view education as an agency of cultural legitimisation, 'in Althusser's case, fettered by ideology' and possessing a rigid and inevitable dependence upon the economic base. Education is simply the handmaiden of economic reproduction, a completely 'determined' process which is denied the ability to challenge existing relations in any way.

It is this debate concerning the relationship of education, culture and ideology to class, the degree of autonomy allowed to moments of the superstructure, that marks the relevance of these recent developments in the sociology of education to explaining contemporary educational practices in Wales. We can argue that it was not until the sociology of education developed the concept of 'culture' in an analytic sense that a comprehensive explanation of education in Wales was made possible. Yet this is a potential form of explanation that remains unrealised by and large. It is clearly far simpler to apply such an explanation to the historical emergence of mass schooling in Wales and the role of the Welsh language and culture in that schooling[6] than it is to explain current practice in terms of the interplay of class and culture. This is probably a consequence of the difficulty of translating a body of fairly abstract theoretical literature into a series of concrete research objectives. Nevertheless, precedents for such initiatives are now beginning to emerge albeit outside Wales, with the recent growth of interest in 'culturalist' forms of explanation which are concerned to analyse specific cultural practices as 'lived' reality rather than as the abstractions of some prior social class reality.[7]

Another essentially important area which has been entirely neglected in the Welsh situation is the curriculum. Bernstein's seminal work on the classification and framing of educational knowledge (Bernstein, 1977), coupled with recent developments in the sociology of education in the U.S.A., has highlighted the way in which the selction and organisation of knowledge is related to societal principles of social control. If, as neo-Marxist sociology of education suggests, education is concerned to purvey particular views of the world and if, as Bernstein suggests, an essential aspect of this process concerns the definition and distribution of knowledge, then clearly there are pungent ramifications for analysing the curriculum in Wales. If this is then coupled with the realisation that the curriculum in Wales is characterised _a priori_ by the existence of two distinct languages and views of the world, the emergence of the curriculum as a central area of investigation and explanation needs no further justification.

To conclude, what this paper has sought to argue is that education in Wales is a heavily under-researched area. The little research available has all too often subscribed to the notion of education as an unquestioned public and individual utility thus leading to analyses of education which obviate the need to view it in terms of its structural relationships to other aspects of the social formation, particularly the organisation of production. It was suggested that this situation was in part fostered by the inability of traditional sociology of education to move beyond a theoretical reliance on a mechanistic theory of stratification in social class terms. However, it was argued that current developments within the sociology of education and cultural studies have generated new theoretical insights by seeking to reconcile and synthesise class and culture to provide a dynamic account of the parameters of education. It is clear that, in the abstract, at least, these developments could provide a far more rigorous framework for the analysis of education in Wales. The problem, however, is whether this potential will be realised given the limited number of research workers focussing on education in Wales. As a cautionary note in conclusion, we might usefully refer to an unheeded statement written almost thirty years ago with reference to the analysis of education and language in Wales:

> Research of a more formal character requires to be undertaken too. In the first place, there are problems that belong to the sociology of bilingualism. We have seen how difficult it is to enumerate or to assess the factors involved in the bilingual situation, and it has been pressed home to us by the experience of this enquiry that the analysis of social forces working for and against bilingualism, ... are among the first projects to be undertaken. This work, too, as we have shown, has been attempted elsewhere, but no formula that is approprite to other countries is suitable to Wales without considerable modification (CACE, Wales, 1953 : 70).

Notes

Chapter 1

1. It is axiomatic that the concept of region pre-supposes the existence of a totality of which the region is a subordinate part. The place from which the discourse on the region generally emanates is the centre of this totality. Within this discourse in Britain the tendency is to make Wales and Scotland co-terminus with the English regions thereby elevating England to something more than either Wales or Scotland. Since England is seen to be a nation this makes Scotland and Wales something less than nations. It means that a discourse on region and the discourse on nation emanating from Wales as a place of power are incompatible. This much is evident in the use of an English county name rather than 'Welcome to England' as one enters England from Wales or Scotland, the effect being to place Wales and Scotland at the same level as an English county. See Williams, (In press, b).

2. This is a strange question in that if it can be asked then Wales must surely exist! For a discussion of 'why is Wales?' which is an issue of theory as discourse see Williams n.d. and for a discussion of 'what is Wales?' see Williams, (In Press, b).

3. There is a reason to believe that the non-Welsh private sector bourgeoisie associated with 'regional development' is practising similar selective ethnic recruitment from among the non-Welsh in-migrants.

Chapter 2

1. This paper was previously delivered to a Day School held at Coleg Harlech in February, 1980. Readers seeking more detailed data on sources, a fuller bibliography and bibliographic material are referred to Michael (1981). I am grateful to the following for their readiness to share knowledge of A. W. Ashby - David Bateman, Emrys Bowen, Janes Morgan Jones, the late J. R. E. Phillips and Mr and Mrs E. Llewellyn Harry, two important sources on the associations discussed by the journal _Welsh Outlook_ and _Welsh Housing and Development Yearbook_, whilst essential background reading is provided by Stead (1980) and Smith (1980). Finally, my gratitude is extended to Neil Evans for advice given to an inept intruder into the field of Welsh history.

2. In addition to the Report, see Ashby & Anderson (1974).

3. The Welsh Agricultural Co-operative Movement is one of the successes in the checkered history of social economic movements in the British Isles. Directly inspired by the delegation of Welsh County Councillors, visiting Plunkett and A. E. in Ireland early in the century, it survived where its English counterpart perished. By the 1920s it was encountering major administrative and commercial difficulties. After Ashby contracted to provide from his department expertise in accounting, research, education, under his astute guidance, enthusiastic membership never looked back.

4. For critiques of Rees and his followers, see Day & Fitton (1975) and Day (1979). On Owen Edwards' thesis see Jones (1971).

Chapter 3

1. Of course, there are still substantial obstacles and the need for much care and caution. Some discussion of the factors as well as more detailed guidance on the basis for the figures is given in Williams and Boyns (1977).

2. Evidence of John Griffiths in Report of Select Committee 1886.

Chapter 4

1. See for example Therborn (1983).

2. This could be read as an argument about '.... discontinuity of the flow of goods and information between the firm and its environment in contrast to the continuity of this flow within the firm' (Murray, 1972 : 216). Murray's argument refers specifically to the peripheral areas in the world system, but may legitimately be transferred to spatially discreet units within large economies. These discontinuities consisting of barriers of 'risk', 'costs of acquiring information', market scale etc., are the spatial manifestation of the deeper contradictions of private enterprise capitalism: the contradiction between the nationality of organisation within the firm and the anarchy which reigns in its external environment.

3. See the relevant data in <u>Welsh Economic Trends</u> and the <u>Digest of Welsh Statistics</u>.

4. A distinction must be drawn between the multiples which are usually owned and controlled by the United Kingdom or overseas firms and the smaller independents.

5. The greatest linkage arose in the clothing, automobiles and engineering sectors.

6. This proportion is arrived at by recklessly treating the monopolistic sector as manufacturing establishments employing over a hundred, plus all overseas owned establishments and central government employment.

Chapter 6

1. I am endebted to Professor Maurice Broady for his comments on an earlier draft of this paper. Most of the fieldwork for the study of in-migration to Newtown was carried out by members of Le Centre de Recherches en Civilisation Britainnique, France. Expenses incurred by the author were covered by a grant from the Pantyfedwen Trust.

Chapter 7

1. This chapter was written before the results of the 1981 Census of Population were available. We would like to thank Phil Cooke, John Urry and Glyn Williams for comments on an earlier version.

2. In effect, we are referring here almost exclusively to the major work of Professor Brinley Thomas.

3. In doing so, we are not adopting the position that the differences between, say, a neo-classical and a Keynesian analysis or a functionalist and a 'social construction' perspective are not real; nor, indeed, that it is not possible to distinguish between them in terms of their theoretical quality and usefulness. Rather, our argument is simply that these differences are irrelevant to the present discussion.

4. In fact, the coal industry was to some extent insulated from the influence of the reserve army in that between 1876 and 1902 wage levels were related directly to the f.o.b. price of coal through the 'sliding scale'. There were, however, numerous disputes over the precise conditions set out in the 'sliding scale'. See Morris and Williams (1960).

5. There is, then, substantial evidence to support the message of Gwyn Thomas' story which has a graveyard in the Rhondda of the depression with tomb-stones showing 'Not dead, but gone to Slough'.

6. Sir Syndham Portal reported : 'At many meetings which I attended I found a measure of resentment that the young and able-bodied should be in necessity of leaving the district to find employment . . . the view was held that the Government should, as an alternative to transference, take any essential steps to obtain control and direction in the allocation of new industries, having regard to the claims of the depressed areas. I am not in agreement with these representations.' (Ministry of Labour, 1933/4)

7. Admittedly, other considerations were significant as well; as, for example, the need to maintain levels of consumption of the goods produced by Department II industries (Carney, Lewis and Hudson, 1977).

8. Caution is necessary because the figures are based on the Registrar General's Mid-year Estimates and 'Net Migration' is simply a residual calculated from the other two columns. Census of Population data is probably more accurate in that migration is measured directly; unfortunately, however, it is very limited in its time-span.

9. Clearly, the story needs to be much more complex than this and certainly needs to take into account the political struggles over fuel policies: see, for example, Francis and Howells (1980).

10. A number of the points which follow have been clarified by Massey (1980).

11. The complexities here are considerable, as it is difficult to sort out the separate effects of occupational and geographical mobility.

Chapter 8

1. Despite the importance of the Masonic Order few studies have managed to make more than passing reference to it. One important exception to this is Margaret Stacy's account at Banbury. Frankenburg (1966 : 170) in summarising this wrote as follows:

   > "The upper Conservative territory is associated with the Chestnut Bowling Club and the Parish Church; the lower with the bowls, the Conservative Club and the British Legion. The members of the Chestnut Bowls are 90% Conservatives, which includes three Conservative ex-Mayors and two Conservative Borough Councillors. It is closely associated with Rotary (a link with the Liberal connection) and the Freemasons.
   >
   > The Gentry and farmers from outside the town are brought into this charmed circle by their association with the sports which is made up of the rugger, squash, cricket, tennis and hunting group. Here again, there are many links with the Freemasons".

   We are not told, however, how many Lodges there were in Banbury.

2. > "The set of which the 'King' was a member is found within the category of 'locals' and 'spiralist-locals'. The group is of particular importance and might be called 'the King's Set'. Through its members it is closely linked to Rotary, the Conservative Party and the Masons. Not only do members of this set meet in a wide range of associations and through their businesses, but they also have other links, for example a number of them live in one particular street in West Banbury. Several go on holiday together . . ." M. Stacey, E. Batstone, C. Bell, A. Murcott (1975).

Chapter 11

1. See particularly his contributions in Y Celt and Y Genhinen.

2. For his views on Kosuth see Y Celt, 7th March, 1890.

3. He also complained about the manner in which the constitution permitted what he regarded as an unwarranted royal interference in the democratic process such as it was.

4. This view is in sharp contrast with that expressed in the Report of the Commission on Education in Wales (1843) where it was claimed that the monoglot Welsh took advantage of his ignorance of English in the law courts to the disadvantage of the justices and judges. The same source claims that it was a knowledge of the Welsh language which restricted the growth of a bourgeoisie in Wales.

Chapter 12

1. This paper is based in part on work carried out during a year of doctoral research in Wales during 1976-77. The author wishes to acknowledge the financial support received during that year from the Social Science Research Council (New York) and the Wenner-Gren Foundation for Anthropological Research.

Chapter 13

1. The first portion of the paper represents a substantial re-working of material originally written in 1976. A version was published in 1978 (Rawkins, 1978). The analysis of culture in the latter part of the paper derives primarily from a paper presented at the Canada/Israel Workshop on Political Cleavages at Sde Bokar, Israel, in December, 1979.

2. For a detailed examination of these developments see Poulantzas (1974), Mandel (1970, 1973), Levitt (1972), and Hymer (1972).

3. For an examination of the factors responsible for the failure of regional policy in western Europe, and a consideration of some British case-studies see Holland (1975). More generally see Poulantzas (1974) and Mandel (1973).

4. See Nairn (1977). For a documentation of these trends see Carter (1972), Mayo (1974), Milner (1973) and Rawkins (1975).

5. Ulster represents an exception.

6. For a refined theoretical analysis see Williams (1981); for patterns of nationalist support see Rawkins and Balsom (1981); for differential regional recruitment to nationalist activities see Rawkins (1979).

7. For recent analyses of these three cases, see Ken Roberts and Dale Postgate (1980), Oriol Pi-Sunyer (1980) and Robert Clark (1980).

Chapter 14

1. The emergence of a distinctive Welsh sociology is borne out by the Welsh Joint Education Committee's proposals for an 'A' level sociology syllabus which includes the Sociology of Wales as a discrete option.

2. A noteable exception is, however, to be found in the introduction to the Report of the CACE, Wales (1953). This represents arguably one of the most useful texts on the development of education in Wales and the associated treatment of the Welsh language.

3. In this context 'national' is taken to be synonomous with 'British'.

4. This is not to imply that the 'common sense' which informs most so-called objective historiography is not in itself theoretical.

5. For an extended discussion of the historical and contemporary conceptualisations of culture see Williams (1980).

6. A brief attempt to accomplish this is presented in Williams and Roberts (1981).

7. This form of analysis has been promoted particularly by the Centre for Contemporary Cultural Studies. See Hall and Jefferson (1975) and CCCS (1981) for examples.

Bibliography

ABRAMS, P. — Origins of British Sociology : 1834-1914. Univeristy of Chicago Press, Chicago, 1968

ALMOND, G. A. and S. VERBA — The Civic Culture. Little Brown, Boston. 1965

ALTHUSSER, L. — Lenin and Philosophy and other Essays. New Left Books London, 1971

AMIN, S. ed. — Modern Migrations in Western Africa. Oxford University Press, London, 1971

APPLE, M. — Ideology and Curriculum. Routledge and Kegan Paul, London, 1979

ARNOLD, M. — Evidence to Royal Commission on Education H.M.S.O. London, 1853

ASHBY, M. K. — Joseph Ashby of Tysoe. Merlin, London, 1974

ASHBY, E. and M. ANDERSON — Portrait of Haldene at Work on Education. Macmillan, London, 1974

BACON, F. — Novum Organum. George Ball, London, 1879

BACON, F. and W. ELTIS. — Britain's Economic Problem Macmillan, London, 1976

BARKE, E. M. and D. E. WILLIAMS — A Further Study of the Comparative Intelligence of Certain Schoolchildren in Bilingual Schools in South Wales. British Journal of Educational Psychology. Vol. 8, 1938, pp. 62-67

BARNES, F. A. — Settlement and Landscape Changes in a Caernarfonshire Slate-quarrying village. In P. OSBORNE, et.al. eds. Geographical Essays in Honour of K. C. Edwards. University of Nottingham Press, Nottingham, 1970

BARNET, R. and R. E. MULLER — Global Reach : The Power of the Multinational Corporations. Simon and Schuster, New York, 1972

BELL, D. — The Coming of Post-Industrial Society Basic Books, New York, 1973

BELL, D. — Ethnicity and Social Change. In N. GLAZER and D. MOYNIHAN eds. Ethnicity : Theory and Experience. Harvard University Press, New Haven, 1975

BENDIX, F. — National Building and Citizenship. John Wiley, New York, 1964

BENEWITZ, M. C. — Migrant and non-migrant Occupational Pattern . Industrial and Labour Relations Review. Vol. 9, 1956, pp. 235-240

BERNSTEIN, B. — Class, Codes and Control. Vol. 3, Routledge and Kegan Paul, London, 1977

BETTS, C. Culture in Crisis. Ffynnon Press, Wirral, 1976.

BEYNON, H. Working for Ford. Penguin, Harmondsworth, 1973

BIRNBAUM, N. Towards a Critical Sociology, Oxford University Press, Oxford, 1979

BLUM, A. The Corpus of Knowledge. In M. YOUNG ed. Knowledge and Control. Macmillan, London, 1971 pp. 117-133

BOURDIEU, P. Cultural Reproduction and Social Reproduction. In R. BROWN ed. Knowledge, Education and Cultural Change. Tavistock, London, 1973, pp. 71-112

BOURDIEU, P. The School as a Conservative Force.: Scholastic and Cultural Inequalities. In R. DALE et.al. eds. Schooling and Capitalism. Routledge and Kegan Paul, London, 1976, pp. 110-119

BOURDIEU, P. and R. PASSERON Reproduction in Education, Society and Culture. Sage, London, 1977

BOWLES, S. and H. GINTIS Schooling in Capitalist America. Routledge and Kegan Paul, London, 1976

BRACKEN, I. and D. HUME Problems and Issues in Structure Planning : Industrial South Wales. Department of Town Planning, U.W.I.S.T., Mineo, 1979

BRAUDEL, F. The Mediterranean and the Mediterranean World in the Age of Phillip II. Weidenfeld and Nicolson, London, 1973

BRUCE, M. The Coming of the Welfare State. Batsford, London, 1968

BRUNER, J. S. Culture, Politics and Pedagogy. Saturday Review. May 18th, 1968

BURKE, E. The Correspondence of Edmund Burke. University of Chicago Press, Chicago, 1959

BUTT, J. Working Class Housing in Glasgow 1900-1939. In I. McDougal Essays in Scottish Labour History MacDougall, Edinburgh, 1979, pp. 143-169

BUTT PHILLIP, A. The Welsh Question : Nationalism in Welsh Politics 1945-1970. University of Wales Press, Cardiff, 1974

CARNEY, J. and J. LEWIS Accumulation, the Regional Problem and Nationalism In P. W. J. BATEY, ed. Theory and Method in Urban and Regional Analysis. Pion, London, 1978, pp.67-81

CARNEY, J., J. LEWIS and R. HUDSON Coal Combines and Inter regional Uneven Development in the U.K. In D. MASSEY and P.W.J. BATEY eds. Alternative Frameworks for Analysis. Pion, London. 1976

CARTER, H. and W. DAVIES eds. Geography, Culture and Habitat : Selected Essays (1925-1975) of E. G. BOWEN. Gomer, Llandyssul, 1976

CARTER H. and S. W. WILLIAMS Aggregate Studies of Language and Culture Change in Wales. In G. WILLIAMS, ed. Social and Cultural Change in Contemporary Wales. Routledge and Kegan Paul, London, 1978, pp. 143-166.

CARTER, I. — The Highlands of Scotland as an Underdeveloped Region. In E. DEKADT and G. WILLIAMS eds. Sociology and Development. Tavistock, London, 1974, pp. 279-315

CENTRE FOR CONTEMPORARY CULTURAL STUDIES — On Ideology. Hutchinson, London, 1978

CENTRE FOR CONTEMPORARY CULTURAL STUDIES — Unpopular Education. Hutchinson, London, 1981

CENTRAL ADVISORY COUNCIL FOR EDUCATION (ENGLAND) — Children and Their Primary Schools (The Plowden Report) H.M.S.O., London, 1967

CENTRAL ADVISORY COUNCIL FOR EDUCATION (WALES) — The Place of Welsh and English in the Schools of Wales (The Aaron Report) Introduction by E.G. Lewis H.M.S.O., London, 1967

CENTRAL ADVISORY COUNCIL FOR EDUCATION (WALES) — Primary Education in Wales (The Gittens Report). H.M.S.O., London, 1967

CLARK, R. — Euzkadi: Basque Nationalism since the Civil War In C. FOSTER, ed. Nations Without State. Praeger, New York, 1980, pp. 75-100

CLAESON, C. F. — Interzonal Differences in Age Structure. Geografiska Annaler. Series B. 50, 1968, pp. 14-22

CLAPHAM, J. — A Concise Economic History of Britain. Cambridge University Press, Cambridge, 1966

CLARKE, J., C. CRITCHER, and R. JOHNSON eds. — Working Class Culture : History and Theory. Hutchinson, London, 1979

CLAYTON, P. — Domain and Register in the Use of Welsh. In G. WILLIAMS ed. Social and Cultural Change in Contemporary Wales. Routledge and Kegan Paul, London, 1978, pp. 206-219

COHEN, I. J. — On Hechter's Interpretation of Weber. American Journal of Sociology. Vol. 81, No. 5, 1976, pp.1160-1162

COMMISSION OF ENQUIRY INTO INDUSTRIAL UNREST IN SOUTH WALES — Report of the Commission. H.M.S.O., London, 1917

COMMITTEE ON WELSH AFFAIRS — The Role of the Welsh Office and Associated Bodies in Developing Employment Opportunities in Wales. Vol. 1, H.M.S.O., London, 1980

CONNOR, W. — Ethnonationalism in the First World : The Present in Historical Perspective. In M. ESMAN, ed. Ethnic Conflict in the Western World. Cornell University Press, Ithica, 1977, pp. 19-46

COOKE, P. — Capital Relations and State Dependency : An Analysis of Urban Development Policy in Cardiff. In G. REES and T. L. REES, eds. Poverty and Social Inequality in Wales. Croom Helm, London, 1980a, pp. 206-230

COOKE, P. — Class Relations and Uneven Development in Wales. In G. DAY ed. _Diversity and Decomposition in the Labour Market_. Gower, Farnborough, 1982a, pp.147-178

COOKE, P. — Dependency, Supply Factors and Uneven Development in Wales and other Problem Regions. _Regional Studies_. Vol. 16, 1982b, pp. 187-204

COOKE, P. — Class Interests, Regional Restructuring and State Formation in Wales. _International Journal of Urban and Regional Research_. Vol. 16, 1982c, pp. 187-204

COOKE, P. — Dependent Development in U.K. Regions with Particular Reference to Wales. _Progress in Planning_. Vol. 15 No. 1, 1980b, pp.1-63

CORDEY-HAYES, M. and D. GLEAVE — Migration Movements and the Differential Growth of City Regions in England and Wales. _C.E.S. Research Papers_, No.1, 1973

CREWE, I. — Why the Conservatives Won. In H. PENNIMAN, ed. _Britain at the Polls, 1979._ American Enterprise Institute, Washington D.C., 1979, pp. 263-305

DAVIES, D. H. — _The Welsh Nationalist Party 1925-1945 : A Search for Identity_. Unpublished M.Sc. (Econ.) Thesis, University of Wales, 1979

DAVIES, E. T. — _Religion in the Industrial Revolution in south Wales_. University of Wales Press, Cardiff, 1965

DAVIES, G. and I. THOMAS — _Overseas Investment in Wales, the Welcome Invasion_ Christopher Davies, Swansea, 1976

DAVIES, J. — The End of the Great Estates and the Rise of Freehold Farming in Wales. _Welsh History Review_, Vol. 7, 1974, pp. 186-212

DAVIES, R. — _The Withered Root_. Holt, New York, 1927

DAVIES, T. — _Our National Language_. Fishman and Unwin, London, 1914

DAY, G. — Underdeveloped Wales. _Planet_. Nos. 33/34, 1978, pp. 102-110

DAY, G. — The Sociology of Wales, Issues and Perspectives. _Sociological Review_. Vol. 27, No.3, 1979, pp. 447-474

DAY, G. and M. FITTON — Religion and Social Status in Rural Wales : 'Buchedd' and its Relevance for concepts of Stratification. _Sociological Review_, Vol. 23, No.4, 1975, pp. 867-891

DEUTSCH, K. — _Nationality and Social Communication_. M.I.T. Press, Cambridge, 1966

DEVELOPMENT CORPORATION FOR WALES — _Annual Report_. D.C.W., Cardiff, 1978-1979

DICTIONARY OF WELSH BIOGRAPHY — _Y Bywgraffiadur Cymreig hyd 1940_. Honourable Society of Cymmrodorion, London, 1953

DODSON, C. J. — The Bilingual Method. University College of Wales, Aberystwyth, 1962

DODSON, C. J. — Foreign and Second Language Learning in Primary Schools. University College of Wales, Aberystwyth, 1966

DODSON, C. J. E. PRICE and I. T. WILLIAMS — Towards Bilingualism. University of Wales Press, Cardiff, 1951

DODD, A. H. — The Industrial Revolution in north Wales. University of Wales Press, Cardiff, 1951

EDUCATION COMMISSION — The State of Popular Education in England. H.M.S.O., London, 1861

EDWARDS, L. — Traethodau Llenyddol. Hughes a'i Fab, Wrecsam, n.d.

EISENSTADT, S. N. — Social Differentiation and Stratification. Scott Foresman, London, 1971

EISENSTADT, S. N. — Tradition, Change and Modernization. Prentice Hall, New York, 1975

EMMANUEL, A. — Unequal Exchange. Monthly Review Press, New York, 1972

ESLAND, G. — Teaching and Learning as the Social Organisation of Knowledge. In M. YOUNG, ed. Knowledge and Control : New Directions for the Sociology of Education. Collier-Macmillan, London, 1971, pp. 70-117

EVANS, M. — Karl Marx. Aldine, London, 1975

EVANS, G. — Diwedd Prydeindod Y Lolfa, Talybont, 1981

FISHMAN, J. A. — The Sociology of Language. Newbury House, Rowley, 1972

FLETCHER, C. — Regional Community in the Era of Regional Aid. In G. WILLIAMS, ed. Social and Cultural Change in Contemporary Wales. Routledge and Kegan Paul, London, 1978, pp. 32-49

FRANCIS, H. and K. HOWELLS — The south Wales Coalfield Research Project. Llafur, No. 3, 1980, pp. 97-98

FRANCIS, H. and D. SMITH — The Fed : A History of the south Wales Miners in the Twentieth Century. Lawrence and Wishart, London, 1980

FRANKENBERG, R. — Communities in Britain. Penguin, Harmondsworth, 1966

FREIRE, P. — Cultural Activity for Freedom. Penguin, Harmondsworth 1977.

FRIEDLANDER, D. — The Spread of Urbanization in England and Wales. Population Studies, Vol. 24, No.3, 1970,

FRIEDLANDER, D. and P. ROSHIER — A Study of Internal Migration in England and Wales. Population Studies, Vol. 20, 1965/1966, pp. 45-59, 239-280

FRIEDMAN, A. L. — Industry and Labour : Class Struggle at Work, Macmillan, London, 1977

FURTADO, C. — The Concept of Dependence in the Study of Underdevelopment. In C. K. WILBER, ed. *The Political Economy of Underdevelopment.* Random House, New York, 1974

GALPIN, G. C. — *Social Anatomy of a Rural Community*. Wisconsin Agricultural Experimental Station, 1916

GALTUNG, J. — A Structural Theory of Imperialism. *Journal of Peace Research*. Vol. 2, 1971,

GARBET, G. K. and B. KAPFERER — Theoretical Orientations in the Study of Labour Migration. *The New Atlantis*, Vol. 1, 1970, pp.179-197

GELLNER, E. — *Thought and Change*. Weidenfeld and Nicholson, London, 1964

GELLNER, E. — *Legitimation of Belief*. Cambridge University Press, Cambridge, 1974

GERTH, H. and C. W. MILLS — *From Max Weber*. Oxford University Press, London, 1946

GIDDENS, A. — *Politics and Sociology in the Thoughts of Max Weber.* Macmillan, London, 1971

GIDDENS, A. — *A Contemporary Critique of Historical Materialism.* Macmillan, London, 1981

GILLETTE, F. — *Constructive Rural Sociology*, 1915

GOLDBERG, I. — *The Wonder of Words.* Ungar, New York, 1958

GOLDTHORPE, J. — *Social Mobility and Class Structure in Modern Britain.* Clarendon, Oxford, 1980

GRAMSCI, A. — *Selections from Prison Notebooks.* Lawrence and Wishart, London, 1971.

GRANT, G. — *A Social Atlas of Gwynedd.* Unpublished m.s.

GREENWOOD, M. J. — An Analysis of the Determinants of Geographic Labour Mobility in the U.S.A. *Review of Economics and Statistics*. Vol. 51, 1969, pp. 189-194

GREENWOOD, M. J. — Lagged Response in the Decision to Migrate. *Journal of Regional Science.* Vol. 4, 1970, pp. 375-384

GUMPERTZ, J. — Types of Language Communities. *Anthropological Linguistics*, Vol. 4, No. 1, 1962, pp. 28-40

HABERMAS, J. — *Towards a Rational Society*. Heinemann, London, 1971

HALL, P. et.al. — *The Containment of Urban England.* Allen & Unwin, London, 1973.

HALL, S. — Culture, the Media and the Ideological Effect. In J. CURRAN, M. GUREVITCH and J. WOOLLACOTT eds. *Mass Communication and Society*. Arnold, London, 1977

HALL, S. and T. JEFFERSON — *Resistance Through Ritual*. Hutchinson, London, 1975

HALLIDAY, R. J. — The Sociological Movements, the Sociological Society and the Genesis of Academic Sociology in Britain. *Sociological Review*, Vol. 16, 1968, pp. 377-398

HARRISON, G., W. BELLIN and B. PIETTE — *Bilingual Mothers in Wales and the Language of their Children.* Board of Celtic Studies Social Science Monographs, No. 6, University of Wales Press, Cardiff, 1981

HARRISON, J. Thatcherism : is it Working? Marxism Today, July, 1982

HART, R. A. A model of Inter-regional Migration in England and Wales. Regional Studies, Vol. 4, 1970, pp. 279-296

HECHTER, M. Internal Colonialism : The Celtic Fringe in British National Development 1536-1966. Routledge and Kegan Paul, London, 1975

HECHTER, M. Group Formation and the Cultural Division of Labour. American Journal of Sociology, Vol. 84, No.2, 1978, pp. 293-318

HELLEINER, G. Manufactured Exports for Less Developed Countries and Multinational Firms. Economic Journal. Vol. 82, 1972

HERBERT, D. T. Population Mobility and Social Change in south Wales. Town Planning Review, Vol. 43, 1972, pp. 327-343

HIMMELWEIT, H. et.al. How Voters Decide. Academic Press, London, 1981

HIRSCHMAN, A. D. The Strategy of Economic Development. Yale University Press, New Haven, 1958

HOBSBAWM, E. J. Industry and Empire : an Economic History of Britain since 1750. Weidenfeld and Nicholson, London, 1968

HODGES, T. M. The Peopling of the Hinterland of the Port of Cardiff 1801-1914. Economic History Review. Vol.17, 1947 pp. 62-72

HOFSTADER, R. The Age of Reform. Vintage Books, New York, 1955.

HOLDING, S. Evidence Presented to the Llantrisant New Town Public Enquiry In J. A. EDWARDS and W. THOMAS, eds. Llantrisant New Town : The Case Against. Thomas and Partners, Cardiff, 1972.

HOLLAND, S. The Socialist Challenge. Quartet Books, London, 1975

HOLLAND, S. Britain : A Suitable Case for Treatment? I.D.S. Bulletin, Vol.9, No.2, 1977, pp. 23-28

HOPPER, E. ed. Readings in the Theory of Educational Systems. Hutchinson, London, 1971

HOWELL, D. Land and People in Nineteenth Century Wales. Routledge and Kegan Paul, London, 1977.

HUGHES, E. C. et.al. eds. The Collected Papers of Robert Ezra Park. Vol.1, The Free Press, Glencoe, 1950

HYMER, S. The Multinational Corporation and the Law of Uneven Development. In J. N. BAGWATTI, ed. Economics and World Order from the 1970s to the 1990s. Macmillan, New York, 1972

HYMER, S. The Multinational Corporation : Your Home is our Home. Canadian Dimension, Vol. 8, No. 6, 1972, pp. 29-35

HYMER, S. The Multinational Corporation : A Radical Analysis. Cambridge University Press, Cambridge, 1979

IVERSON, R. Inter-Regional Input-Output Tables for Wales and the Rest of the U.K. Welsh Council, Cardiff, 1973

JONES, T. Leeks and Daffodils. W. Griffiths, Newtown, 1942.

JONES, W. R. Attitude Towards Welsh as a Second Language : A Preliminary Investigation. British Journal of educational Psychology, Vol. 19, 1949, pp.44-52

JONES, W. R. Attitude Towards Welsh as a Second Language : A Further Investigation. British Journal of educational Psychology, Vol.20, 1950, pp. 117-132.

JONES, W. R. Bilingualism and Intelligence. University of Wales Press, Cardiff, 1955.

JONES, W. R. A Critical Study of Bilingualism and Non-Verbal Intelligence. British Journal of Psychology, Vol.30, 1960, pp.71-76

JONES, W. R. Bilingualism in Welsh Education. University of Wales Press, Cardiff, 1966.

KALDOR, M. The Baroque Arsenal. Deutsch, London, 1960.

KEDDIE, N. Classroom Knowledge. In M. YOUNG, ed. Knowledge and Control : The New Sociology of Education. Macmillan, London, 1971, pp.133-161.

KEDOURIE, E. Nationalism. Hutchinson, London, 1960.

KEOWN, P. A. The Career Cycle and the Stepwise Migration Process. New Zealand Geographer, Vol.27, 1971, pp.175-184

KHLEIF, B. B. Ethnic Awakening in the First World : The Case of Wales. In G. WILLIAMS, ed. Social and Cultural Change in Contemporary Wales. Routledge and Kegan Paul, London, 1978, pp.102-120.

LACLAU, E. Feudalism and Capitalism in Latin America. New Left Review, No.67, 1971, pp.19-38.

LEE, E. A Theory of Migration. Demography, Vol.3, 1966, pp. 47-57.

LENSKI, E. E. Status Crystalization : A Non-vertical Dimension of Social Status. American Sociological Review, Vol. 19, 1954, pp. 405-413

LERNER, D. The Passing of Traditional Society. Free Press, New York, 1958.

LEVITT, K. Towards Decolonization : Canada and Quebec. Canadian Forum, Vol. 51, No.614, 1972, pp.2-3

LEWIS, E. G. Migration and Language in the U.S.S.R. International Migration Review, Vol.5, 1971, pp.147-159

LEWIS, E. G. Multilingualism in the Soviet Union. Mouton, The Hague, 1972.

LEWIS, E. G. Migration and the Decline of the Welsh Language. In J. A. FISHMAN, ed., Advances in the Study of Societal Multilingualism. Mouton, The Hague, 1978a, pp. 263-353

LEWIS, E. G. Bilingualism in Education in Wales. In B. SPOLSKY and R. L. COOPER, eds., Case Studies in Bilingual Education. Newbury House, Rowley, 1978b.

LEWIS, E. G. — A Comparative Study of Language Contact : The Influence of Demographic Factors in Wales and the Soviet Union. In W. McCORMACK, S. WURM, eds. Language and Society : Papers Delivered at the 19th International Congress of Anthropological and Ethnographical Sciences. Chicago, 1978c, pp. 331-358

LINDSAY, J. — A History of the north Wales Slate Industry. David and Charles, Newton Abbot, 1974.

LIPIETZ, A. — Towards a Global Fordism? New Left Review, No. 132, 1982.

LOVERING, J. — The Theory of Internal Colony and the Political Economy of Wales. Review of Radical Political Economics, Vol. 10, 1978a, pp. 55-67

LOVERING, J. — Dependence and the Welsh Economy. Economic Research Papers, No.22, Institute of Economic Research, C.P.G.C./U.C.N.W., Bangor, 1978b.

LOWRY, I. S. — Migration and Metropolitan Growth : The Analytical Models. Institute of Government and Public Affairs, U.C.L.A., Los Angeles, 1966.

MANDEL, E. — Europe Versus America : Contradictions of Imperialism, New Left Books, London, 1970.

MANDEL, E. — Capitalism and Regional Disparities. New Hogtown Press, Toronto, 1973.

MANDEL, E. — Late Capitalism. New Left Books, London, 1975.

MACMILLAN, H. — Industrial Reconstruction : A Plea for a National Policy. Macmillan, London, 1933.

MACKAY, R. — Regional Policy, Its Impact, Declining Effect and Uncertain Future. Unpublished m.s., 1979

MADGWICK, P. and P. RAWKINS — The Welsh Language in the Policy Process. In P. MADGWICK and R. ROSE, eds. The Territorial Dimension in British Politics. Macmillan, London, 1982

MANNERS, G. — South Wales in the Sixties : Studies in Industrial Geography. Macmillan, New York, 1964.

MANNHEIM, K. — Man and Society in the Age of Reconstruction. Harcourt, Brace, New York, 1940.

MARGOLIOUTH, M. — (Quoted in R. F. JONES, The Triumph of the English Language. Oxford University Press, Oxford, 1953.)

MASSER, I. — The Test of Some Models for Predicting inter Metropolitan Movement of Population in England and Wales. Centre for Environmental Studies, Working Papers, No.9, 1970

MASSEY, D. — Regionalism : Some Current Issues. Capital and Class, Vol. 6, 1978, pp. 106-125.

MASSEY, D. — In What Sense a Regional Problem? Regional Studies, Vol. 13, 1979, pp. 233-244.

MASSEY, D. — Industrial Restructuring as Class Restructuring: Some Examples of the Implications of Industrial Change for Class Structure. Centre for Environmental Studies, Working Papers, No.604, 1980.

MASSEY, D. and R. MEEGAN — The Anatomy of Job Loss. Methuen, London, 1982

MATHIAS, D. — The First Industrial Nation. Macmillan, London, 1969

MAYO, P. E. — The Roots of Identity. Allen Lane, London, 1974

McCRONE, G. — Regional Policy in Britain. Allen and Unwin, London, 1969

McNABB, R. — Segmented Labour Markets, Female Employment and Poverty in Wales. In G. REES and T. L. REES, eds., Poverty and Social Inequality in Wales, Croom Helm, London, 1980, pp. 156-168

McROBERTS, K. and D. POSTGATE — Quebec : Social Change and Political Crisis. McLelland and Steward, Toronto, 1980.

MELLOR, J. R. — Urban Sociology in an Urbanized Society. Routledge and Kegan Paul, London, 1977.

MICHAEL, D. — Before Alwyn : Early Social Thought, Action and Research in Wales. In N. EVANS, I. HUGHES and D. MICHAEL, eds. Wales, Aspects of Change, Occasional Papers in Welsh Studies, No. 1, Coleg Harlech, Harlech, 1981, pp.9-35

MIDDLEMAS, K. — Politics in an Industrial Society. Deutsch, London, 1979

MIDDLETON, A. — International Capital and Internal Migration in Equador. : A Historico-Structural Analysis. Paper presented at the I.S.A. World Congress of Sociology, Upsala, 1978

MILIBAND, R. — The State in Capitalist Society. Weidenfeld and Nicolson, London, 1969.

MILIBAND, R. — State Power and Class Interests. New Left Review, No. 138, 1983, pp. 57-69.

MILNER, B. — The French Far West. New Society, October 25th, 1973, pp. 197-198

MINISTRY OF EDUCATION, WELSH DEPARTMENT — Welsh in Education and Life : Report of the Departmental Committee, H.M.S.O., London, 1927.

MINISTRY OF HOUSING AND LOCAL GOVERNMENT — Depopulation in mid Wales. (Beecham Report), H.M.S.O., London, 1964

MINISTRY OF HOUSING AND LOCAL GOVERNMENT — The Needs of New Communities : Report on Social Provision in New and Expanding Communities, H.M.S.O., London, 1967

MINISTRY OF LABOUR — Reports of Investigations into the Industrial Conditions in Certain Depressed Areas : Report on South Wales and Monmouthshire. H.M.S.O., London, 1933/1934

MITCHELL, J. C. — Problems in Sociological Analysis of Economic Behaviour. Paper presented to Conference on Urban Development in Africa. I.D.S. University of Sussex, 1971

MOORE, W. E. — The Impact of Industry. Prentice Hall, Englewood Cliffs, 1964.

MOORE, J. and B. RHODES — Regional Policy and the Economy of Wales. Cyngor Cymru /Welsh Council, Caerdydd/ Cardiff, 1975

MORGAN, K. State Regional Interventions and Industrial Reconstruction in Post-War Britain : The Case of Wales. Urban and Regional Studies Working Papers, No.16, University of Sussex, 1980

MORGAN, K. O. Wales in British Politics 1868-1922. University of Wales Press, Cardiff, 1963.

MORGAN, K. O. Rebirth of a Nation : Wales 1880-1980. Oxford University Press and University of Wales Press, Oxford and Cardiff, 1981.

MORGAN, R. H. Non-Response in Postal Questionnaire Surveys. Area, Vol. 6, No.4, pp. 309-314

MORRIS, J. H. and J. WILLIAMS The South Wales sliding Scale. Manchester School of Economic and Social Studies, Vol. 28, 1960, pp.161-176

MOSELEY, M. J. Growth Centres in Spatial Planning. Pergamon, Oxford, 1974.

MURRAY, R. Underdevelopment, International Firms and the International Division of Labour. In SOCIETY FOR INTERNATIONAL DEVELOPMENT, Towards a New World Economy. Society of International Development, Rotterdam, 1971.

MYRDAL, G. M. Economic Theory and Underdeveloped Regions. Duckworth, London, 1957.

NAIRN, T. The Modern Janus. New Left Review, No.94, 1975 pp. 3-31.

NAIRN, T. The Break-up of Britain. New Left Books, London, 1977

NAIRN, T. Britain's Perenial Crisis, New Left Review, Nos. 113-114 1979

OSMOND, J. Creative Conflict. Routledge and Kegan Paul, London, 1977.

OWEN, T. M. Peasant Weddings in Nineteenth Century Wales. Paper presented to the Peasants Seminar, Centre for International and Area Studies, University of London, 1976.

PAGE, A. C. State Intervention in the Inter-War Period : The Special Areas Acts 1936-1937. British Journal of Law and Society. Vol.4, 1977, pp. 175-203.

PI-SUNYER, O. Dimensions of Catalan Nationalism. In C. FOSTER, ed. Nations Without States. Praeger, New York, 1980, pp. 101-115.

POKSHISHEVSKIY, V. V. Urbanization and Ethnographical Processes. Mytl, Moscow, 1971.

POLYANI, W. Words, Conceptions and Science. Twentieth Century, 1955.

POULANTZAS, N. Internationalisation of Capitalist Relations and the Nation State. Economy and Society, Vol.3, No.2, 1974 pp. 145-179.

POULANTZAS, N. Classes in Contemporary Capitalism. New Left Books, London, 1975.

PYE, L. W. and W. ROSTOW — Political Culture and Political Development. Princeton University Press, Princeton, 1965.

QUIJANO OBREGON, A. — The Marginal Pole of the Economy and the Marginalized Labour Force. Economy and Society, Vol. 3, No.4, 1974, pp. 393-428

RANDALL, P. J. — Wales in the Structure of Central Government. Public Administration Journal, Vol. 50, 1972, pp.352-372

RAWKINS, P. — Nationalist Mobilization in England and Wales. In A. COTRELL and J. ROSS eds. The Mobilization of Collective Identity : Comparative Perspectives. University Press of America, Washington D.C., 1978

RAWKINS, P. — The Implementation of Language Policy in the Schools of Wales. Studies in Public Policy, No.40, 1979

RAWKINS, P. — Living in the House of Power : Welsh Nationalism and the Dilemmas of Anti-System Politics. In E. TIRYAKIN and R. ROGOWSKI, eds. The New Nationalisms of the Developed West : Towards Explanation. Allen and Unwin, New York, 1983.

REES, A. D. — Life in a Welsh Countryside. University of Wales Press, Cardiff, 1950.

REES, G. — Uneven Development, State Intervention and the Generation of Inequality : the Case of Industrial south Wales. In G. REES and T. L. REES, eds. Poverty and Social Inequality in Wales. Croom Helm, London, 1980, pp. 185-206.

REES, G. and J. LAMBERT — Nationalism as Legitimation? Notes Towards a Political Economy of Regional Development in south Wales. In M. HARLOWE, ed. New Perspectives in Urban Change and Conflict. Heineman, London, 1981, pp. 122-137

REES, G. and T. L. REES eds. — Poverty and Social Inequality in Wales. Croom Helm, London, 1980

REES, T. L. — The Origin and Destination of Migrants to and from the Valleys of south Wales. Glyncorwg C.D.P. Research Team Working Paper, No.17, U.W.I.S.T., Cardiff, 1976a

REES, T. L. — A Demographic and Socio-Economic Profile of Migrants to and from the south Wales Valleys. Glyncorrwg, C.D.P. Research Team Working Papers, No.16, 1976b.

REES, T. L. — Population and Industrial Decline in the south Wales Coalfield. Regional Studies, Vol. 12, 1978, pp.69-77

REVEL, J. and C. TOMKINS — Personal Wealth and Finance in Wales. Cyngor Cymru /Welsh Council, Caerdydd/ Cardiff, 1974

ROGERS, A. — A Regression Analysis of Inter-regional Migration in California. Review of Economics and Statistics, Vol. 17, 1966, pp.205-224.

ROGERS, A. — Demometrics of Migration and Settlement. International Institute for Applied Systems Analysis, Luxembourg, 1976.

ROKKAN, S. ed. — Comparative Research Across Culture. Mouton, The Hague, 1968.

ROSS, J. — A Framework for the Comparative Analysis of the Mobilization of Ethnic Identity. In J. ROSS, A. COTTRELL, P. RAWKINS and R. ST. CYR eds. _The Mobilization of Collective Identity_. University of America, Washington D. C., 1980, pp. 1-30

ROSTOW, W. W. — _The Stages of Economic Growth_. Cambridge University Press, Cambridge, 1960.

ROWLANDS, D. — _At y Methodistiaid Calfiniaidd ym Mhatagonia_. P. M. Evans, Treffynon, n.d.

ROYAL COMMISSION ON EDUCATION IN ENGLAND AND WALES — _Report of Commissioners of Inquiry into the State of Education in Wales_, H.M.S.O., London, 1847

ROYAL COMMISSION ON THE UNIVERSITY OF WALES — _Report of the Commissioners of Inquiry_. H.M.S.O., London, 1916

SADLER, P., B. ARCHER and C. OWEN — _Regional Income Multipliers_. Institute of Economic Research, C.P.G.C./U.C.N.W., Bangor, 1974

SAER, D. J. — An Enquiry into the Effects of Bilingualism on the Intelligence of Young Children. _Journal of Experimental Pedagogy_. Vol.1, 1922.

SAER, D. J. — Psychological Problems of Bilingualism. _Welsh Outlook_, No.15, 1928, pp.131-134, 161-163

SAER, D. J. — The Effect of Bilingualism in Intelligence. _British Journal of Educational Psychology_. Vol.14, 1932, pp.25-38 266-274

SCHOOLS COUNCIL COMMITTEE FOR WALES — _Development of Bilingual Education in Wales_. Methuen, London, 1972.

SCHOOLS COUNCIL COMMITTEE FOR WALES — _Bilingual Education in Wales, 5 - 11_. Methuen, London, 1978

SCOTT, J. — _Corporations, Classes and Capitalism_. Hutchinson, London, 1979.

SEERS, D. — The Periphery of Europe. In D. SEERS, B. SCHAEFFER, and M. L. KILJUNEN, eds. _Underdeveloped Europe : Studies in Core-Periphery Relations_. Harvester, London, 1979.

SELWYN, P. — Some thoughts on Cores and Peripheries. In D. SEERS, B. SHAEFFER and M. L. KILJUNEN, eds. _Underdeveloped Europe : Studies in Core-Periphery Relations_. Harvester, London, 1979.

SHARP, D., B. THOMAS, E. PRICE, G. FRANCIS, and I. DAVIES — _Attitudes to Welsh and English in the Schools of Wales_. Macmillan, London, 1973.

SHARP, R. and A. GREEN — _Education and Social Control_. Routledge and Kegan Paul, London, 1975.

SILVERT, K. H. — _Discussions at Bellagio : The Political Alternatives to Development_. American University Press, Washington D. C., 1964

SMITH, A. D. — _Theories of nationalism_. Duckworth, London, 1971.

SMITH, D. ed. — A People and a Proletariat. Pluto, London, 1980

SMITH, F. — Bilingualism and Mental Development. British Journal of Psychology, Vol. 13, 1923, pp. 271-282.

SOROKIN, P. and C. ZIMMERMAN — Source Book of Rural-Urban Sociology. University of Minnesota Press, Minneapolis, 1930.

SOROKIN, P. and C. ZIMMERMAN — Principles of Rural-Urban Sociology. Holt, New York, 1929

STACEY, M., E. BATSTONE, C. BELL, and A. MURCOTT — Power Resistance and Change : A Second Study of Banbury. Routledge and Kegan Paul, London, 1975

STACEY, M. — Tradition and Change. Oxford University Press, Oxford, 1960

STEAD, P. — Coleg Harlech : The First Fifty Years. University of Wales Press, Cardiff, 1972

STEPAN, N. — The Idea of Space in Science. Cambridge University Press, Cambridge, 1982

SWANN, D. — The Economics of the Common Market. Penguin, Harmondsworth, 1975

TABOURET-KELLER, A. — A Contribution to the Sociological Study of Language and Language Shift. In J. FISHMAN, ed. Advances in The Sociology of Language. Vol.2, Mouton, The Hague, 1972, pp. 365-377.

TARVER, J. — Occupational Migration Differentials. Social Forces, Vol. 43, 1964, pp. 536-547.

TAYLOR, P. J. and N. SPENCE — Classification Procedures. In C. BOARD, et.al. eds, Progress in Geography. Vol. 2, Arnold, London, 1969.

THERBORN, G. — The Travail of Latin American Democracy. New Left Review, No. 138, 1983, pp. 37-57

THOMAS, B. — The Migration of Labour into the Glamorganshire Coalfield, 1861-1911. Economica, Vol. 10, 1930, pp. 275-294.

THOMAS, B. — Migration and Urban Development : A Reappraisal of British and American Long Cycles. Methuen, London, 1972.

THOMAS, D. — England's Golden West. New Society, Vol. 64, No. 1069, May, 1983, pp. 209

THOMAS, D. S. — Research Memorandum on Migration Differentials. Bulletin, No. 43, S.S.R.C., New York, 1958

THOMAS, D. S. — Age and Economic Differentials in Interstate Migration. Population Index, Vol. 24, 1938, pp.213-225

THOMAS, E. R. ed. — Farmers Together. Welsh Agricultural Organising Society, Aberystwyth, 1972

THOMAS, N. — Education in Wales. In R. BELL and R. FOWLER, eds., Education in Great Britain and Ireland. Routledge and Kegan Paul, London, 1973,

THOMAS, R. S. — The Times. In *'H'm.* Macmillan, London, 1972, p.25

TOMKINS, C. — *Income and Expenditure Accounts for Wales, 1965-1968* Cyngor Cymru/Welsh Council, Caerdydd, Cardiff, 1972

TOMKINS, C. and J. LOVERING — *Location, Size, Ownership and Control Tables for Welsh Industry.* Cyngor Cymru/Welsh Council, Caerdydd/Cardiff, 1973

TOWN, S. W. — *After the Mines : Changing Employment Opportunities in a south Wales Valley.* Board of Celtic Studies Social Science Monograph No.4, University of Wales Press, Cardiff, 1978

TOWNSEND, A. — Recession and the Regions of Great Britain, 1976-1980 Analysis of Redundancy Data. *Environment and Planning.* Vol. 14, 1982, pp. 1389-1404

TREASURY DEPARTMENT — *Rural Depopulation.* Inter Departmental Report. London, 1976

TREMENHEERE, J. — *The State of Elementary Education in the Mining Districts of south Wales, 1839—1840.* Appendix to Report of Committee of Education of the Privy Council, H.M.S.O., London, 1840

TURNER, G. — *Business in Britain.* Penguin, Harmondsworth, 1971

URRY, J. — Location, Regions and Social Class. *International Journal of Urban and Regional Research,* Vol.5, 1981 pp. 455-474

VEBLEN, T. — *The Theory of the Leisure Class.* Allen and Unwin, London, 1971

VERNON, R. — *Sovereignty at Bay.* Penguin, Harmondsworth, 1975

VERDERY, K. — Ethnicity and Local Systems : The Religious Organization of Welshness. In C.A.SMITH, ed. *Regional Analysis : Social Systems.* Vol.2, Academic Press, London, 1976, pp.191-227

WALLERSTEIN, I. — World System Analysis : Theoretical and Interpretive Issues. In B. H. KAPLAN, ed. *Social Change in the Capitalist World Economy.* Sage, Beverley Hills, 1978, pp. 219-236

WALLERSTEIN, I. — *The Capitalist World Economy.* Cambridge University Press, Cambridge, 1979.

WARREN, K. — *The British Iron and Steel Industry Since 1840.* Bell, London, 1970

WATSON, J. D. — *The Double Helix : A Personal Account of the Discovery of DNA.* Weidenfeld and Nicolson, London, 1968

WELSH COUNCIL — *Growth Centres in mid Wales.* H.M.S.O., London, 1971

WELSH OFFICE — *Wales : The Way Ahead.* Cmnd. 3334, H.M.S.O., London, 1967

WELSH OFFICE — Migration Into, Out of, and within Wales in the 1966-71 period. *Occasional Papers,* No.4, Cardiff, 1979

WHITTY, G. and M. YOUNG, eds. — *Explorations in the Politics of School Knowledge.* Nafferton, Driffield, 1976

WILKINSON, F. ed. — *The Dynamics of Labour Market Segmentation.* Academic Press, London, 1981

WILLIAMS, D. — The History of Modern Wales. Charles, London, 1950

WILLIAMS, G. — The Desert and the Dream : A History of the Welsh Colonization of Patagonia 1865-1915. University of Wales Press, Cardiff, 1975.

WILLIAMS, G. — Towards a Sociology of Wales. Planet, No. 40, 1977, pp. 30-38

WILLIAMS, G. — Industrialization and Ethnic Change in the Lower Chubut Valley, Argentina. American Ethnologist, Vol. 5, No. 3, 1978a, pp. 618-631.

WILLIAMS, G. — Introduction. In G. WILLIAMS, ed. Social and Cultural Change in Contemporary Wales. Routledge and Kegan Paul, London, 1978b, pp. 1-15

WILLIAMS, G. ed. — Social and Cultural Change in Contemporary Wales. Routledge and Kegan Paul, London, 1978c.

WILLIAMS, G. — Industrialization, Inequality and Deprivation in Rural Wales. In G. REES and T. L. REES, eds. Poverty and Social Inequality in Wales. Croom Helm, London, 1980a, pp. 168-185.

WILLIAMS, G. — Education, Social and Cultural Reproduction in Wales : A Historical Review. Paper presented at the Annual Conference of the British Educational Research Association, Cardiff, 1980b.

WILLIAMS, G. — Economic Development, Social Structure and Contemporary Nationalism in Wales. Review, Vol. 5, No. 2, 1981, pp. 275-311.

WILLIAMS, G. — The Political Economy of Contemporary Nationalism : The Case of Wales. In E. TIRYAKIN and R. ROGOWSKI eds., The New Nationalisms of the Developed West : Towards Explanation. Allen and Unwin, New York, 1983

WILLIAMS, G. ed. — The Sociology of Welsh. Mouton, The Hague, In Press, a.

WILLIAMS, G. — What is Wales? The Discourse of Devolution. Journal of Ethnic and Racial Studies. In Press, b.

WILLIAMS, G. and C. ROBERTS — Language and Social Structure in Welsh Education. In J. MEGARRY, S. NISBET and E. HOYLE. eds., World Yearbook of Education 1981 : Education of Minorities. Kogan Page, London, 1981, pp. 147-164

WILLIAMS, G. and C. ROBERTS — Language, Education and Reproduction in Wales. In B. BAIN ed., The Sociogenesis of Language and Human Conduct. Plenum, New York, 1983, pp. 497-515.

WILLIAMS, G. A. — The Merthyr Rising. Croom Helm, London, 1978.

WILLIAMS, G. A. — When Was Wales? B.B.C., Cardiff, 1979

WILLIAMS, G. A. — Land of Our Fathers. Marxism Today. August, 1982.

WILLIAMS, J. L. — Sociology and Education in Contemporary Wales. In SCHOOLS COUNCIL, WELSH COMMITTEE, Educational Research in Wales. H.M.S.O., London, 1968, pp. 35-65

WILLIAMS, J. and T. BOYNS — Occupation in Wales, 1851-1971. Bulletin of Economic Research, Vol. 29, 1977, pp. 71-83

WILLIAMS, R. *The Country and the City*. Chatto and Windus, London, 1973.

WILLIAMS, R. Base and Superstructure in Marxist Cultural Theory. *New Left Review*, No. 82, 1973, pp. 3-16.

WILLIAMS, R. *Culture*. Fontana, London, 1980

WILLIAMS, R. B. *Y Wladfa*. University of Wales Press, Cardiff, 1962

WILMOTT, P. Social Research and New Communities. *Journal of the American Institute of Planners*. Vol. 33, 1967, pp. 387-398.

WRIGHT, E. O. Class Boundaries in Advanced Capitalist Societies. *New Left Review*, No. 98, 1976, pp. 3-43

YOUNG, M. ed., *Knowledge and Control*. Macmillan, London, 1971.

Newspapers and Periodicals

Digest of Welsh Statistics.

The Times.

Y Celt.

Y Cenhadwr.

Y Drych.

Y Ddraig Goch.

Y Genhinen.

Young Wales.

Name Index

R

S

T

U

V

W

Y

Z

Subject Index

I

J

L

M

N

O

P

Q

R

S